MS. MARVEL
Best of the Best

WRITER: BRIAN REED
PENCILER: ROBERTO DE LA TORRE
INKER: JIMMY PALMIOTTI

COLORIST: *CHRIS SOTOMAYOR*
LETTERER: *DAVE SHARPE*
COVER ART: *FRANK CHO & JASON KEITH*
GIANT-SIZE MS. MARVEL #1 COVER: *ROBERTO DE LA TORRE, CAM SMITH & CHRIS SOTOMAYOR*
ASSISTANT EDITORS: *MOLLY LAZER & AUBREY SITTERSON*
EDITOR: *ANDY SCHMIDT*

COLLECTION EDITOR: *JENNIFER GRÜNWALD*
ASSISTANT EDITOR: *MICHAEL SHORT*
ASSOCIATE EDITOR: *MARK D. BEAZLEY*
SENIOR EDITOR, SPECIAL PROJECTS: *JEFF YOUNGQUIST*
SENIOR VICE PRESIDENT OF SALES: *DAVID GABRIEL*
BOOK DESIGNER: *PATRICK MCGRATH*
VICE PRESIDENT OF CREATIVE: *TOM MARVELLI*

EDITOR IN CHIEF: *JOE QUESADA*
PUBLISHER: *DAN BUCKLEY*

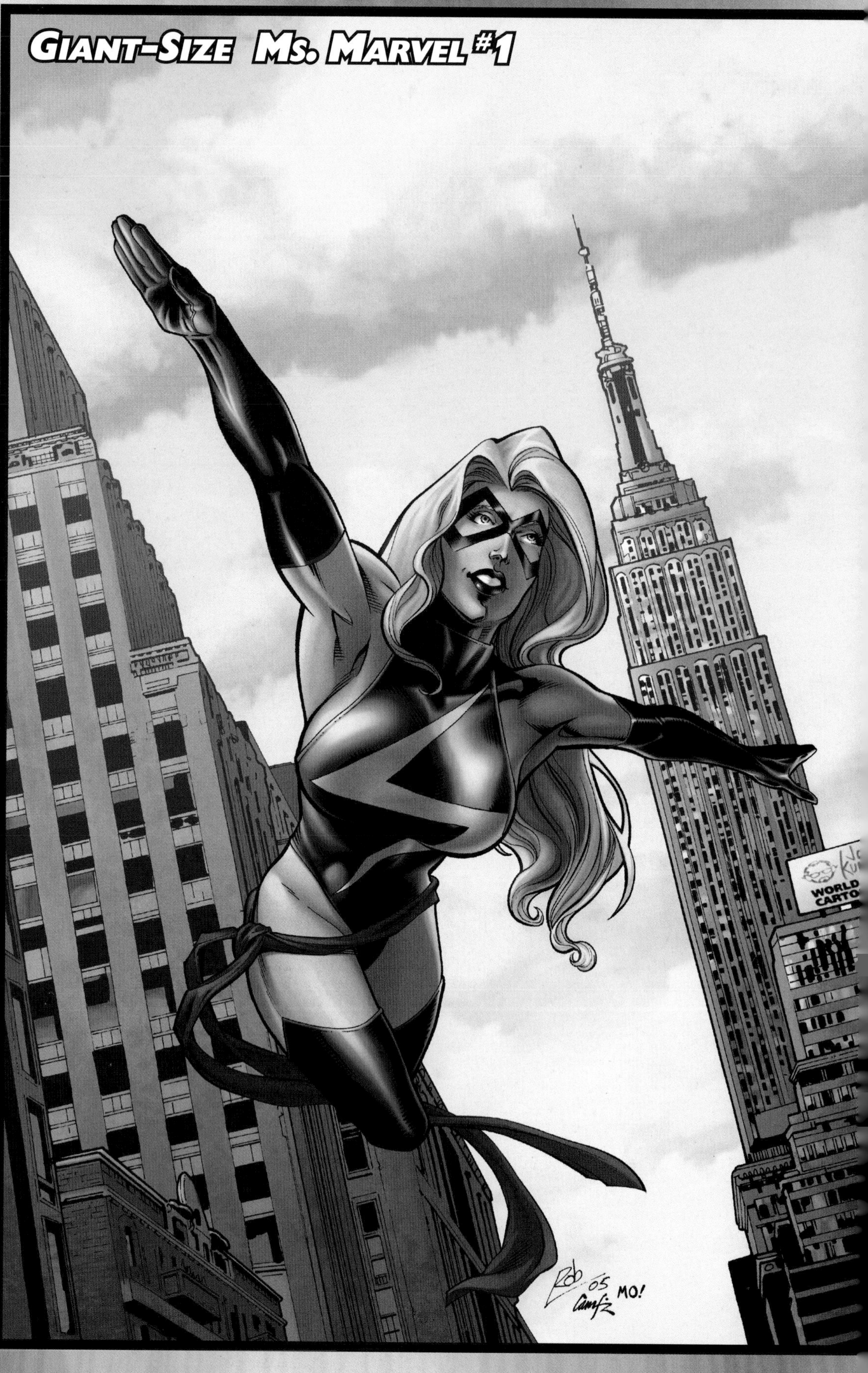
GIANT-SIZE Ms. MARVEL #1

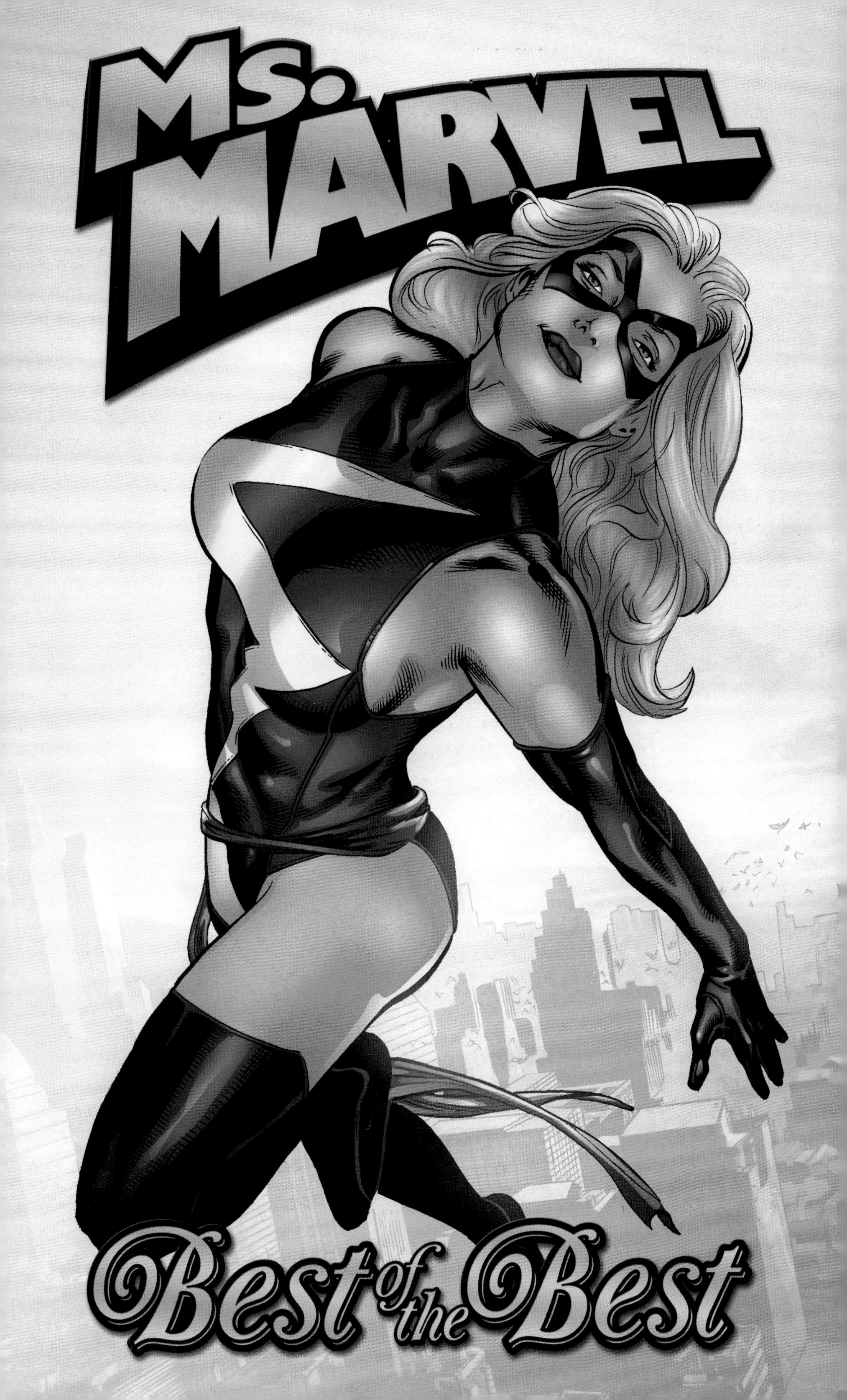
MS. MARVEL
Best of the Best

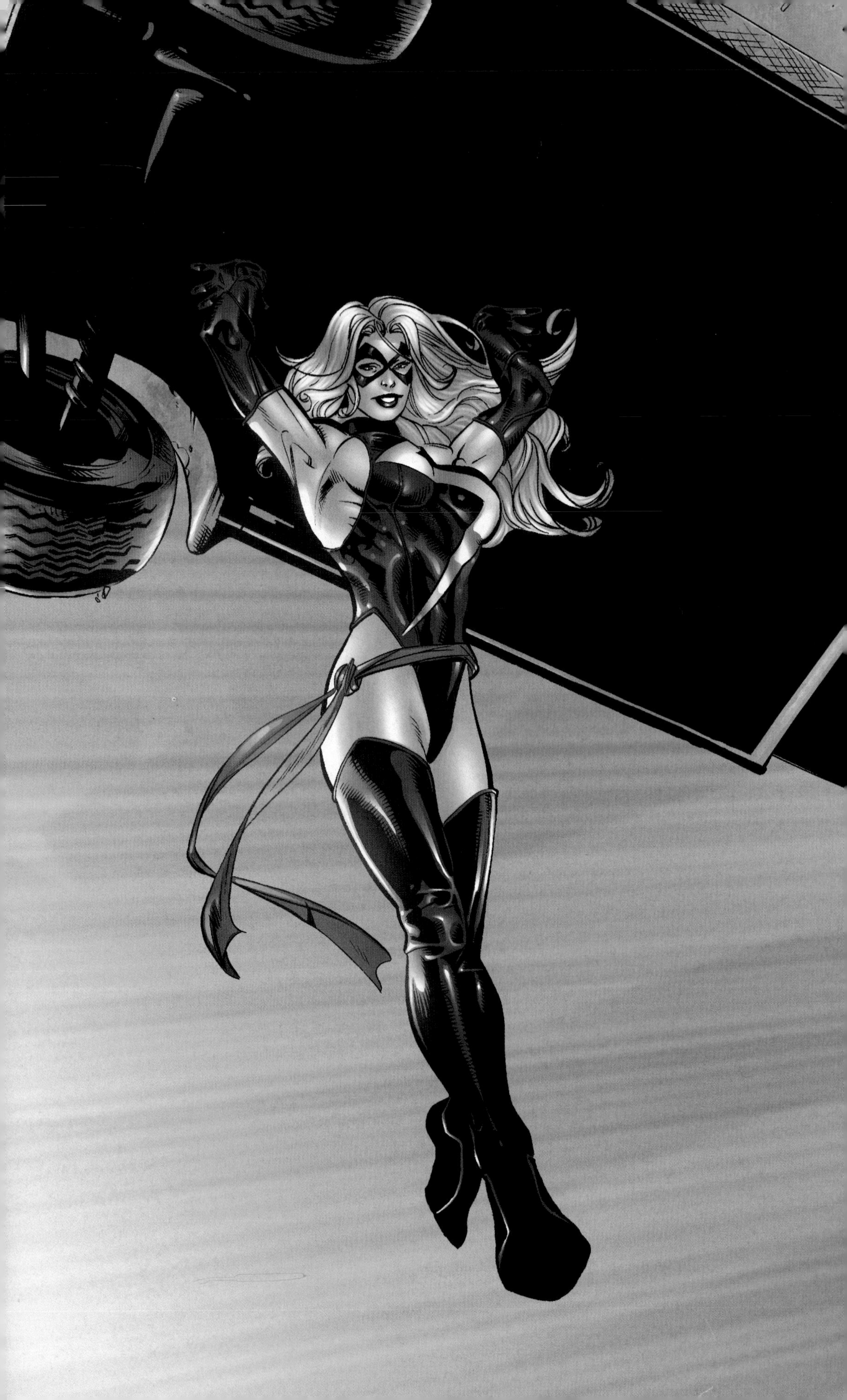

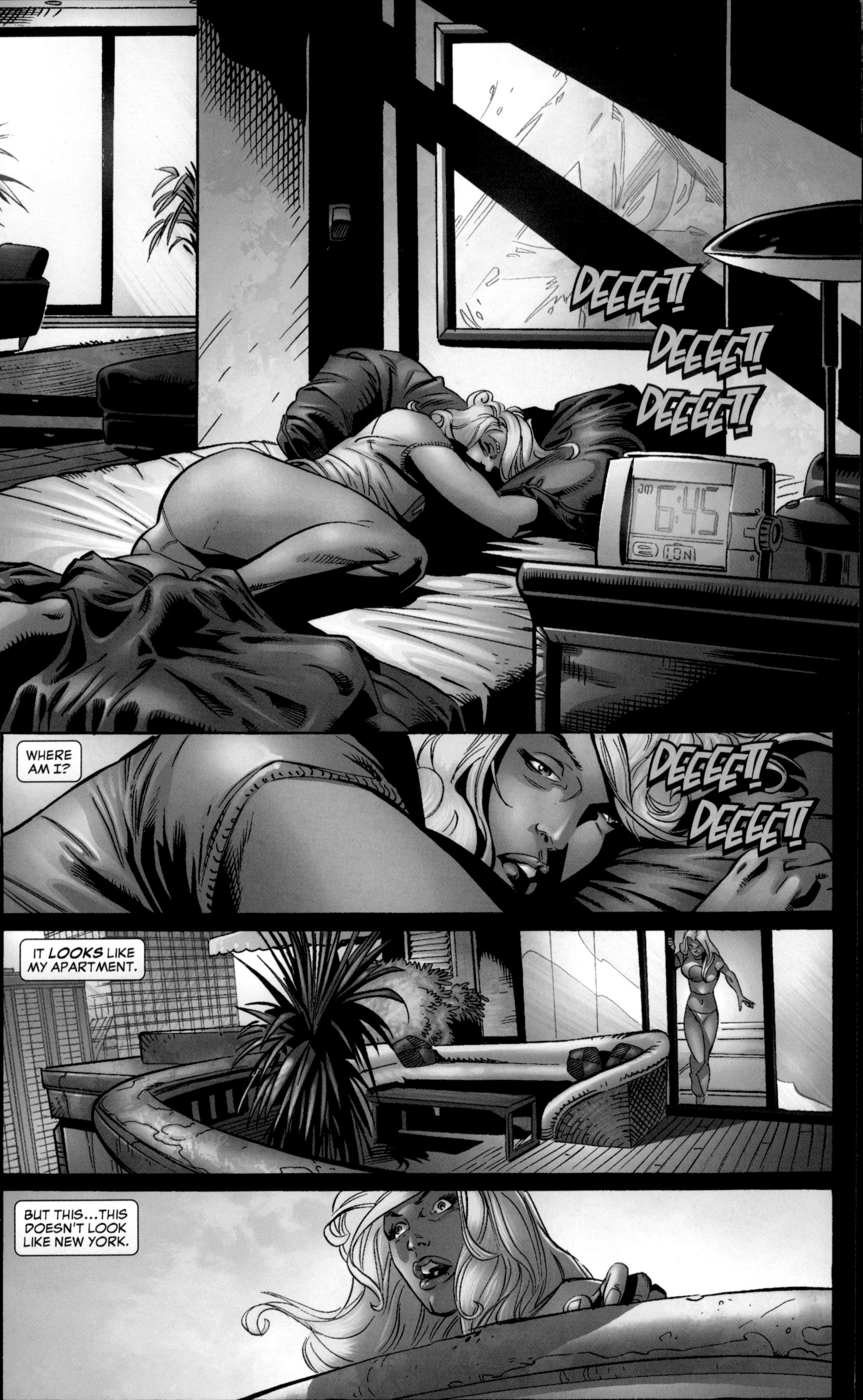
DEEEET!
DEEEET!
DEEEET!
WHERE AM I?
DEEEET!
DEEEET!
IT LOOKS LIKE MY APARTMENT.
BUT THIS...THIS DOESN'T LOOK LIKE NEW YORK.

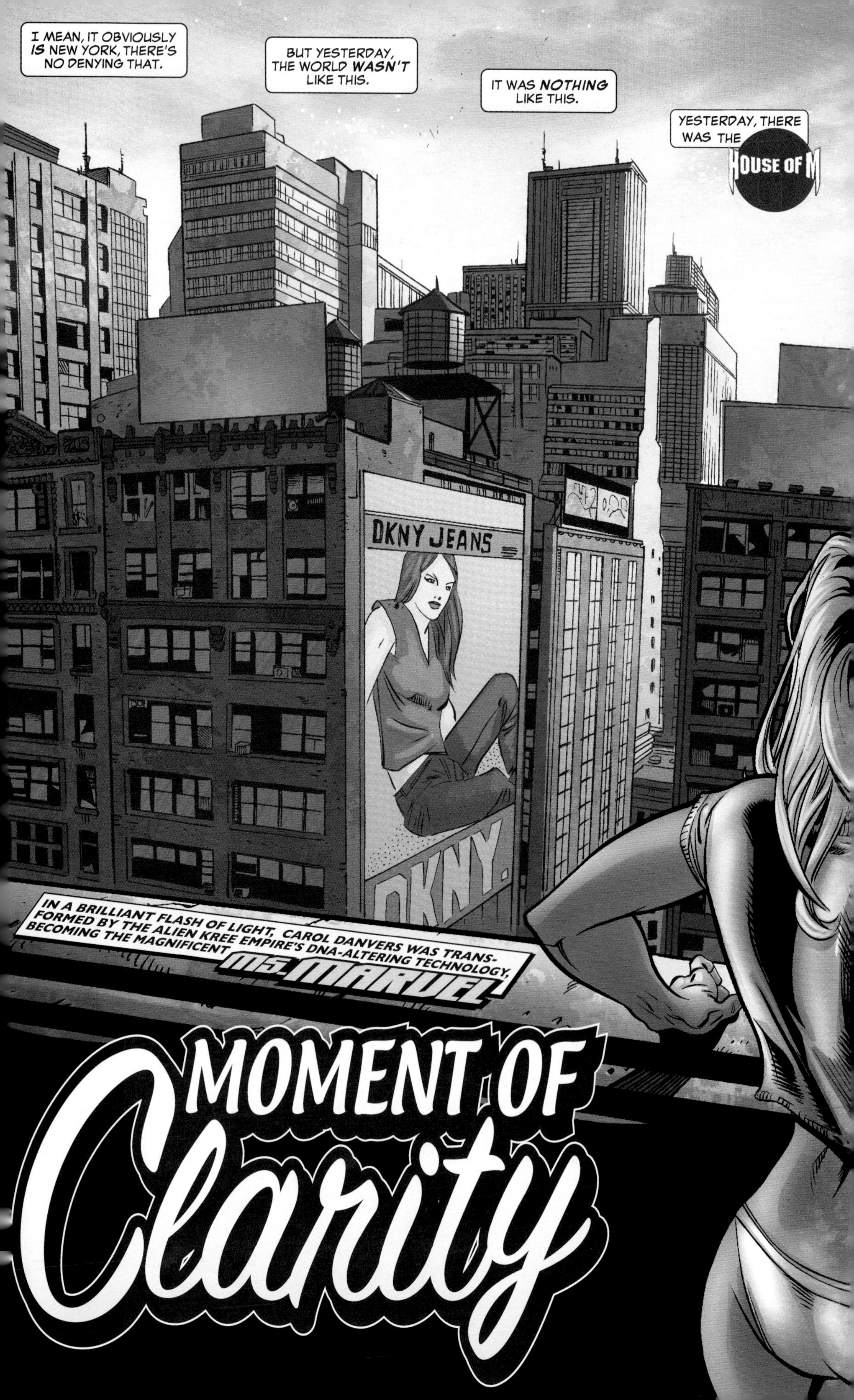

I MEAN, IT OBVIOUSLY IS NEW YORK, THERE'S NO DENYING THAT.
BUT YESTERDAY, THE WORLD WASN'T LIKE THIS.
IT WAS NOTHING LIKE THIS.
YESTERDAY, THERE WAS THE HOUSE OF M
DKNY JEANS
DKNY.
IN A BRILLIANT FLASH OF LIGHT, CAROL DANVERS WAS TRANSFORMED BY THE ALIEN KREE EMPIRE'S DNA-ALTERING TECHNOLOGY, BECOMING THE MAGNIFICENT MS. MARVEL
MOMENT OF Clarity

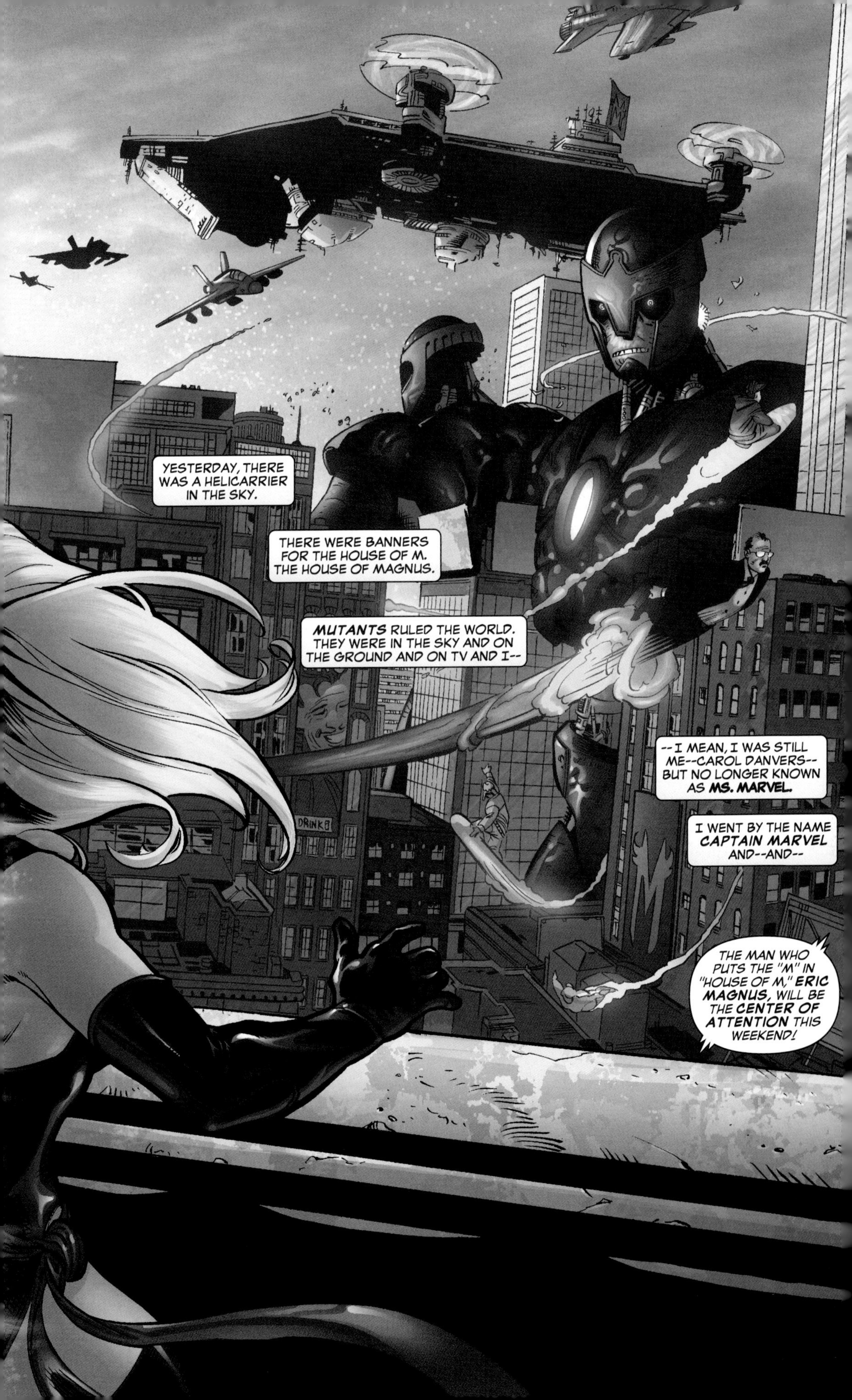
YESTERDAY, THERE WAS A HELICARRIER IN THE SKY.
THERE WERE BANNERS FOR THE HOUSE OF M. THE HOUSE OF MAGNUS.
MUTANTS RULED THE WORLD. THEY WERE IN THE SKY AND ON THE GROUND AND ON TV AND I--
--I MEAN, I WAS STILL ME--CAROL DANVERS--BUT NO LONGER KNOWN AS MS. MARVEL.
I WENT BY THE NAME CAPTAIN MARVEL AND--AND--
THE MAN WHO PUTS THE "M" IN "HOUSE OF M," ERIC MAGNUS, WILL BE THE CENTER OF ATTENTION THIS WEEKEND!
DRINK

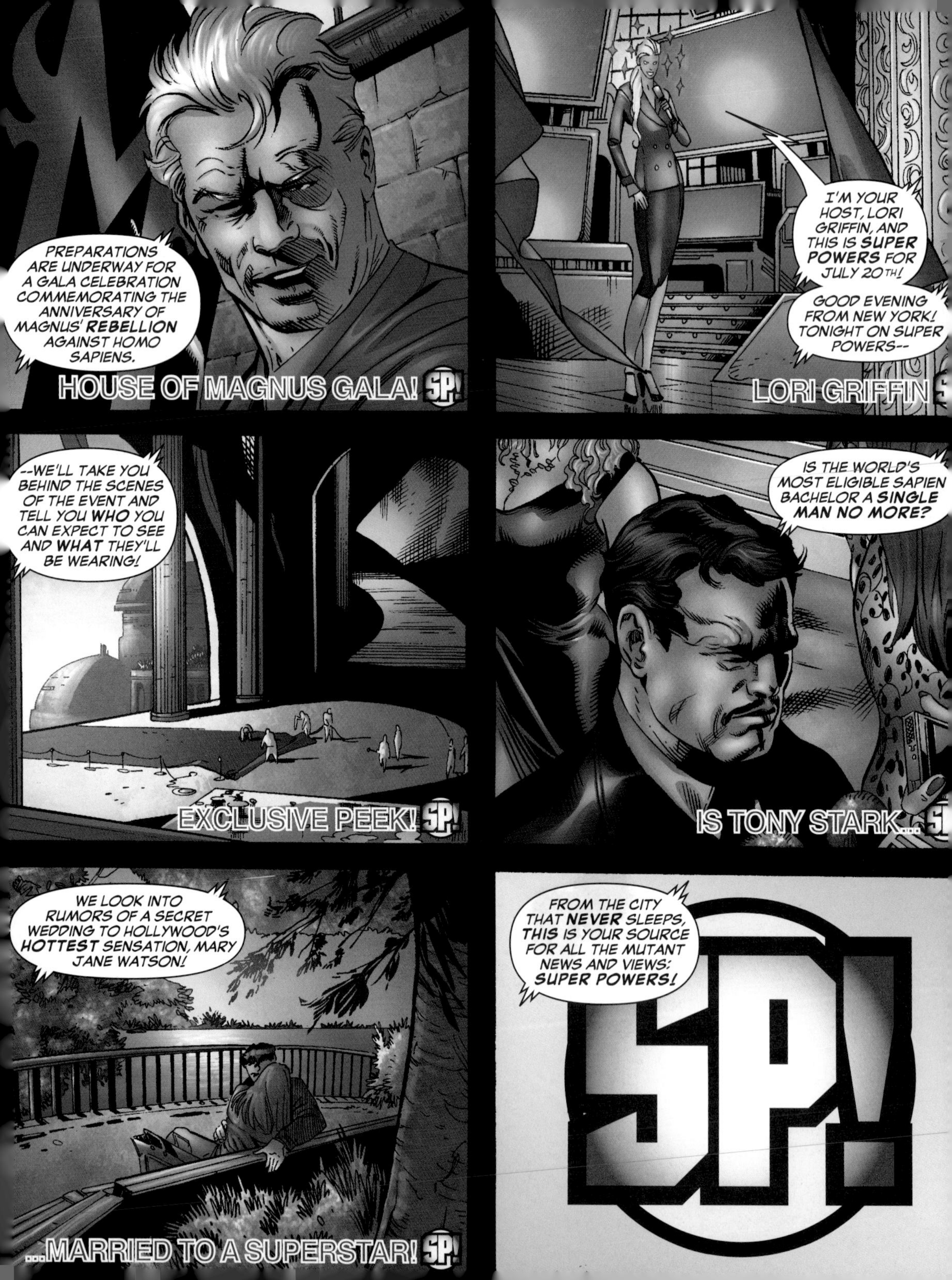
PREPARATIONS ARE UNDERWAY FOR A GALA CELEBRATION COMMEMORATING THE ANNIVERSARY OF MAGNUS' **REBELLION** AGAINST HOMO SAPIENS.
HOUSE OF MAGNUS GALA! SP!
I'M YOUR HOST, LORI GRIFFIN, AND THIS IS **SUPER POWERS** FOR JULY 20TH!
GOOD EVENING FROM NEW YORK! TONIGHT ON SUPER POWERS--
LORI GRIFFIN
--WE'LL TAKE YOU BEHIND THE SCENES OF THE EVENT AND TELL YOU **WHO** YOU CAN EXPECT TO SEE AND **WHAT** THEY'LL BE WEARING!
EXCLUSIVE PEEK! SP!
IS THE WORLD'S MOST ELIGIBLE SAPIEN BACHELOR A **SINGLE MAN NO MORE?**
IS TONY STARK...
WE LOOK INTO RUMORS OF A SECRET WEDDING TO HOLLYWOOD'S **HOTTEST** SENSATION, MARY JANE WATSON!
...MARRIED TO A SUPERSTAR! SP!
FROM THE CITY THAT **NEVER** SLEEPS, **THIS** IS YOUR SOURCE FOR ALL THE MUTANT NEWS AND VIEWS: **SUPER POWERS!**
SP!

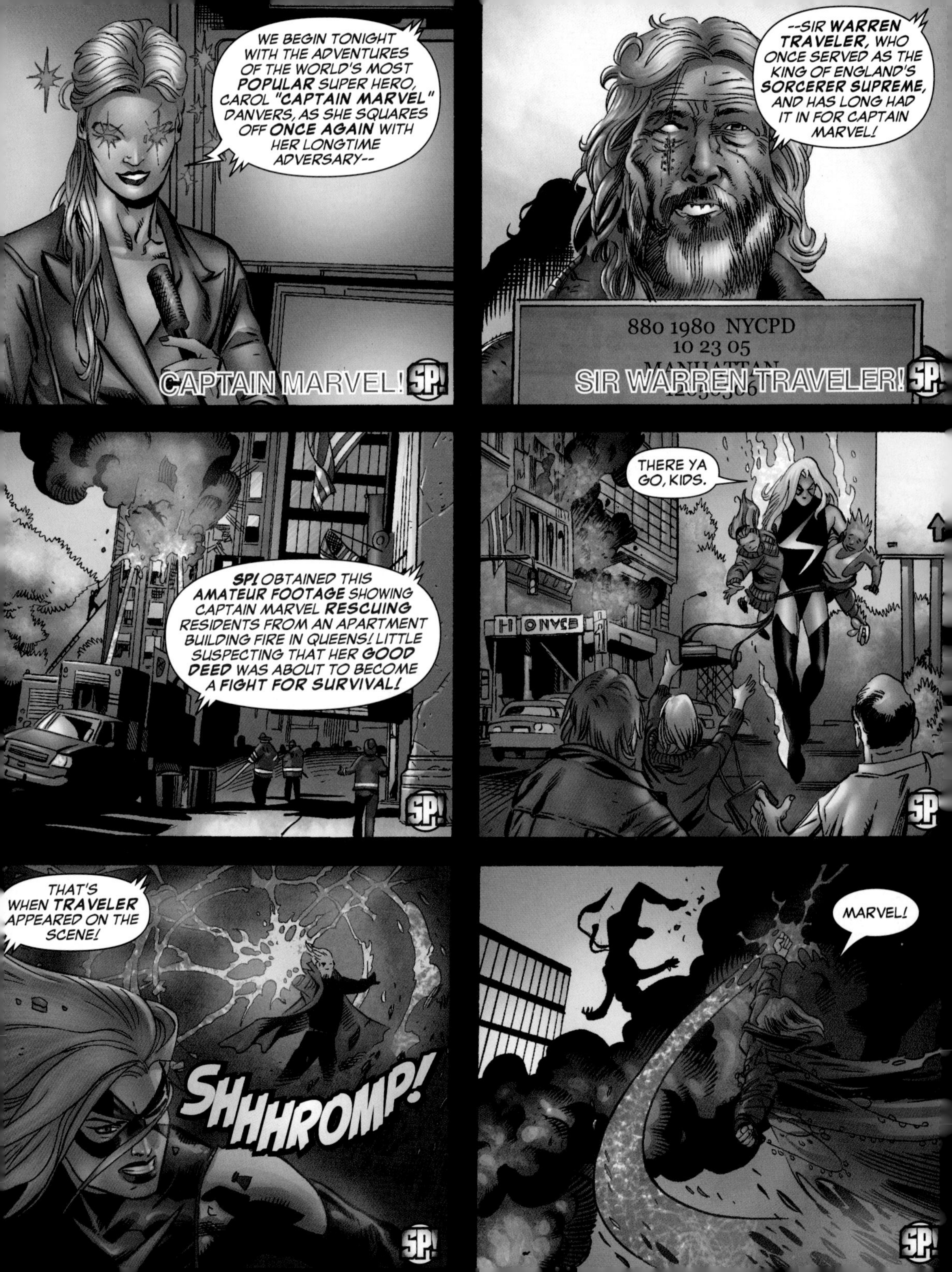

WE BEGIN TONIGHT WITH THE ADVENTURES OF THE WORLD'S MOST POPULAR SUPER HERO, CAROL "CAPTAIN MARVEL" DANVERS, AS SHE SQUARES OFF ONCE AGAIN WITH HER LONGTIME ADVERSARY--
CAPTAIN MARVEL!
SP!
--SIR WARREN TRAVELER, WHO ONCE SERVED AS THE KING OF ENGLAND'S SORCERER SUPREME, AND HAS LONG HAD IT IN FOR CAPTAIN MARVEL!
880 1980 NYCPD
10 23 05
SIR WARREN TRAVELER!
SP!
SP! OBTAINED THIS AMATEUR FOOTAGE SHOWING CAPTAIN MARVEL RESCUING RESIDENTS FROM AN APARTMENT BUILDING FIRE IN QUEENS! LITTLE SUSPECTING THAT HER GOOD DEED WAS ABOUT TO BECOME A FIGHT FOR SURVIVAL!
SP!
THERE YA GO, KIDS.
SP!
THAT'S WHEN TRAVELER APPEARED ON THE SCENE!
SHHHROMP!
SP!
MARVEL!
SP!

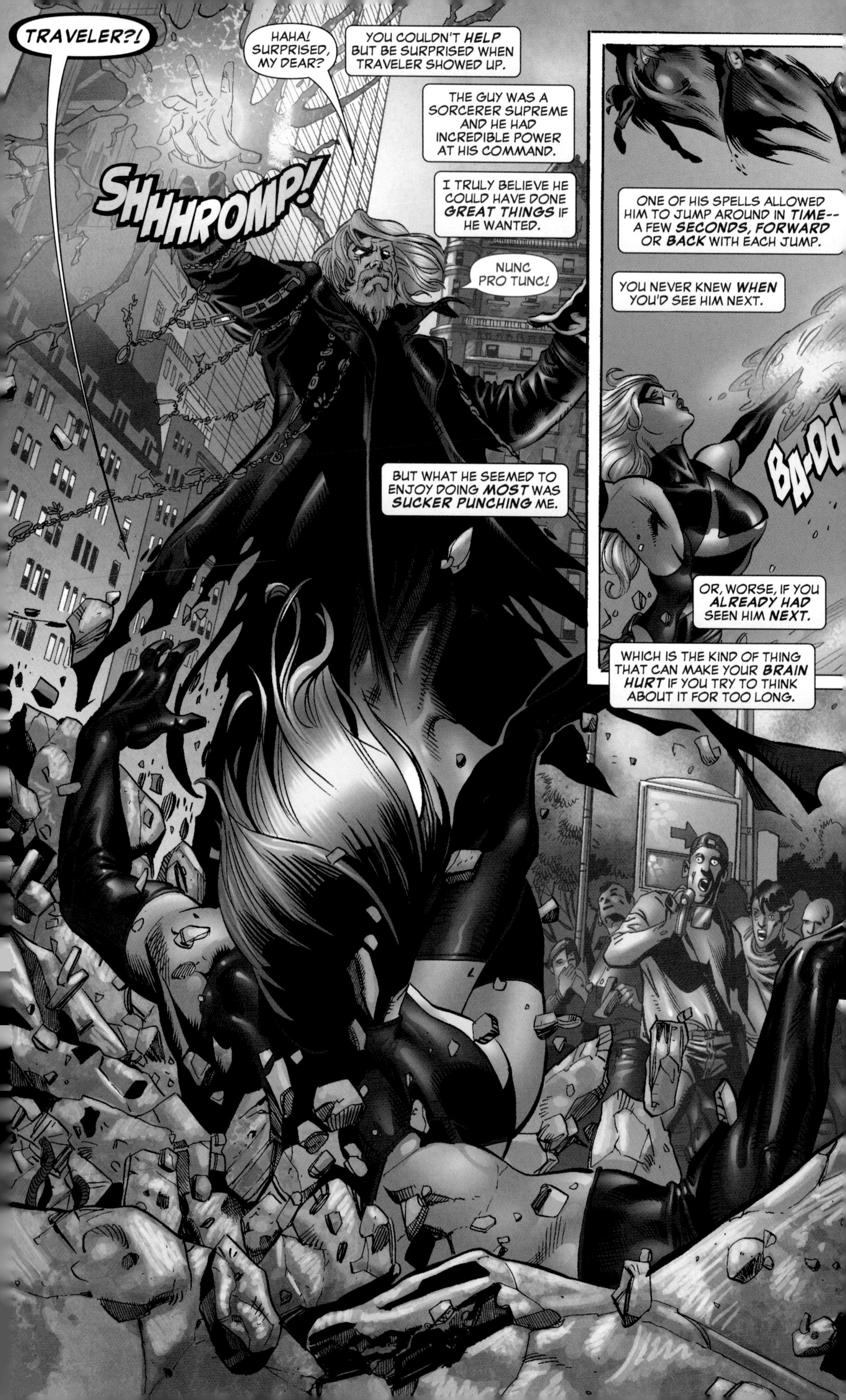

TRAVELER?!
HAHA! SURPRISED, MY DEAR?
YOU COULDN'T HELP BUT BE SURPRISED WHEN TRAVELER SHOWED UP.
THE GUY WAS A SORCERER SUPREME AND HE HAD INCREDIBLE POWER AT HIS COMMAND.
I TRULY BELIEVE HE COULD HAVE DONE GREAT THINGS IF HE WANTED.
SHHHROMP!
NUNC PRO TUNC!
BUT WHAT HE SEEMED TO ENJOY DOING MOST WAS SUCKER PUNCHING ME.
ONE OF HIS SPELLS ALLOWED HIM TO JUMP AROUND IN TIME-- A FEW SECONDS, FORWARD OR BACK WITH EACH JUMP.
YOU NEVER KNEW WHEN YOU'D SEE HIM NEXT.
BA-DO
OR, WORSE, IF YOU ALREADY HAD SEEN HIM NEXT.
WHICH IS THE KIND OF THING THAT CAN MAKE YOUR BRAIN HURT IF YOU TRY TO THINK ABOUT IT FOR TOO LONG.

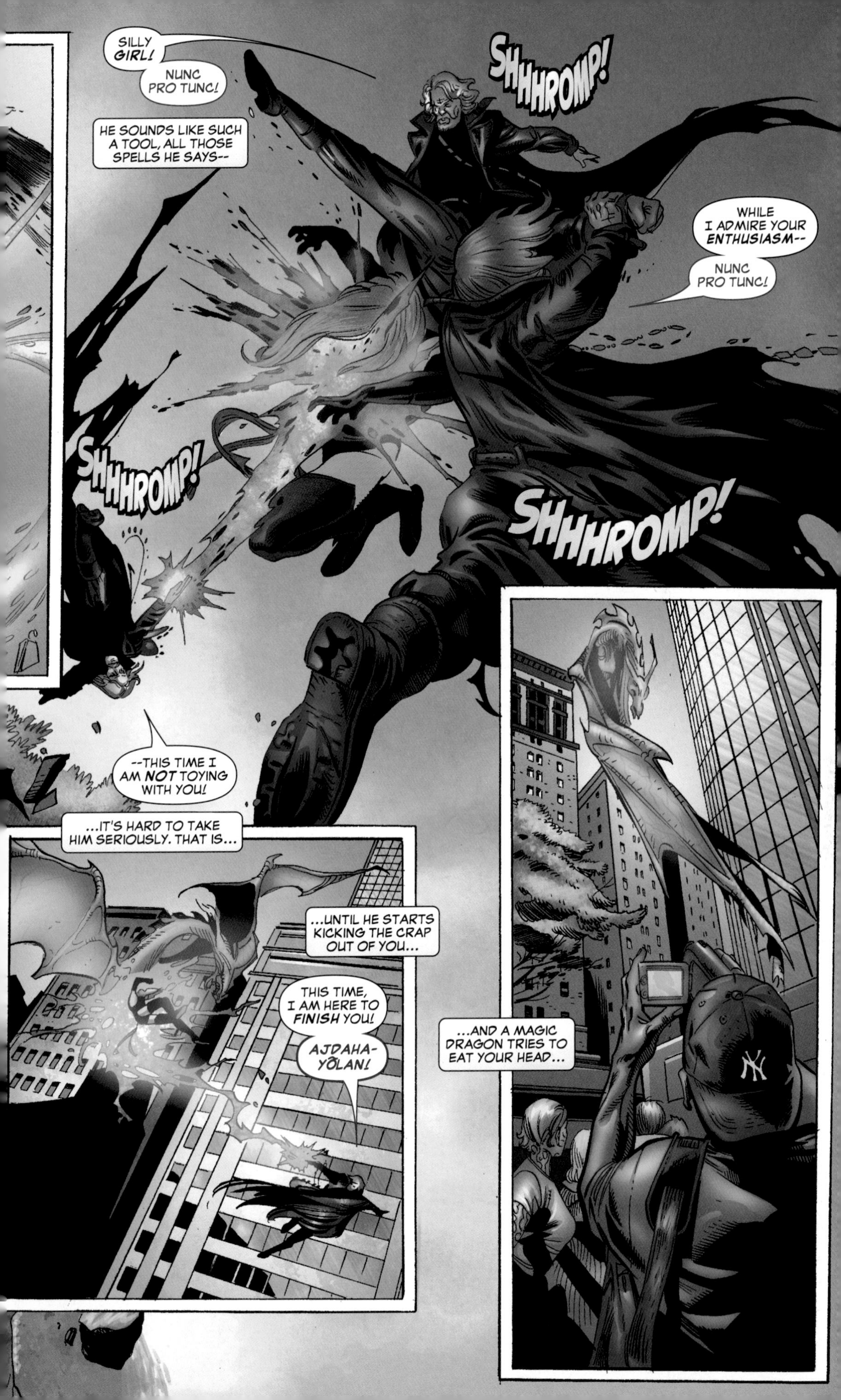
SILLY GIRL!
NUNC PRO TUNC!
HE SOUNDS LIKE SUCH A TOOL, ALL THOSE SPELLS HE SAYS--
SHHHROMP!
WHILE I ADMIRE YOUR ENTHUSIASM--
NUNC PRO TUNC!
SHHHROMP!
SHHHROMP!
--THIS TIME I AM NOT TOYING WITH YOU!
...IT'S HARD TO TAKE HIM SERIOUSLY. THAT IS...
...UNTIL HE STARTS KICKING THE CRAP OUT OF YOU...
THIS TIME, I AM HERE TO FINISH YOU!
AJDAHA-YOLAN!
...AND A MAGIC DRAGON TRIES TO EAT YOUR HEAD...

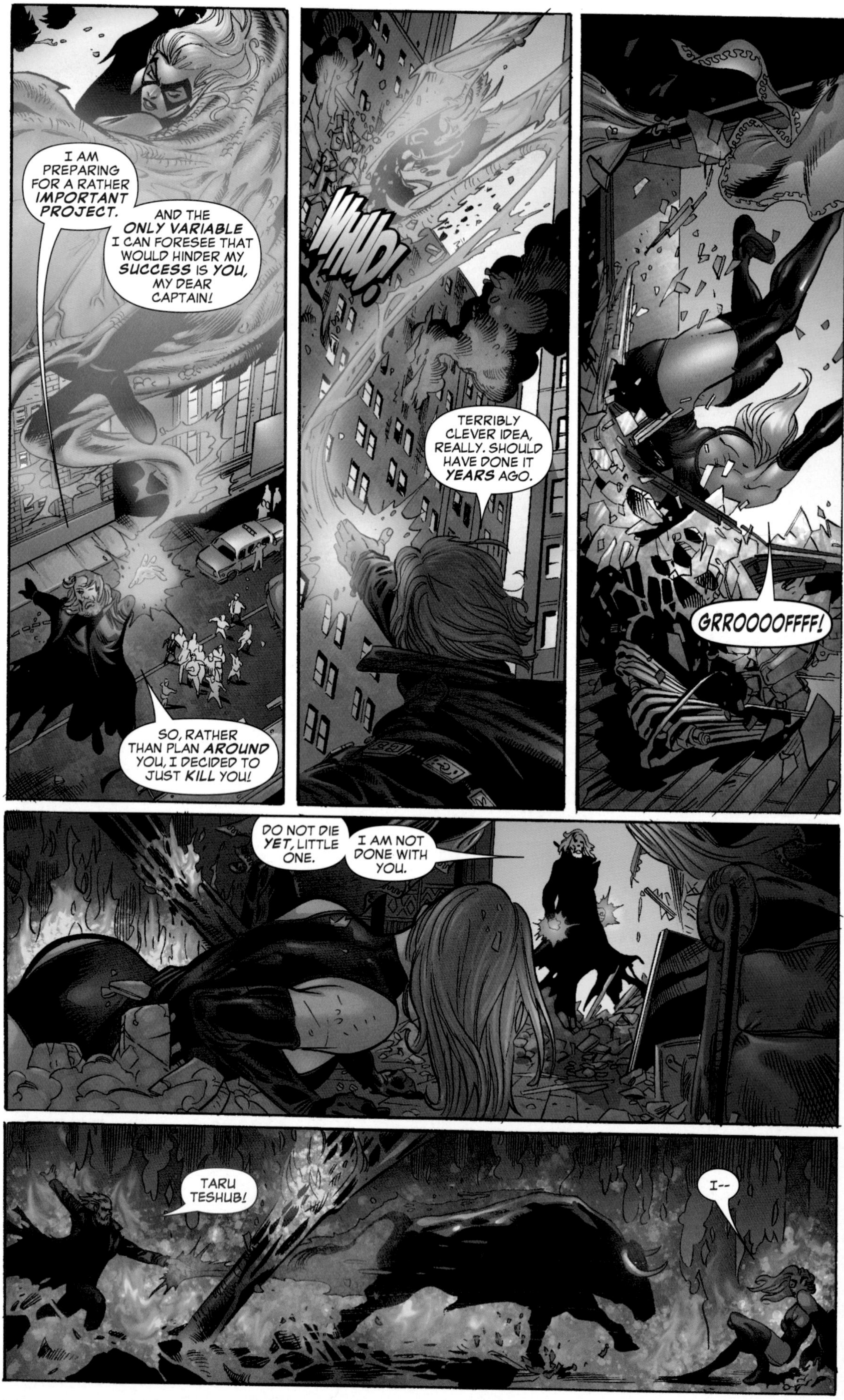
I AM PREPARING FOR A RATHER IMPORTANT PROJECT.
AND THE ONLY VARIABLE I CAN FORESEE THAT WOULD HINDER MY SUCCESS IS YOU, MY DEAR CAPTAIN!
SO, RATHER THAN PLAN AROUND YOU, I DECIDED TO JUST KILL YOU!
WHUD!
TERRIBLY CLEVER IDEA, REALLY. SHOULD HAVE DONE IT YEARS AGO.
GRROOOOFFFF!
DO NOT DIE YET, LITTLE ONE.
I AM NOT DONE WITH YOU.
TARU TESHUB!
I--

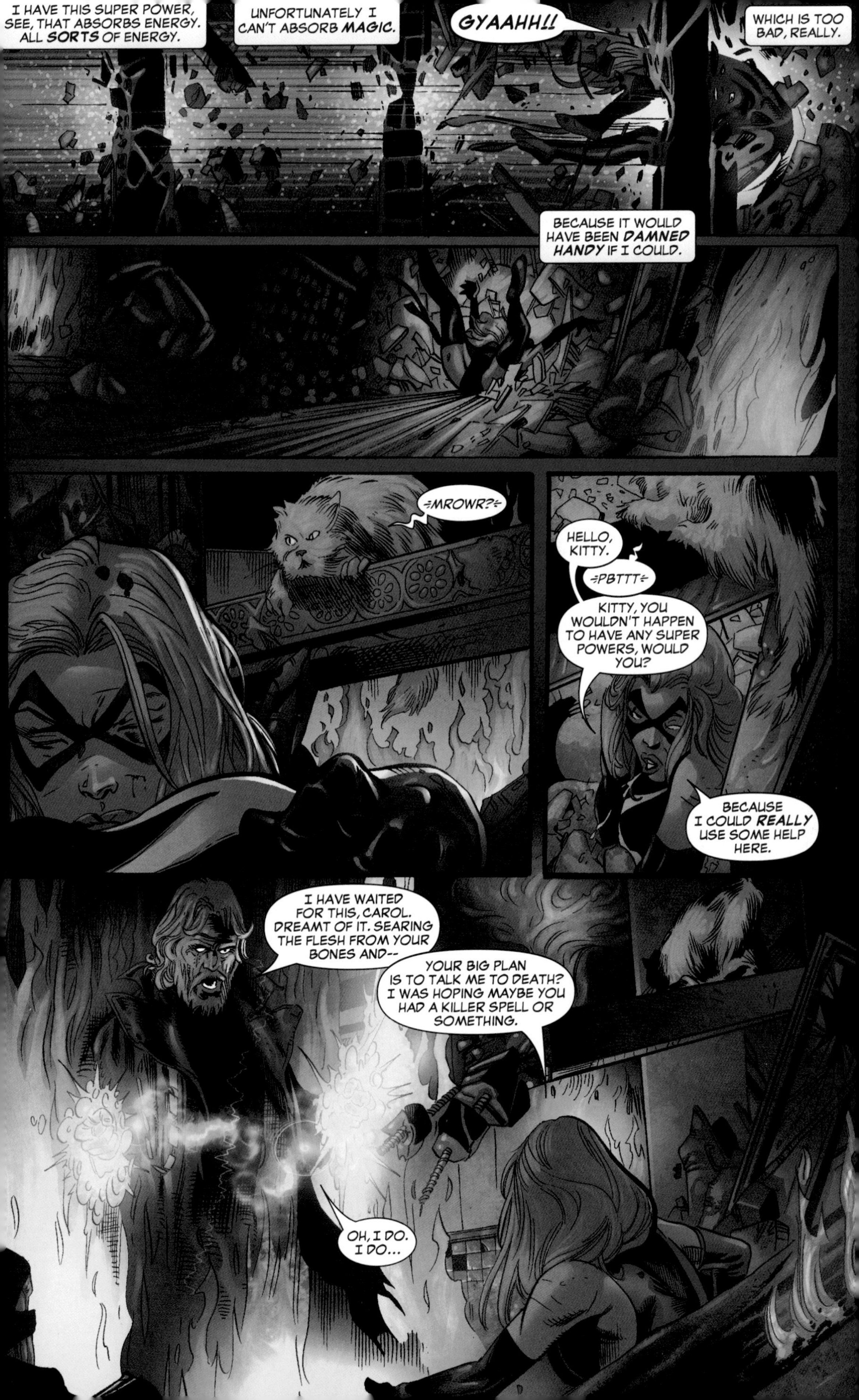
I HAVE THIS SUPER POWER, SEE, THAT ABSORBS ENERGY. ALL SORTS OF ENERGY.
UNFORTUNATELY I CAN'T ABSORB MAGIC.
GYAAHH!!
WHICH IS TOO BAD, REALLY.
BECAUSE IT WOULD HAVE BEEN DAMNED HANDY IF I COULD.
=MROWR?=
HELLO, KITTY.
=PBTTT=
KITTY, YOU WOULDN'T HAPPEN TO HAVE ANY SUPER POWERS, WOULD YOU?
BECAUSE I COULD REALLY USE SOME HELP HERE.
I HAVE WAITED FOR THIS, CAROL. DREAMT OF IT. SEARING THE FLESH FROM YOUR BONES AND--
YOUR BIG PLAN IS TO TALK ME TO DEATH? I WAS HOPING MAYBE YOU HAD A KILLER SPELL OR SOMETHING.
OH, I DO. I DO...

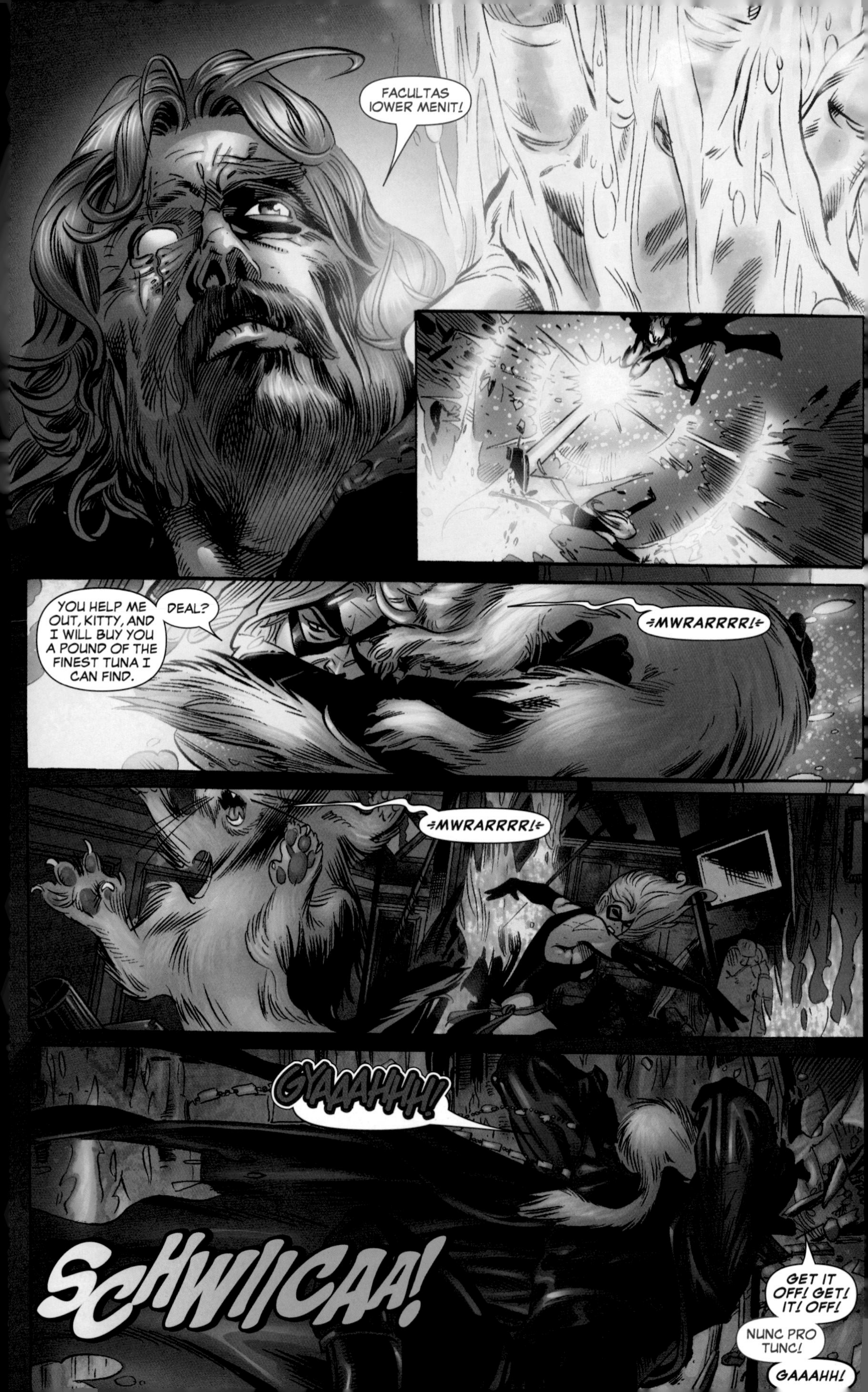
FACULTAS IOWER MENIT!
YOU HELP ME OUT, KITTY, AND I WILL BUY YOU A POUND OF THE FINEST TUNA I CAN FIND.
DEAL?
=MWRARRRR!=
=MWRARRRR!=
GYAAAHHH!
SCHWIICAA!
GET IT OFF! GET! IT! OFF!
NUNC PRO TUNC!
GAAAHH!

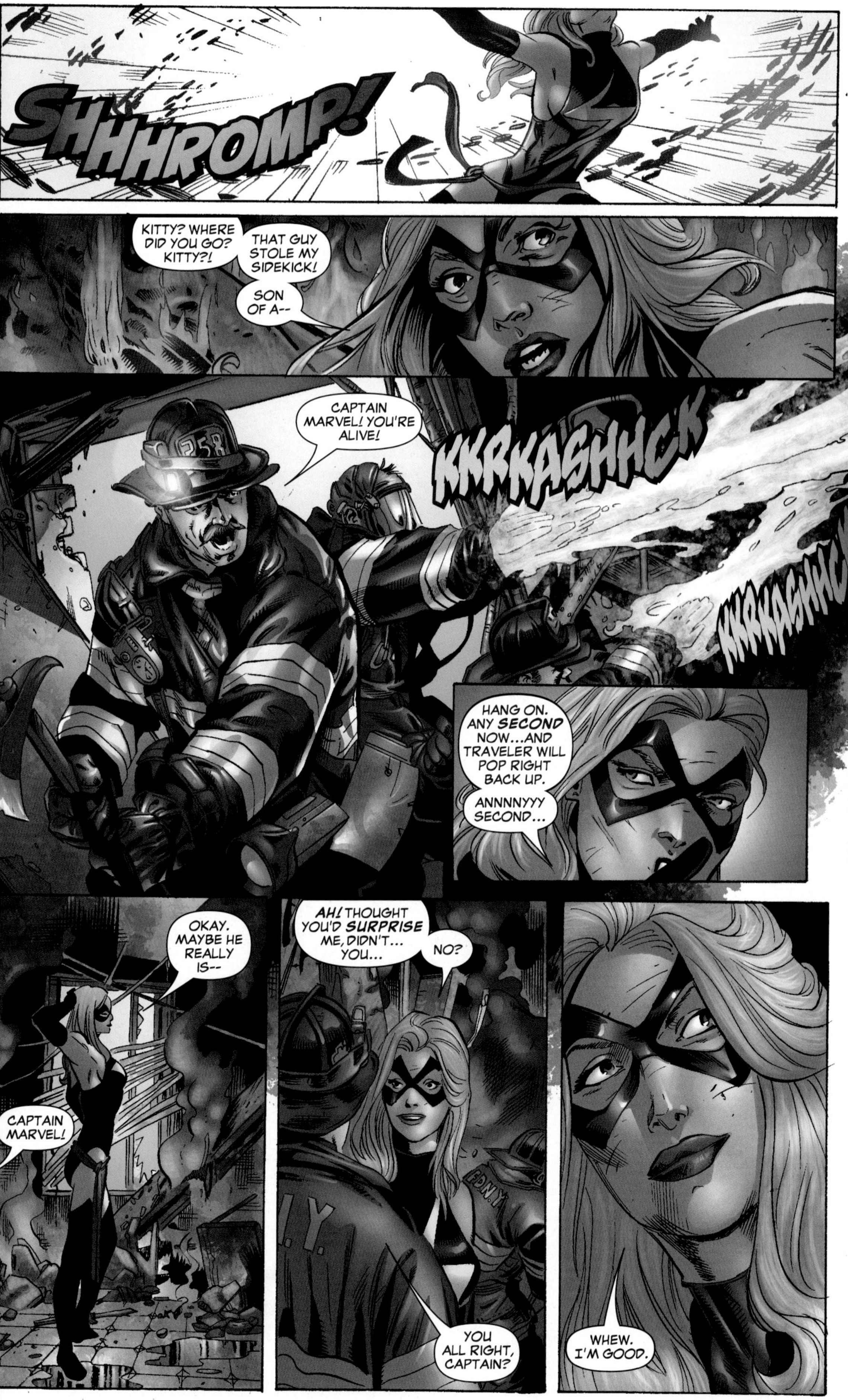
SHHHROMP!
KITTY? WHERE DID YOU GO? KITTY?!
THAT GUY STOLE MY SIDEKICK!
SON OF A--
CAPTAIN MARVEL! YOU'RE ALIVE!
KKRKASHHCK
KKRKASHHCK
HANG ON. ANY SECOND NOW...AND TRAVELER WILL POP RIGHT BACK UP.
ANNNNYYY SECOND...
OKAY. MAYBE HE REALLY IS--
CAPTAIN MARVEL!
AH! THOUGHT YOU'D SURPRISE ME, DIDN'T... YOU...
NO?
YOU ALL RIGHT, CAPTAIN?
WHEW. I'M GOOD.

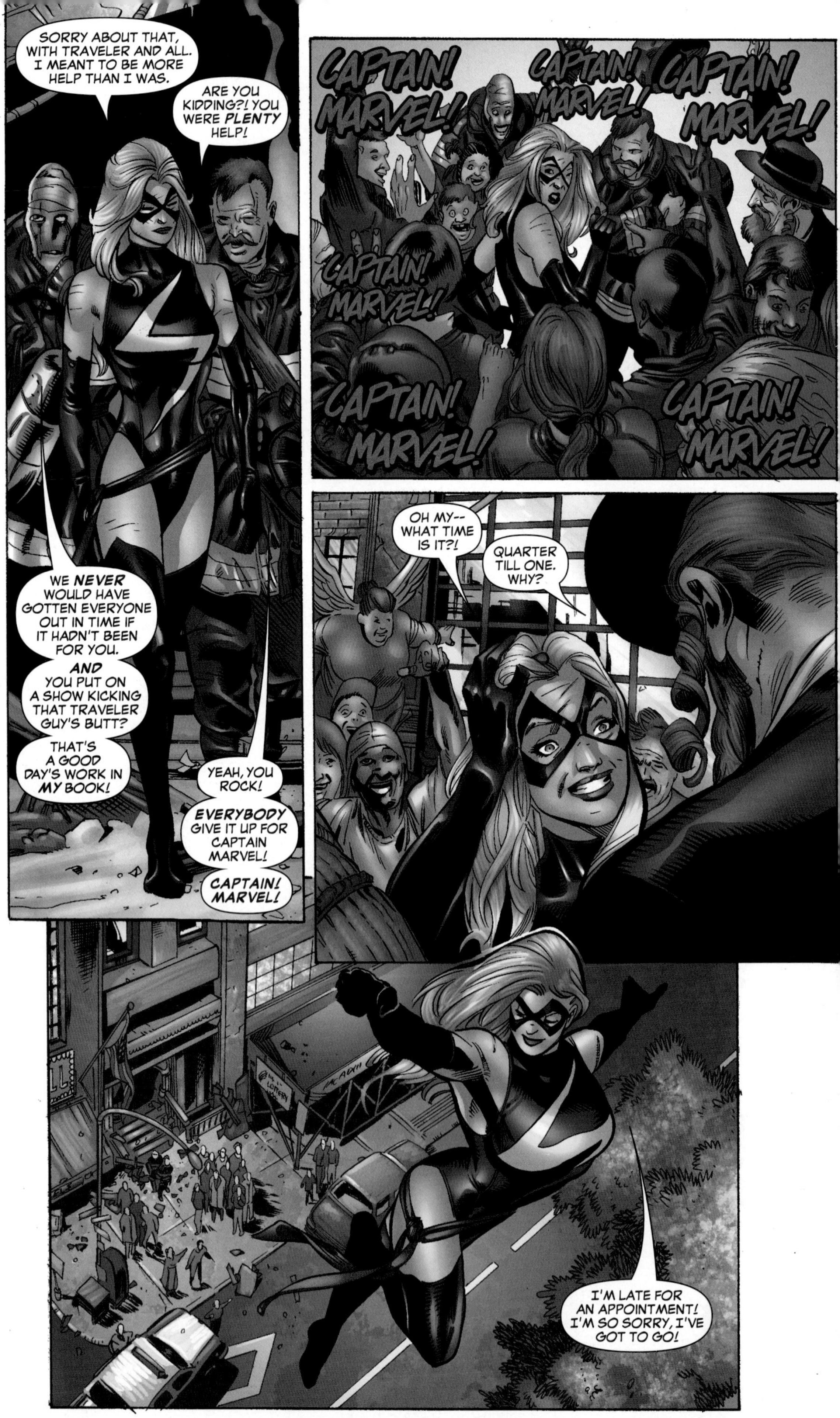

SORRY ABOUT THAT, WITH TRAVELER AND ALL. I MEANT TO BE MORE HELP THAN I WAS.
ARE YOU KIDDING?! YOU WERE PLENTY HELP!
WE NEVER WOULD HAVE GOTTEN EVERYONE OUT IN TIME IF IT HADN'T BEEN FOR YOU.
AND YOU PUT ON A SHOW KICKING THAT TRAVELER GUY'S BUTT?
THAT'S A GOOD DAY'S WORK IN MY BOOK!
YEAH, YOU ROCK!
EVERYBODY GIVE IT UP FOR CAPTAIN MARVEL!
CAPTAIN! MARVEL!
CAPTAIN! MARVEL!
CAPTAIN! MARVEL!
CAPTAIN! MARVEL!
CAPTAIN! MARVEL!
CAPTAIN! MARVEL!
CAPTAIN! MARVEL!
OH MY-- WHAT TIME IS IT?!
QUARTER TILL ONE. WHY?
LOTTERY
I'M LATE FOR AN APPOINTMENT! I'M SO SORRY, I'VE GOT TO GO!

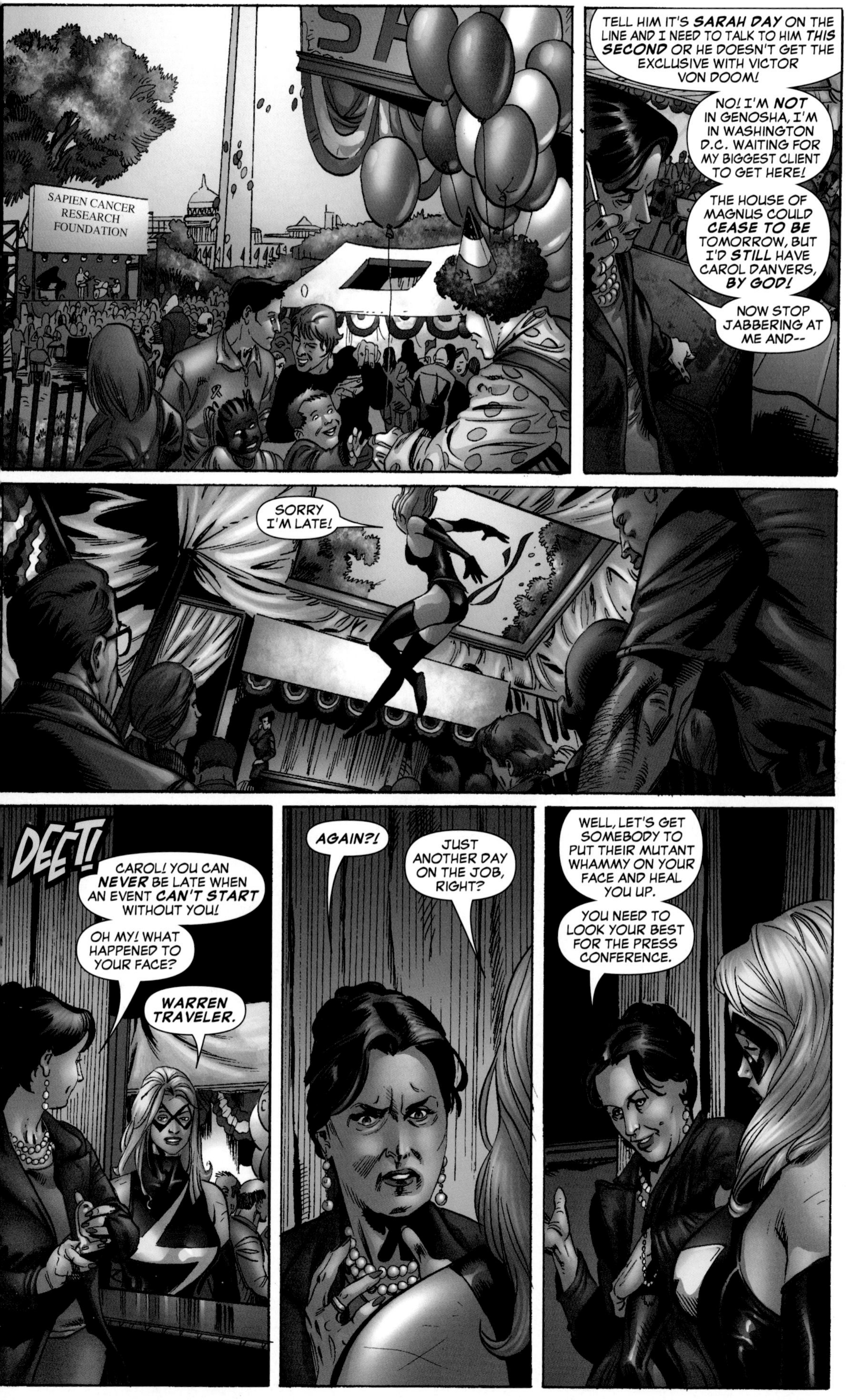
SAPIEN CANCER RESEARCH FOUNDATION
TELL HIM IT'S SARAH DAY ON THE LINE AND I NEED TO TALK TO HIM THIS SECOND OR HE DOESN'T GET THE EXCLUSIVE WITH VICTOR VON DOOM!
NO! I'M NOT IN GENOSHA, I'M IN WASHINGTON D.C. WAITING FOR MY BIGGEST CLIENT TO GET HERE!
THE HOUSE OF MAGNUS COULD CEASE TO BE TOMORROW, BUT I'D STILL HAVE CAROL DANVERS, BY GOD!
NOW STOP JABBERING AT ME AND--
SORRY I'M LATE!
DEET!
CAROL! YOU CAN NEVER BE LATE WHEN AN EVENT CAN'T START WITHOUT YOU!
OH MY! WHAT HAPPENED TO YOUR FACE?
WARREN TRAVELER.
AGAIN?!
JUST ANOTHER DAY ON THE JOB, RIGHT?
WELL, LET'S GET SOMEBODY TO PUT THEIR MUTANT WHAMMY ON YOUR FACE AND HEAL YOU UP.
YOU NEED TO LOOK YOUR BEST FOR THE PRESS CONFERENCE.

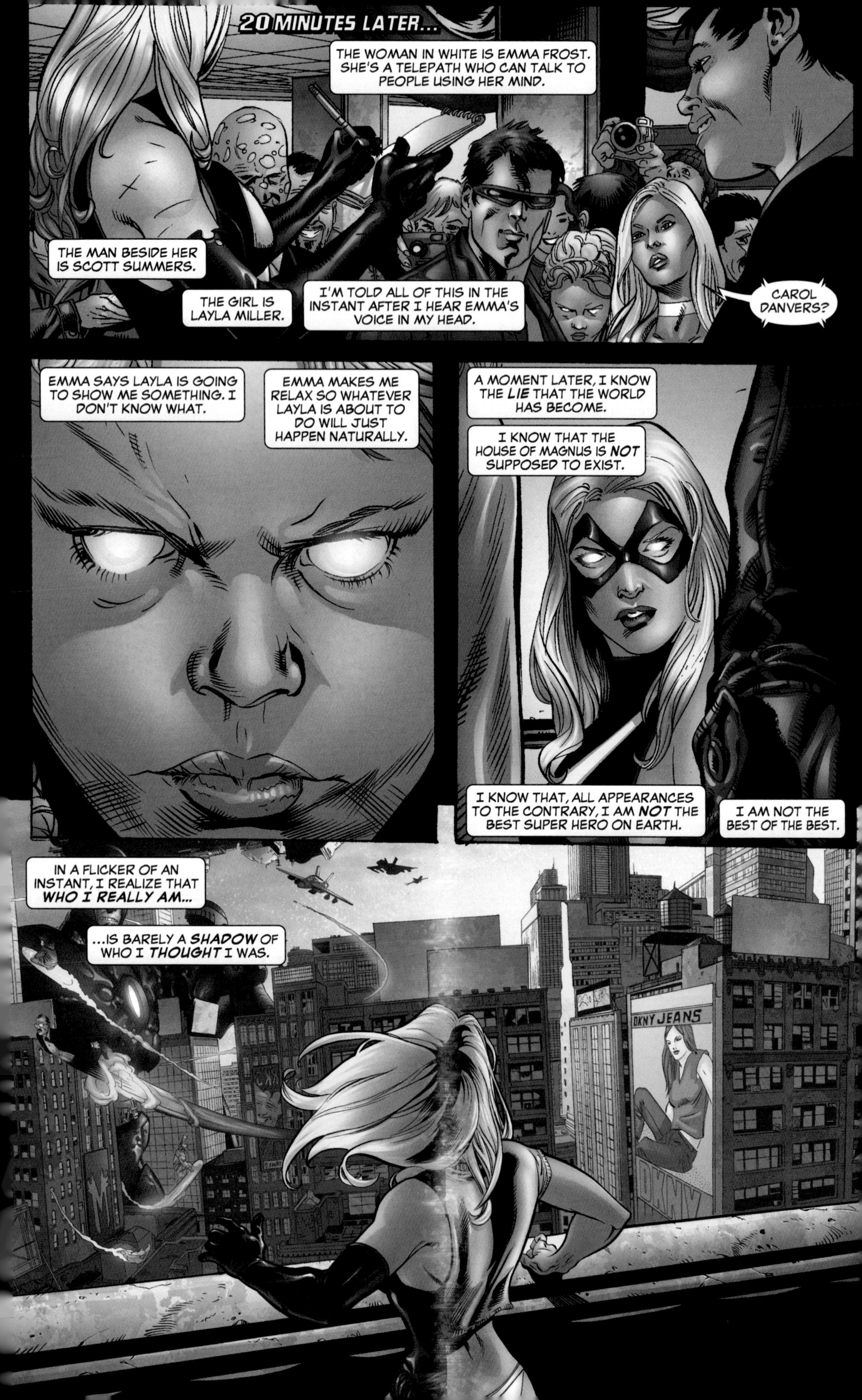

20 MINUTES LATER...
THE WOMAN IN WHITE IS EMMA FROST. SHE'S A TELEPATH WHO CAN TALK TO PEOPLE USING HER MIND.
THE MAN BESIDE HER IS SCOTT SUMMERS.
THE GIRL IS LAYLA MILLER.
I'M TOLD ALL OF THIS IN THE INSTANT AFTER I HEAR EMMA'S VOICE IN MY HEAD.
CAROL DANVERS?
EMMA SAYS LAYLA IS GOING TO SHOW ME SOMETHING. I DON'T KNOW WHAT.
EMMA MAKES ME RELAX SO WHATEVER LAYLA IS ABOUT TO DO WILL JUST HAPPEN NATURALLY.
A MOMENT LATER, I KNOW THE *LIE* THAT THE WORLD HAS BECOME.
I KNOW THAT THE HOUSE OF MAGNUS IS ***NOT*** SUPPOSED TO EXIST.
I KNOW THAT, ALL APPEARANCES TO THE CONTRARY, I AM ***NOT*** THE BEST SUPER HERO ON EARTH.
I AM NOT THE BEST OF THE BEST.
IN A FLICKER OF AN INSTANT, I REALIZE THAT ***WHO I REALLY AM...***
...IS BARELY A ***SHADOW*** OF WHO I ***THOUGHT*** I WAS.
DKNY JEANS

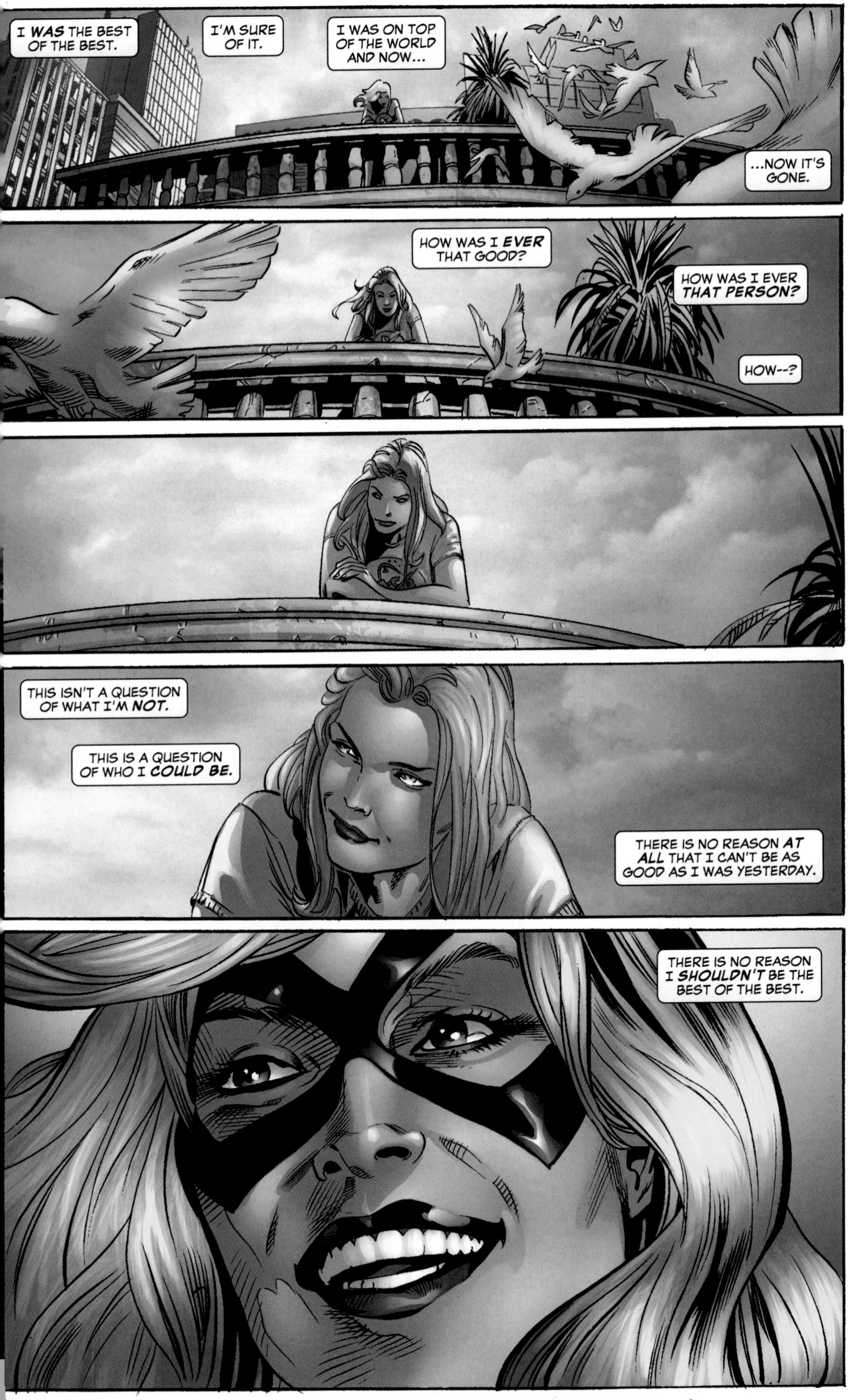
I WAS THE BEST OF THE BEST.
I'M SURE OF IT.
I WAS ON TOP OF THE WORLD AND NOW...
...NOW IT'S GONE.
HOW WAS I EVER THAT GOOD?
HOW WAS I EVER THAT PERSON?
HOW--?
THIS ISN'T A QUESTION OF WHAT I'M NOT.
THIS IS A QUESTION OF WHO I COULD BE.
THERE IS NO REASON AT ALL THAT I CAN'T BE AS GOOD AS I WAS YESTERDAY.
THERE IS NO REASON I SHOULDN'T BE THE BEST OF THE BEST.

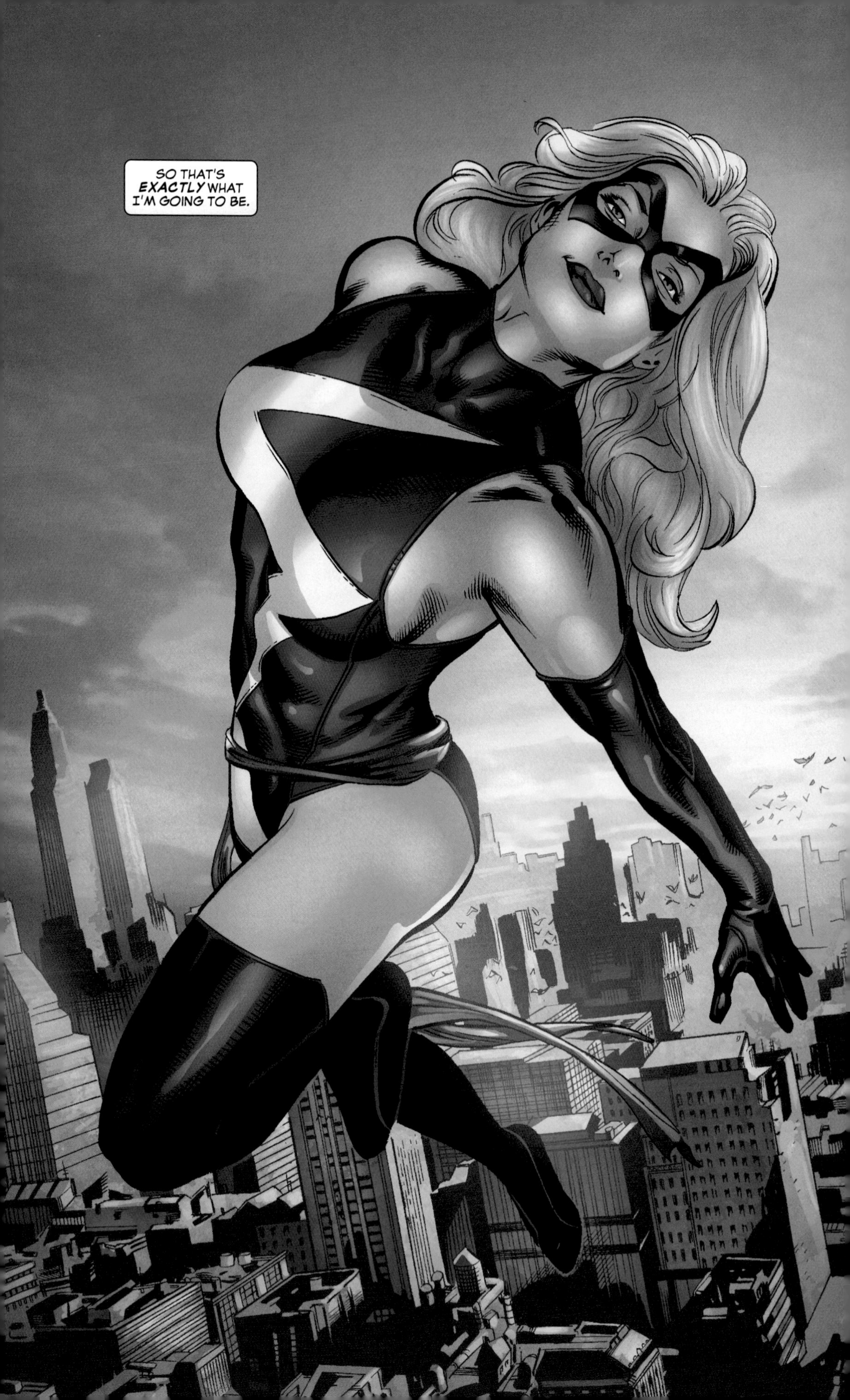
SO THAT'S EXACTLY WHAT I'M GOING TO BE.

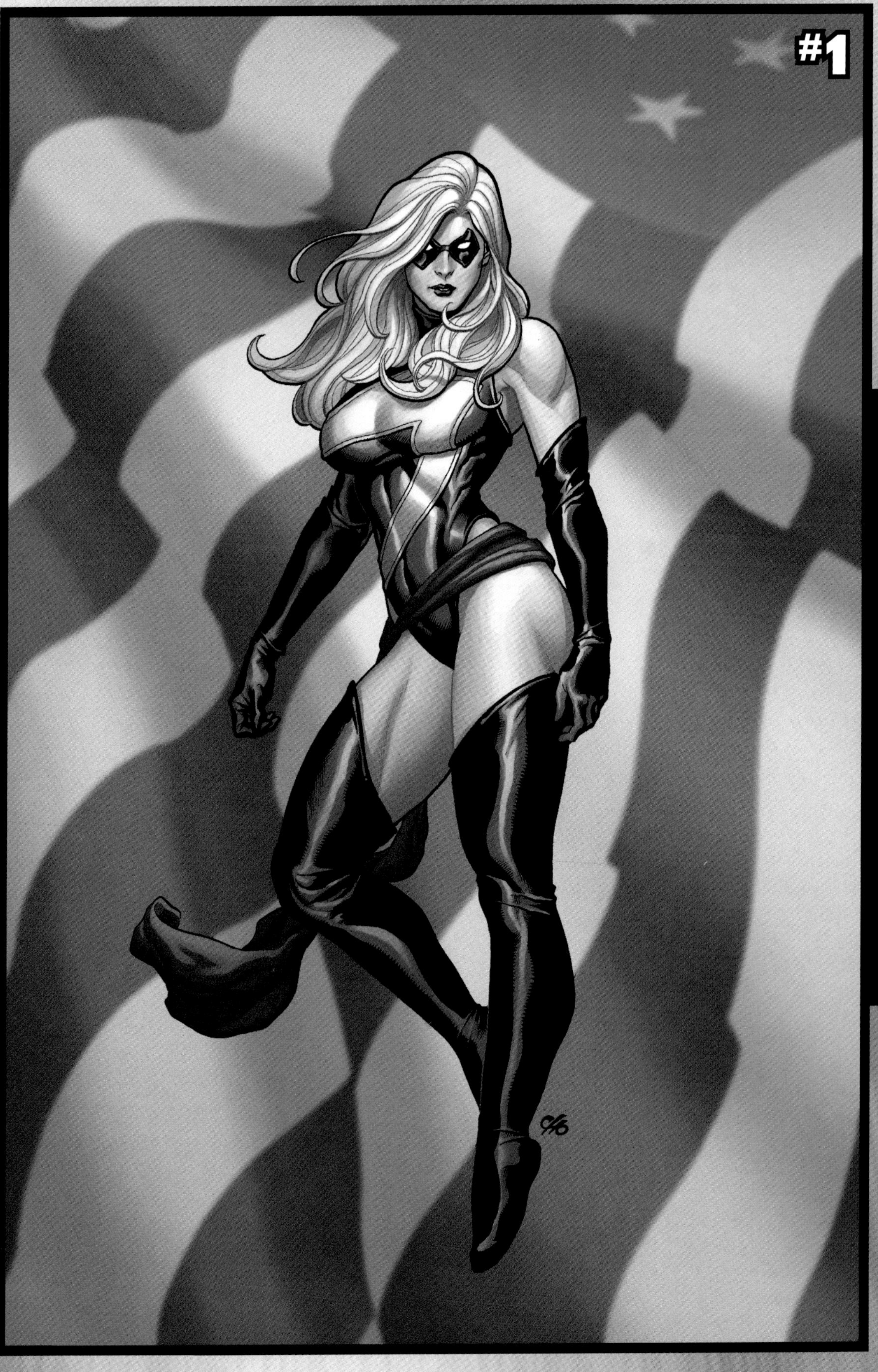
#1

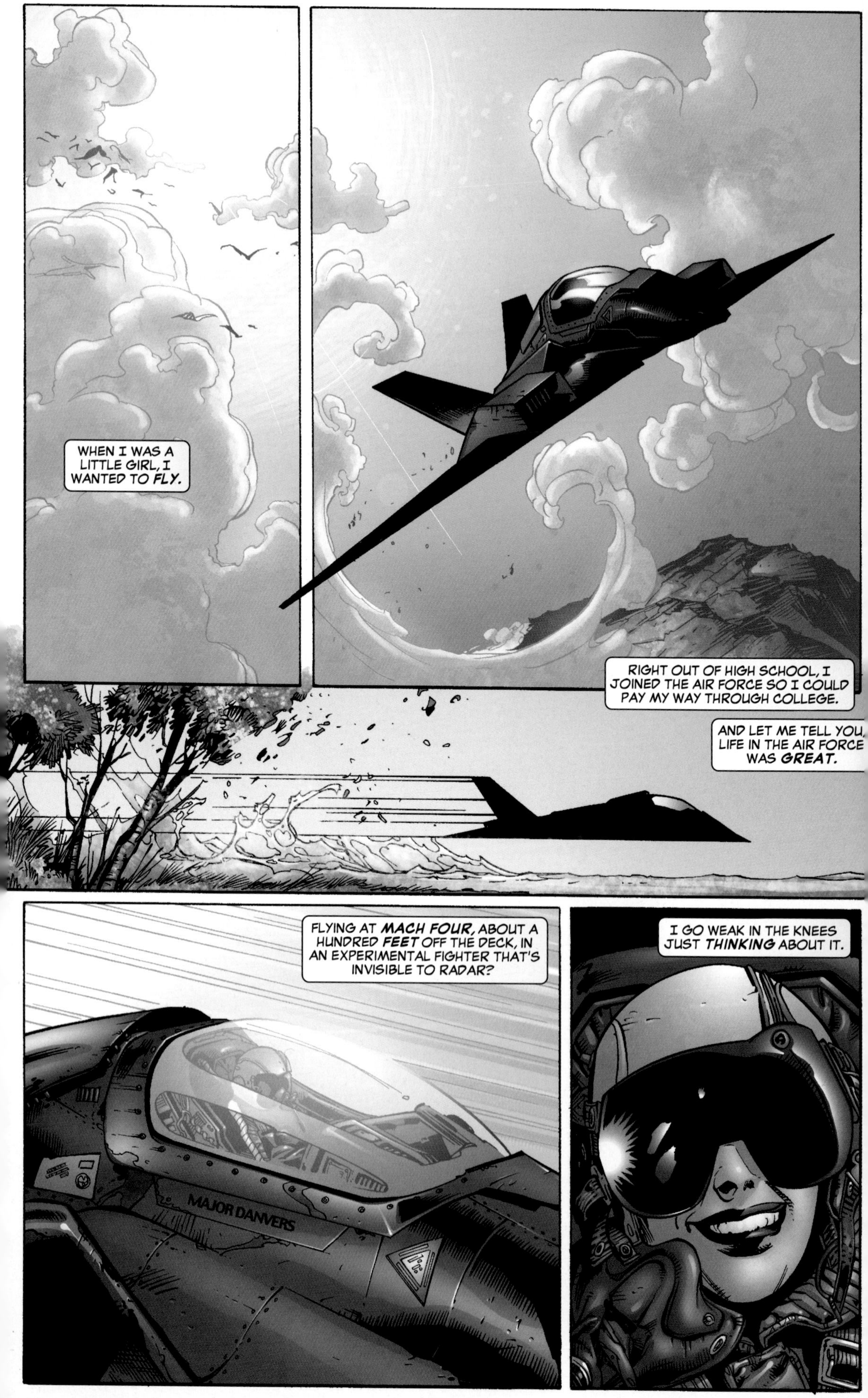
WHEN I WAS A LITTLE GIRL, I WANTED TO *FLY.*
RIGHT OUT OF HIGH SCHOOL, I JOINED THE AIR FORCE SO I COULD PAY MY WAY THROUGH COLLEGE.
AND LET ME TELL YOU, LIFE IN THE AIR FORCE WAS *GREAT.*
FLYING AT *MACH FOUR,* ABOUT A HUNDRED *FEET* OFF THE DECK, IN AN EXPERIMENTAL FIGHTER THAT'S INVISIBLE TO RADAR?
MAJOR DANVERS
I GO WEAK IN THE KNEES JUST *THINKING* ABOUT IT.

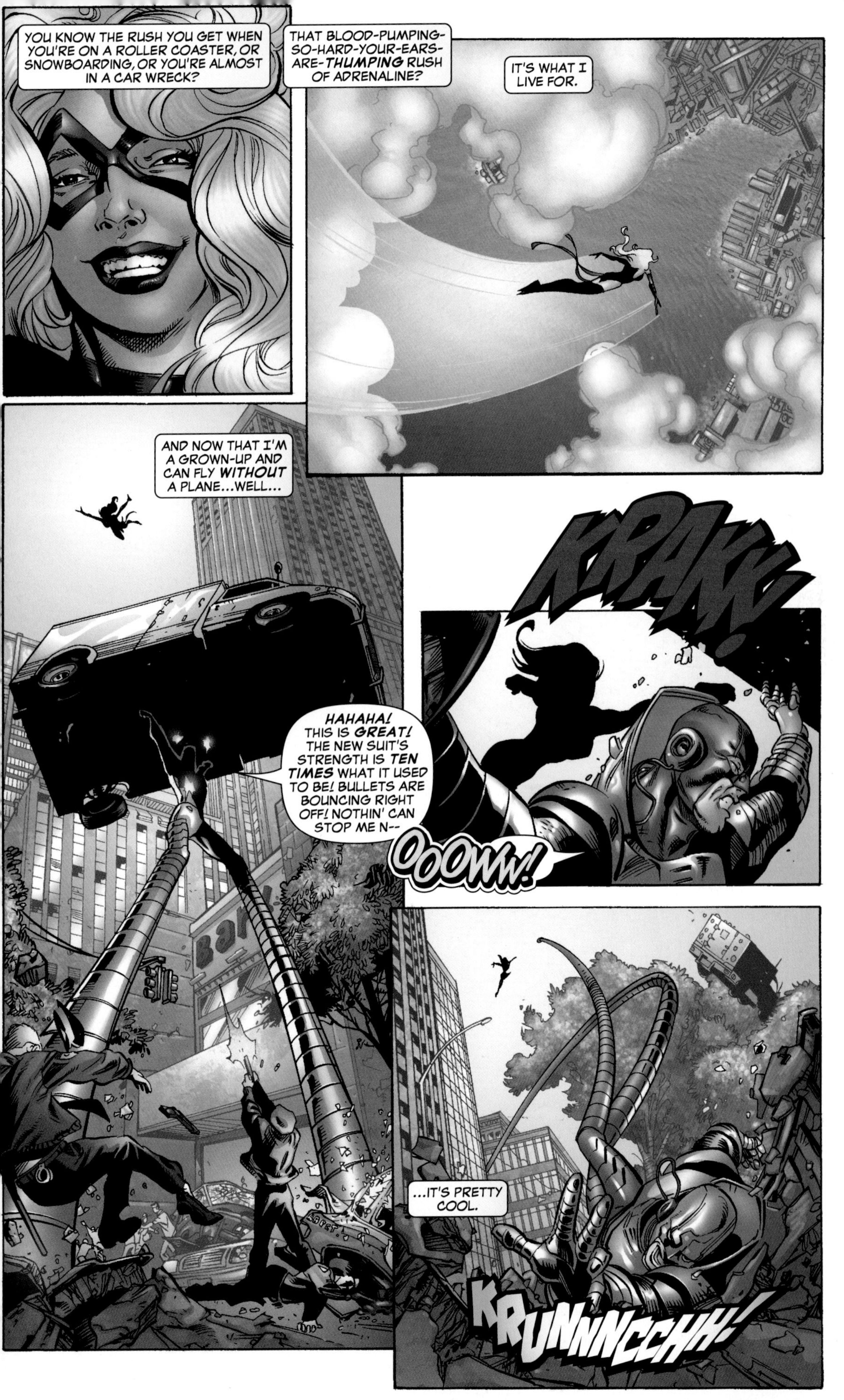

YOU KNOW THE RUSH YOU GET WHEN YOU'RE ON A ROLLER COASTER, OR SNOWBOARDING, OR YOU'RE ALMOST IN A CAR WRECK?
THAT BLOOD-PUMPING-SO-HARD-YOUR-EARS-ARE-*THUMPING* RUSH OF ADRENALINE?
IT'S WHAT I LIVE FOR.
AND NOW THAT I'M A GROWN-UP AND CAN FLY *WITHOUT* A PLANE...WELL...
HAHAHA! THIS IS *GREAT!* THE NEW SUIT'S STRENGTH IS *TEN TIMES* WHAT IT USED TO BE! BULLETS ARE BOUNCING RIGHT OFF! NOTHIN' CAN STOP ME N--
KRAKK!
OOOWW!
...IT'S PRETTY COOL.
KRUNNNCCHH!

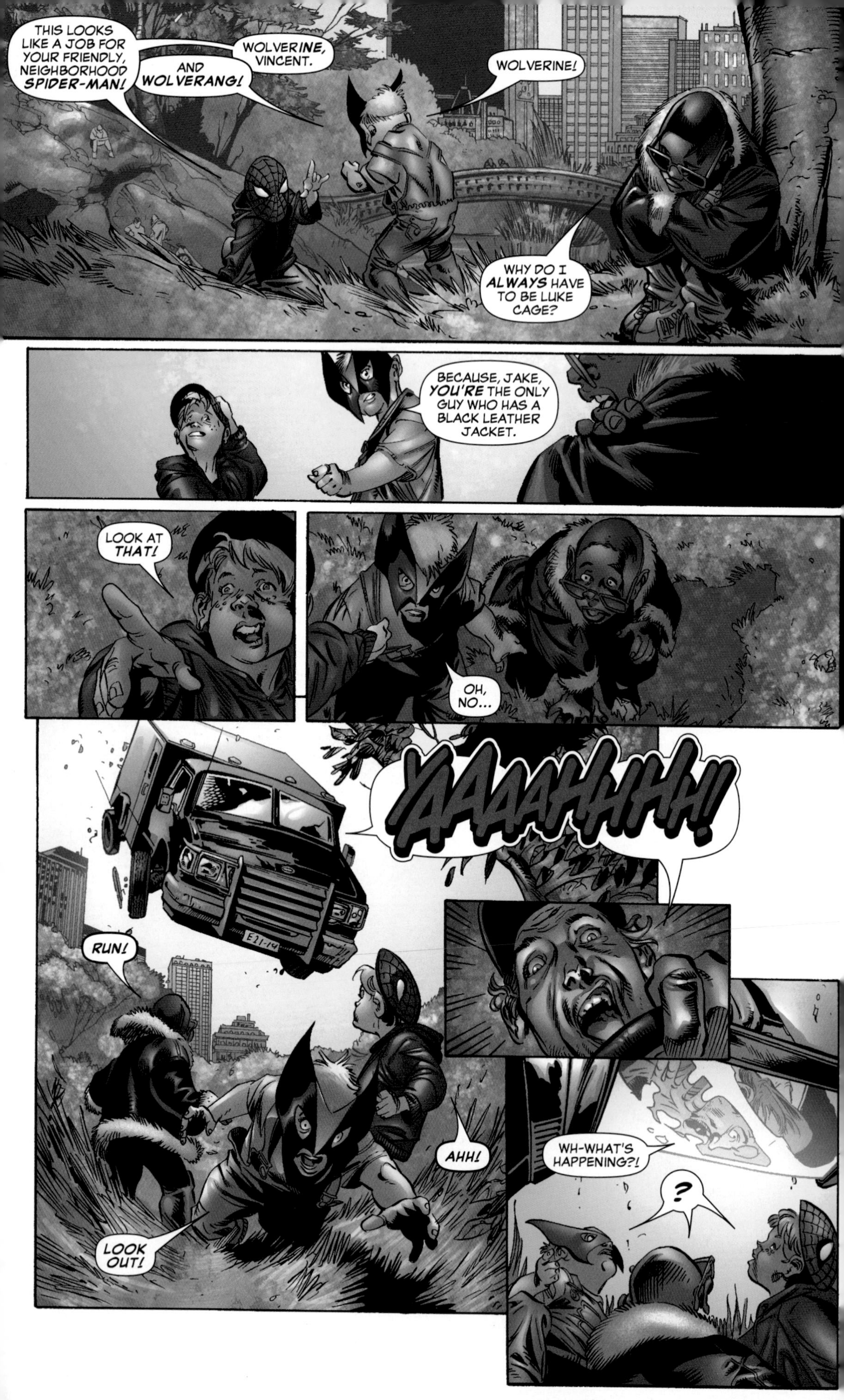
THIS LOOKS LIKE A JOB FOR YOUR FRIENDLY, NEIGHBORHOOD SPIDER-MAN!
AND WOLVERANG!
WOLVERINE, VINCENT.
WOLVERINE!
WHY DO I ALWAYS HAVE TO BE LUKE CAGE?
BECAUSE, JAKE, YOU'RE THE ONLY GUY WHO HAS A BLACK LEATHER JACKET.
LOOK AT THAT!
OH, NO...
YAAAAHHHH!
RUN!
AHH!
LOOK OUT!
WH-WHAT'S HAPPENING?!
?

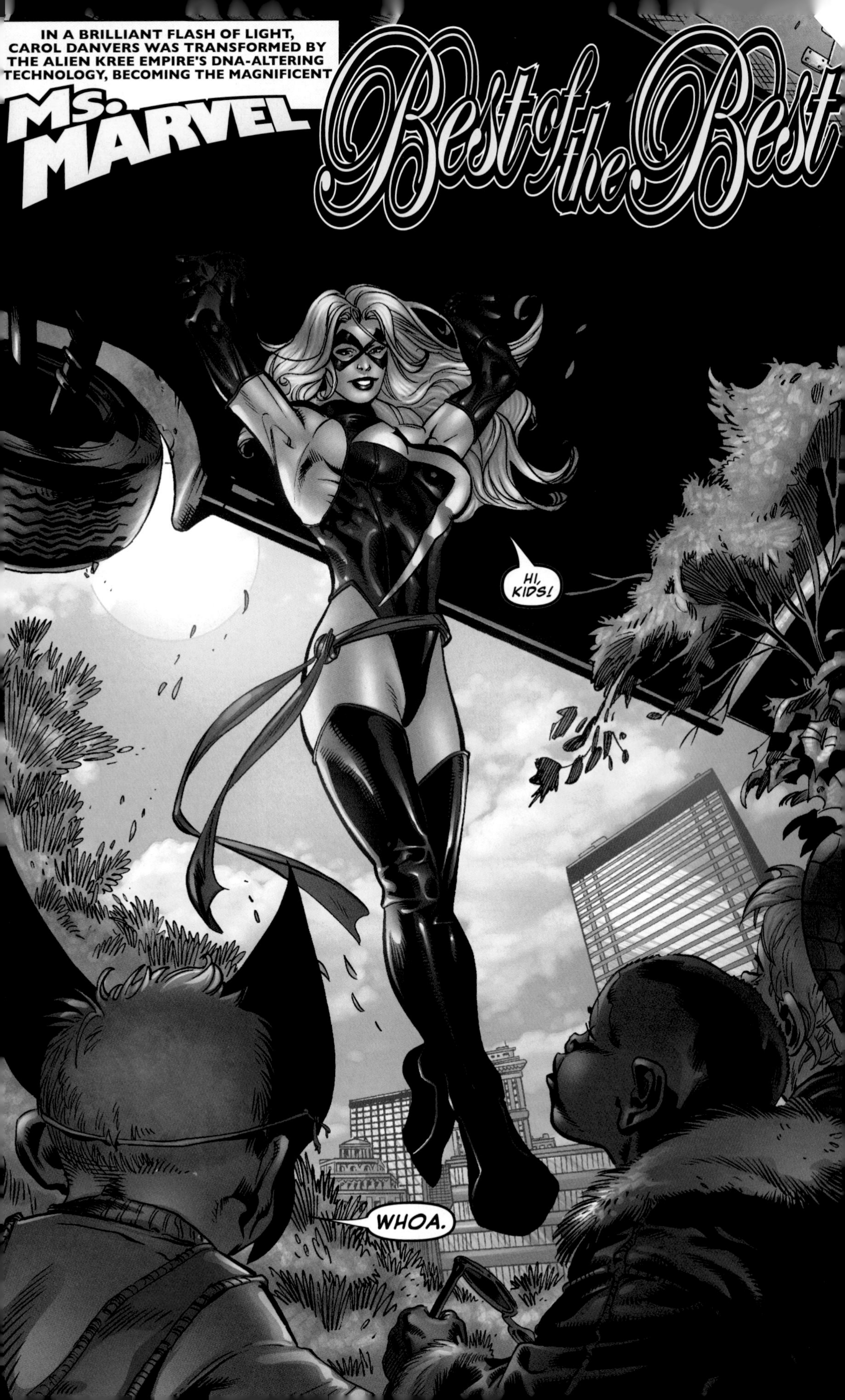
IN A BRILLIANT FLASH OF LIGHT, CAROL DANVERS WAS TRANSFORMED BY THE ALIEN KREE EMPIRE'S DNA-ALTERING TECHNOLOGY, BECOMING THE MAGNIFICENT
MS. MARVEL
Best of the Best
HI, KIDS!
WHOA.

ARE YOU OKAY?

I-- I--

I THOUGHT I WAS GONNA DIE!

YOU NEED TO TAKE A DEEP BREATH NOW, OKAY? AND YOU NEED TO LET GO OF--

BDOOM! BDOOM! BDOOM!

BEHIND YOU!

HANG ON. THERE'S SOME-THING I NEED TO DO.

HEY YOU!

I'M GONNA--

EVERYTHING--

--IS UNDER CONTROL.

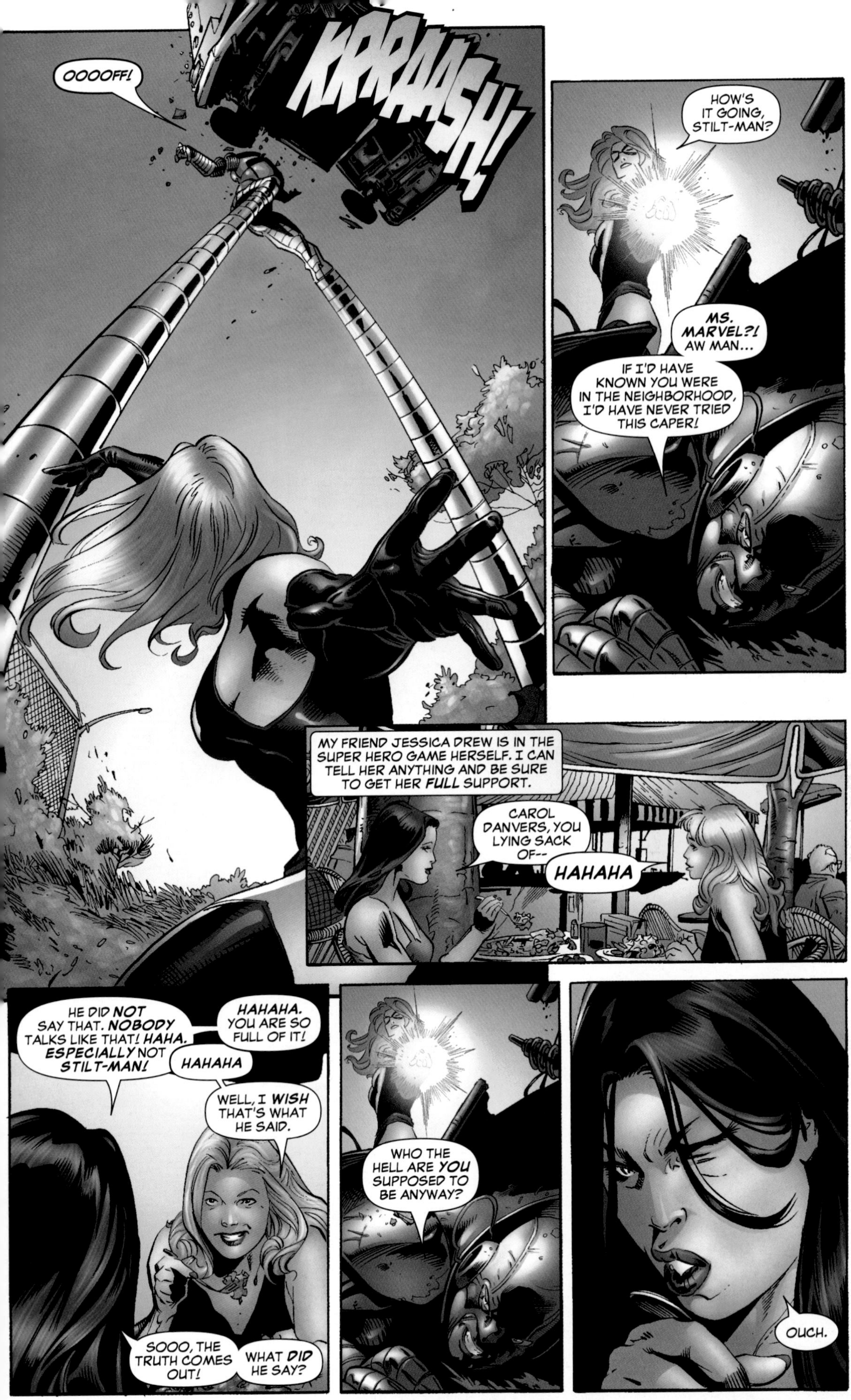
OOOOFF!
KRRAASH!
HOW'S IT GOING, STILT-MAN?
MS. MARVEL?! AW MAN...
IF I'D HAVE KNOWN YOU WERE IN THE NEIGHBORHOOD, I'D HAVE NEVER TRIED THIS CAPER!
MY FRIEND JESSICA DREW IS IN THE SUPER HERO GAME HERSELF. I CAN TELL HER ANYTHING AND BE SURE TO GET HER FULL SUPPORT.
CAROL DANVERS, YOU LYING SACK OF--
HAHAHA
HE DID NOT SAY THAT. NOBODY TALKS LIKE THAT! HAHA. ESPECIALLY NOT STILT-MAN!
HAHAHA. YOU ARE SO FULL OF IT!
HAHAHA
WELL, I WISH THAT'S WHAT HE SAID.
SOOO, THE TRUTH COMES OUT!
WHAT DID HE SAY?
WHO THE HELL ARE YOU SUPPOSED TO BE ANYWAY?
OUCH.

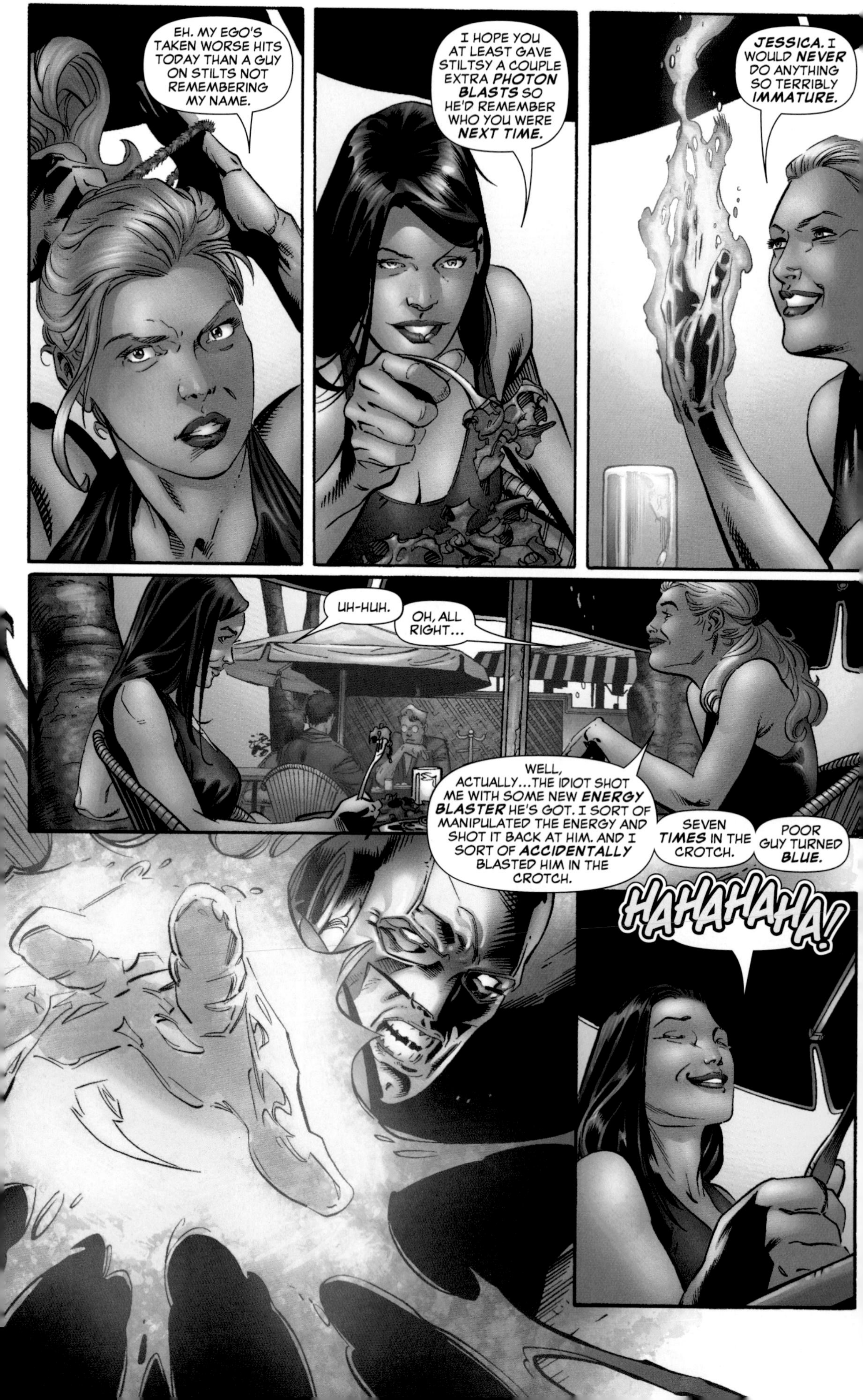
EH. MY EGO'S TAKEN WORSE HITS TODAY THAN A GUY ON STILTS NOT REMEMBERING MY NAME.
I HOPE YOU AT LEAST GAVE STILTSY A COUPLE EXTRA PHOTON BLASTS SO HE'D REMEMBER WHO YOU WERE NEXT TIME.
JESSICA. I WOULD NEVER DO ANYTHING SO TERRIBLY IMMATURE.
UH-HUH.
OH, ALL RIGHT...
WELL, ACTUALLY...THE IDIOT SHOT ME WITH SOME NEW ENERGY BLASTER HE'S GOT. I SORT OF MANIPULATED THE ENERGY AND SHOT IT BACK AT HIM. AND I SORT OF ACCIDENTALLY BLASTED HIM IN THE CROTCH.
SEVEN TIMES IN THE CROTCH.
POOR GUY TURNED BLUE.
HAHAHAHA!

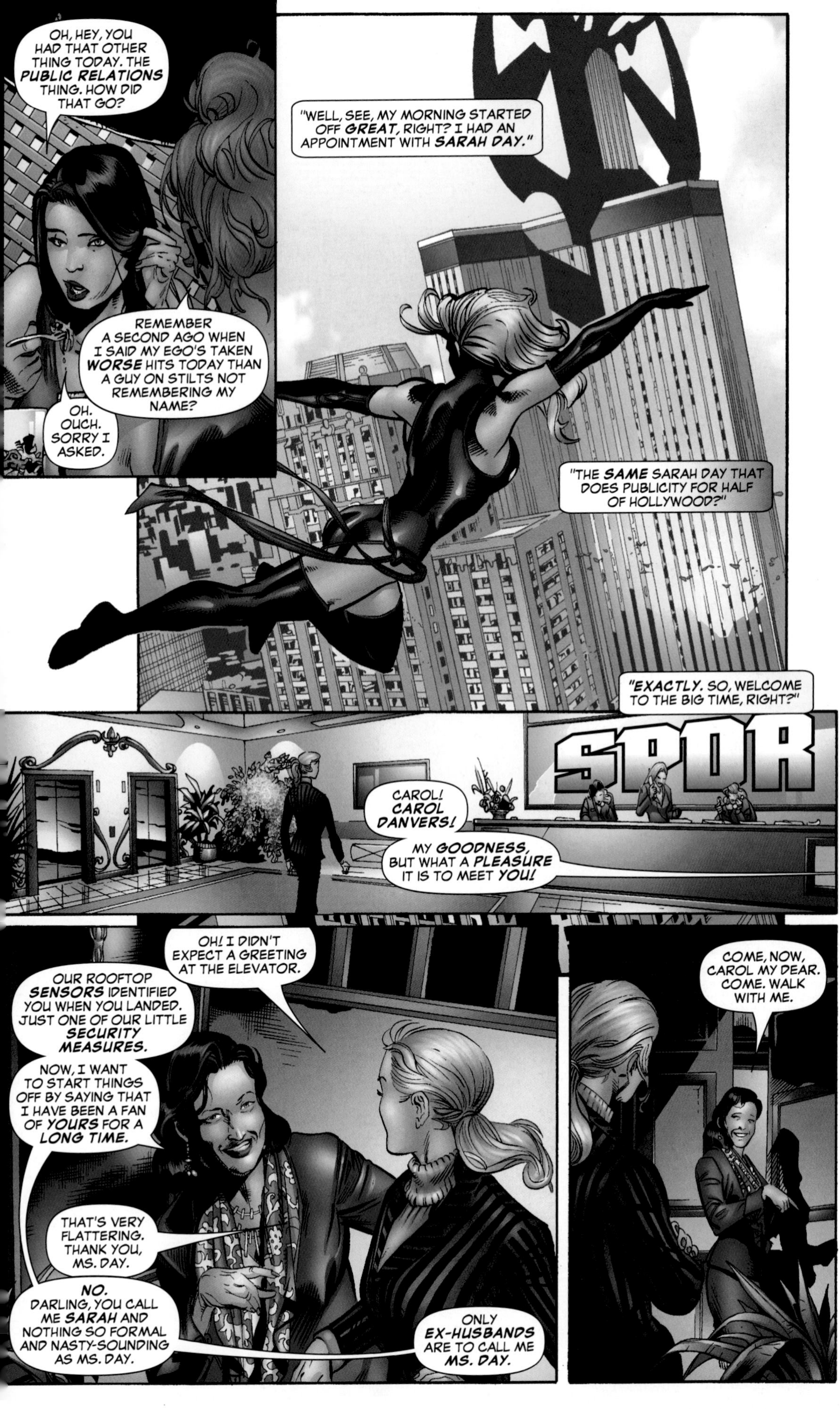
OH, HEY, YOU HAD THAT OTHER THING TODAY. THE PUBLIC RELATIONS THING. HOW DID THAT GO?
"WELL, SEE, MY MORNING STARTED OFF GREAT, RIGHT? I HAD AN APPOINTMENT WITH SARAH DAY."
REMEMBER A SECOND AGO WHEN I SAID MY EGO'S TAKEN WORSE HITS TODAY THAN A GUY ON STILTS NOT REMEMBERING MY NAME?
OH. OUCH. SORRY I ASKED.
"THE SAME SARAH DAY THAT DOES PUBLICITY FOR HALF OF HOLLYWOOD?"
"EXACTLY. SO, WELCOME TO THE BIG TIME, RIGHT?"
SPDR
CAROL! CAROL DANVERS!
MY GOODNESS, BUT WHAT A PLEASURE IT IS TO MEET YOU!
OH! I DIDN'T EXPECT A GREETING AT THE ELEVATOR.
OUR ROOFTOP SENSORS IDENTIFIED YOU WHEN YOU LANDED. JUST ONE OF OUR LITTLE SECURITY MEASURES.
NOW, I WANT TO START THINGS OFF BY SAYING THAT I HAVE BEEN A FAN OF YOURS FOR A LONG TIME.
THAT'S VERY FLATTERING. THANK YOU, MS. DAY.
NO. DARLING, YOU CALL ME SARAH AND NOTHING SO FORMAL AND NASTY-SOUNDING AS MS. DAY.
ONLY EX-HUSBANDS ARE TO CALL ME MS. DAY.
COME, NOW, CAROL MY DEAR. COME. WALK WITH ME.

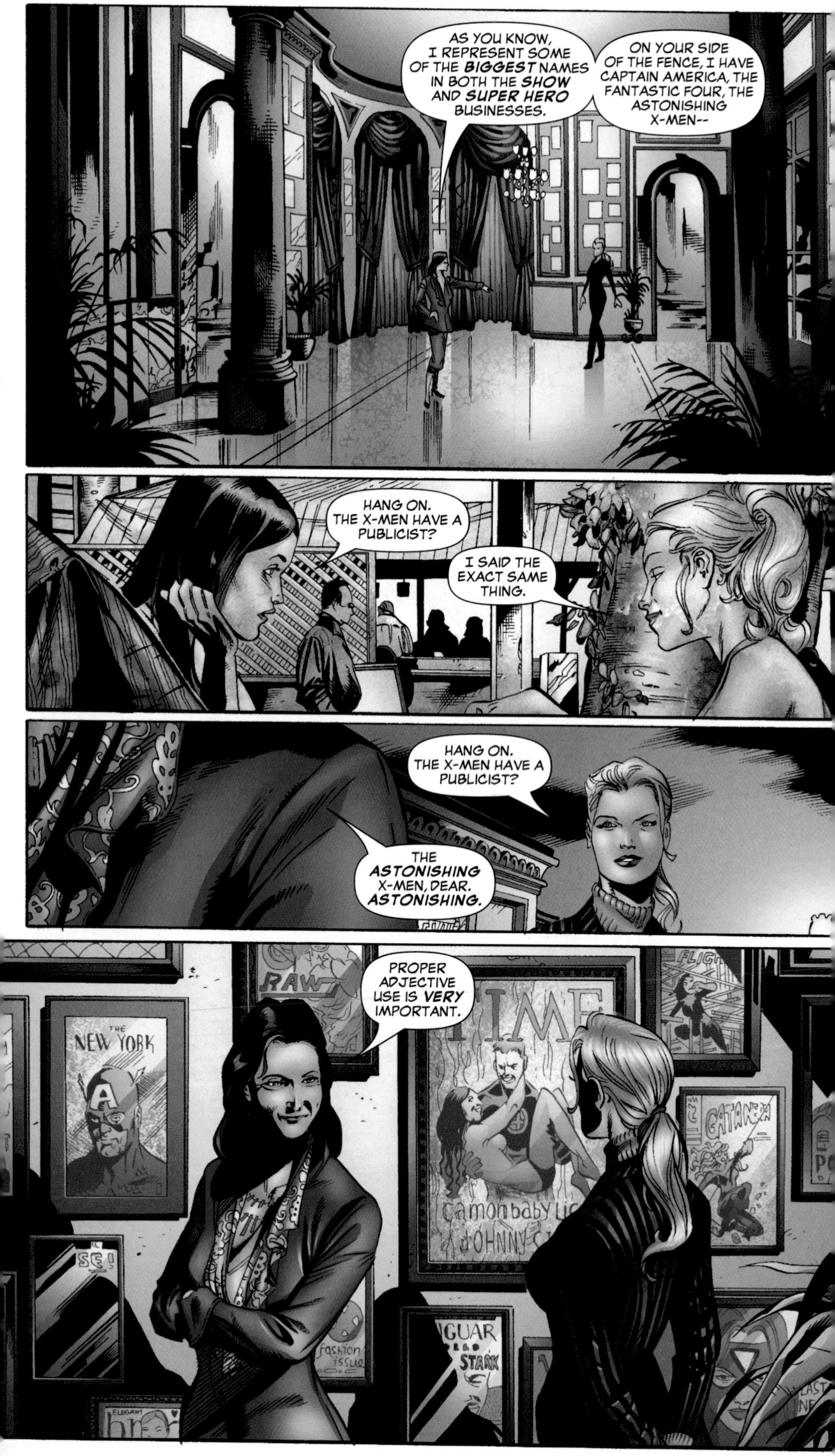
AS YOU KNOW, I REPRESENT SOME OF THE BIGGEST NAMES IN BOTH THE SHOW AND SUPER HERO BUSINESSES.
ON YOUR SIDE OF THE FENCE, I HAVE CAPTAIN AMERICA, THE FANTASTIC FOUR, THE ASTONISHING X-MEN--
HANG ON. THE X-MEN HAVE A PUBLICIST?
I SAID THE EXACT SAME THING.
HANG ON. THE X-MEN HAVE A PUBLICIST?
THE ASTONISHING X-MEN, DEAR. ASTONISHING.
PROPER ADJECTIVE USE IS VERY IMPORTANT.

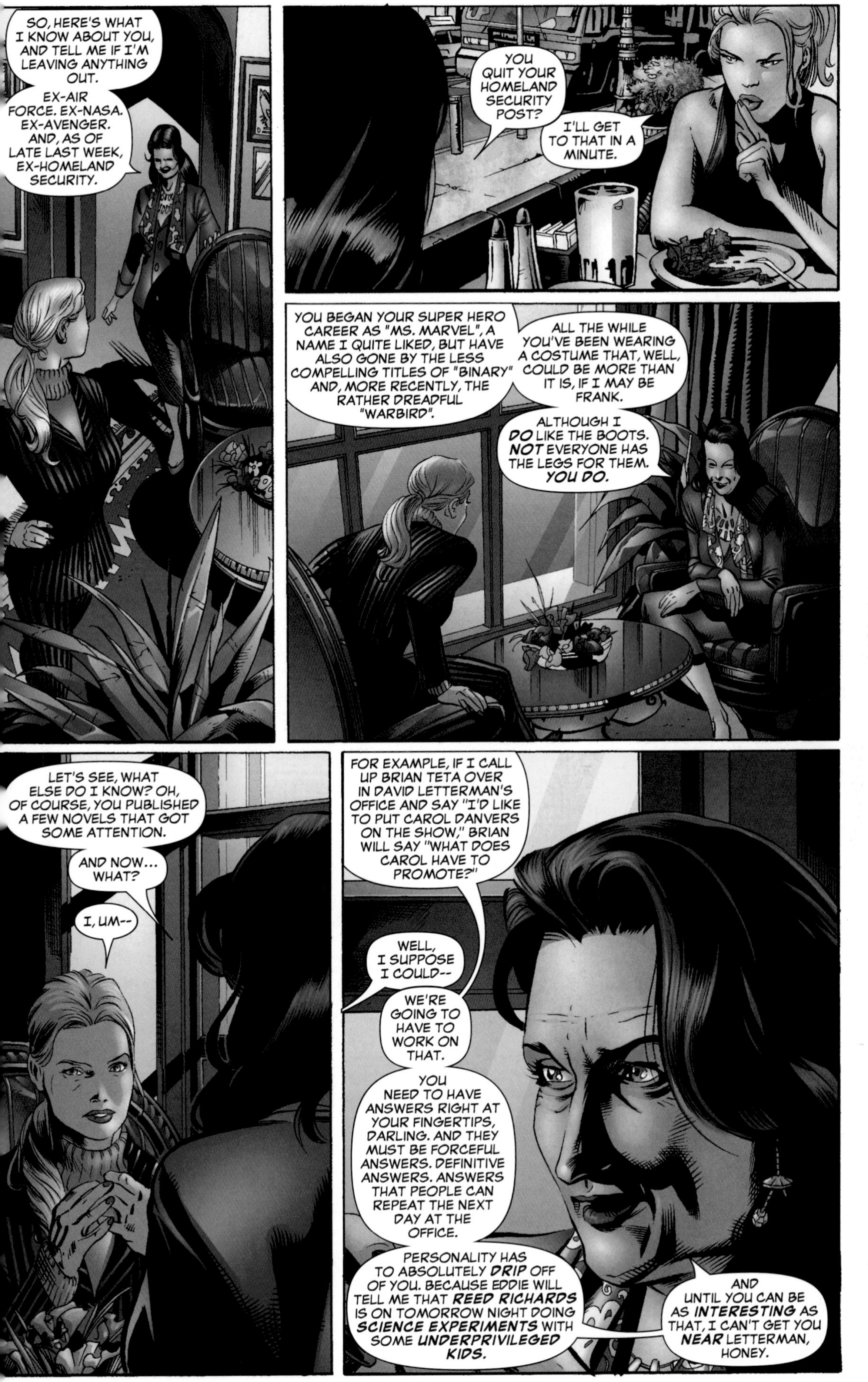
SO, HERE'S WHAT I KNOW ABOUT YOU, AND TELL ME IF I'M LEAVING ANYTHING OUT.
EX-AIR FORCE. EX-NASA. EX-AVENGER. AND, AS OF LATE LAST WEEK, EX-HOMELAND SECURITY.
YOU QUIT YOUR HOMELAND SECURITY POST?
I'LL GET TO THAT IN A MINUTE.
YOU BEGAN YOUR SUPER HERO CAREER AS "MS. MARVEL", A NAME I QUITE LIKED, BUT HAVE ALSO GONE BY THE LESS COMPELLING TITLES OF "BINARY" AND, MORE RECENTLY, THE RATHER DREADFUL "WARBIRD".
ALL THE WHILE YOU'VE BEEN WEARING A COSTUME THAT, WELL, COULD BE MORE THAN IT IS, IF I MAY BE FRANK.
ALTHOUGH I ***DO*** LIKE THE BOOTS. ***NOT*** EVERYONE HAS THE LEGS FOR THEM. ***YOU DO.***
LET'S SEE, WHAT ELSE DO I KNOW? OH, OF COURSE, YOU PUBLISHED A FEW NOVELS THAT GOT SOME ATTENTION.
AND NOW... WHAT?
I, UM--
FOR EXAMPLE, IF I CALL UP BRIAN TETA OVER IN DAVID LETTERMAN'S OFFICE AND SAY "I'D LIKE TO PUT CAROL DANVERS ON THE SHOW," BRIAN WILL SAY "WHAT DOES CAROL HAVE TO PROMOTE?"
WELL, I SUPPOSE I COULD--
WE'RE GOING TO HAVE TO WORK ON THAT.
YOU NEED TO HAVE ANSWERS RIGHT AT YOUR FINGERTIPS, DARLING. AND THEY MUST BE FORCEFUL ANSWERS. DEFINITIVE ANSWERS. ANSWERS THAT PEOPLE CAN REPEAT THE NEXT DAY AT THE OFFICE.
PERSONALITY HAS TO ABSOLUTELY ***DRIP*** OFF OF YOU. BECAUSE EDDIE WILL TELL ME THAT ***REED RICHARDS*** IS ON TOMORROW NIGHT DOING ***SCIENCE EXPERIMENTS*** WITH SOME ***UNDERPRIVILEGED KIDS.***
AND UNTIL YOU CAN BE AS ***INTERESTING*** AS THAT, I CAN'T GET YOU ***NEAR*** LETTERMAN, HONEY.

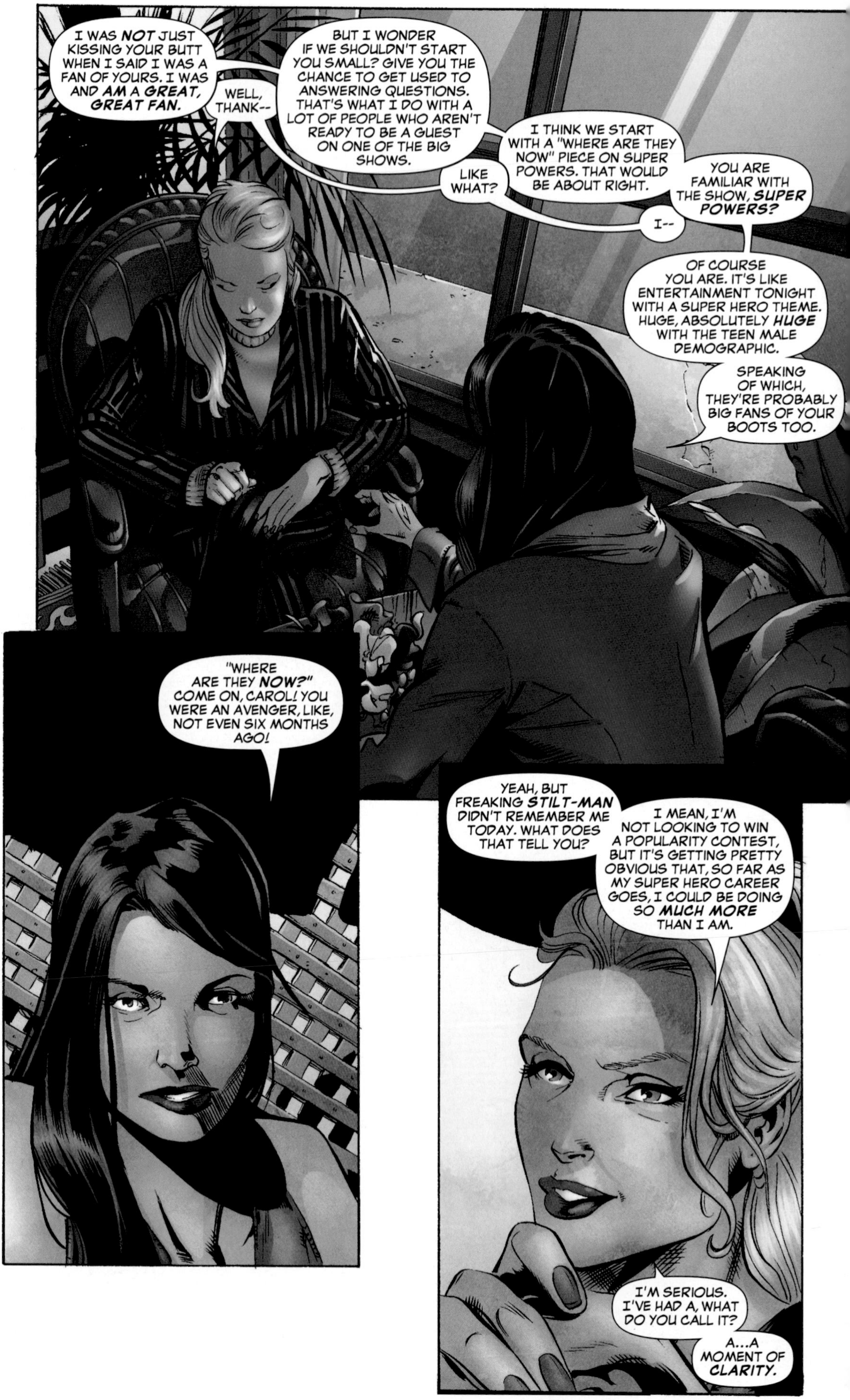
I WAS **NOT** JUST KISSING YOUR BUTT WHEN I SAID I WAS A FAN OF YOURS. I WAS AND **AM** A **GREAT, GREAT FAN.**
WELL, THANK--
BUT I WONDER IF WE SHOULDN'T START YOU SMALL? GIVE YOU THE CHANCE TO GET USED TO ANSWERING QUESTIONS. THAT'S WHAT I DO WITH A LOT OF PEOPLE WHO AREN'T READY TO BE A GUEST ON ONE OF THE BIG SHOWS.
LIKE WHAT?
I THINK WE START WITH A "WHERE ARE THEY NOW" PIECE ON SUPER POWERS. THAT WOULD BE ABOUT RIGHT.
YOU ARE FAMILIAR WITH THE SHOW, **SUPER POWERS?**
I--
OF COURSE YOU ARE. IT'S LIKE ENTERTAINMENT TONIGHT WITH A SUPER HERO THEME. HUGE, ABSOLUTELY **HUGE** WITH THE TEEN MALE DEMOGRAPHIC.
SPEAKING OF WHICH, THEY'RE PROBABLY BIG FANS OF YOUR BOOTS TOO.
"WHERE ARE THEY **NOW?**" COME ON, CAROL! YOU WERE AN AVENGER, LIKE, NOT EVEN SIX MONTHS AGO!
YEAH, BUT FREAKING **STILT-MAN** DIDN'T REMEMBER ME TODAY. WHAT DOES THAT TELL YOU?
I MEAN, I'M NOT LOOKING TO WIN A POPULARITY CONTEST, BUT IT'S GETTING PRETTY OBVIOUS THAT, SO FAR AS MY SUPER HERO CAREER GOES, I COULD BE DOING SO **MUCH MORE** THAN I AM.
I'M SERIOUS. I'VE HAD A, WHAT DO YOU CALL IT?
A...A MOMENT OF **CLARITY.**

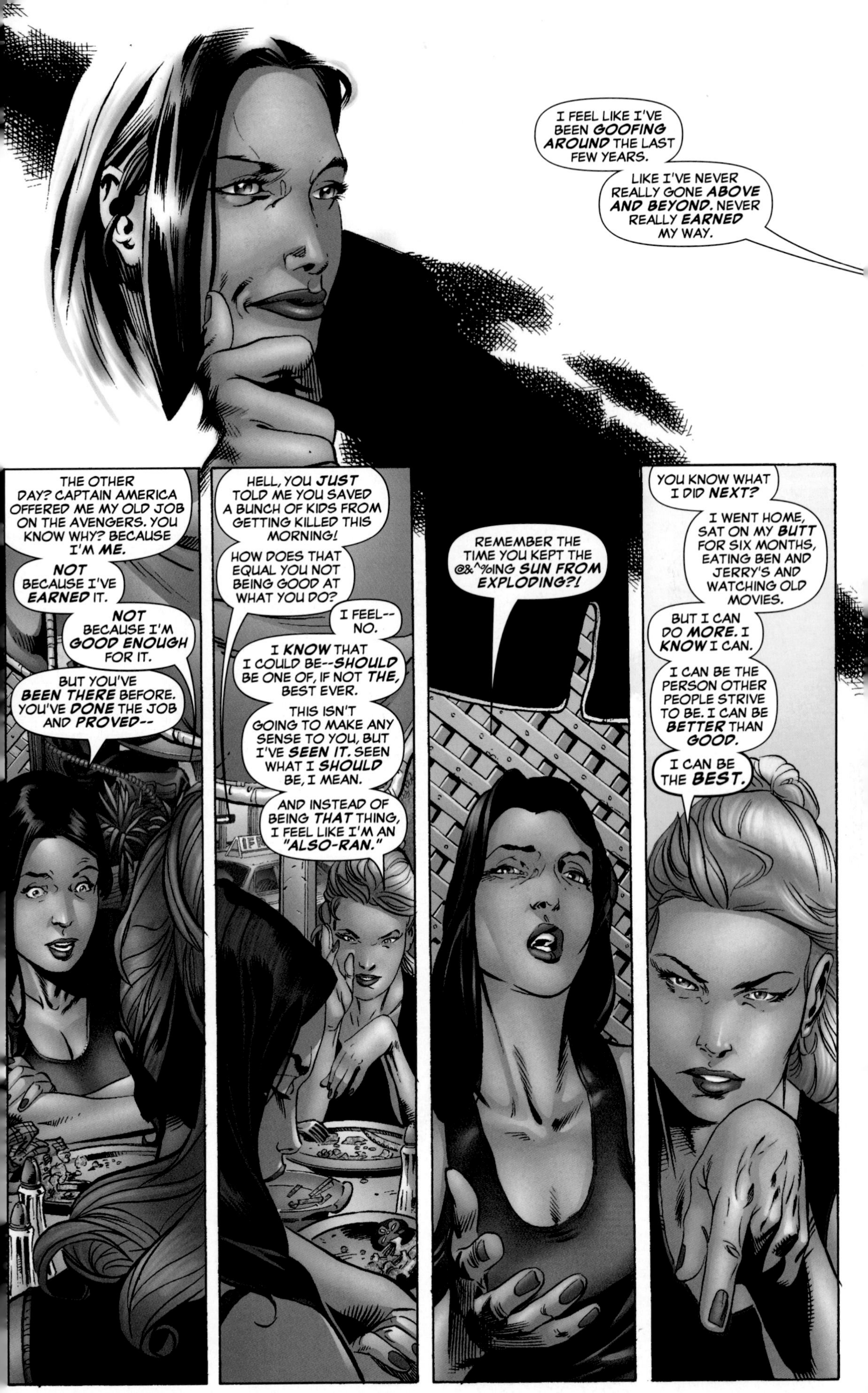

I FEEL LIKE I'VE BEEN GOOFING AROUND THE LAST FEW YEARS.
LIKE I'VE NEVER REALLY GONE ABOVE AND BEYOND. NEVER REALLY EARNED MY WAY.
THE OTHER DAY? CAPTAIN AMERICA OFFERED ME MY OLD JOB ON THE AVENGERS. YOU KNOW WHY? BECAUSE I'M ME.
NOT BECAUSE I'VE EARNED IT.
NOT BECAUSE I'M GOOD ENOUGH FOR IT.
BUT YOU'VE BEEN THERE BEFORE. YOU'VE DONE THE JOB AND PROVED--
HELL, YOU JUST TOLD ME YOU SAVED A BUNCH OF KIDS FROM GETTING KILLED THIS MORNING!
HOW DOES THAT EQUAL YOU NOT BEING GOOD AT WHAT YOU DO?
I FEEL-- NO.
I KNOW THAT I COULD BE--SHOULD BE ONE OF, IF NOT THE, BEST EVER.
THIS ISN'T GOING TO MAKE ANY SENSE TO YOU, BUT I'VE SEEN IT. SEEN WHAT I SHOULD BE, I MEAN.
AND INSTEAD OF BEING THAT THING, I FEEL LIKE I'M AN "ALSO-RAN."
REMEMBER THE TIME YOU KEPT THE @&^%ING SUN FROM EXPLODING?!
YOU KNOW WHAT I DID NEXT?
I WENT HOME, SAT ON MY BUTT FOR SIX MONTHS, EATING BEN AND JERRY'S AND WATCHING OLD MOVIES.
BUT I CAN DO MORE. I KNOW I CAN.
I CAN BE THE PERSON OTHER PEOPLE STRIVE TO BE. I CAN BE BETTER THAN GOOD.
I CAN BE THE BEST.

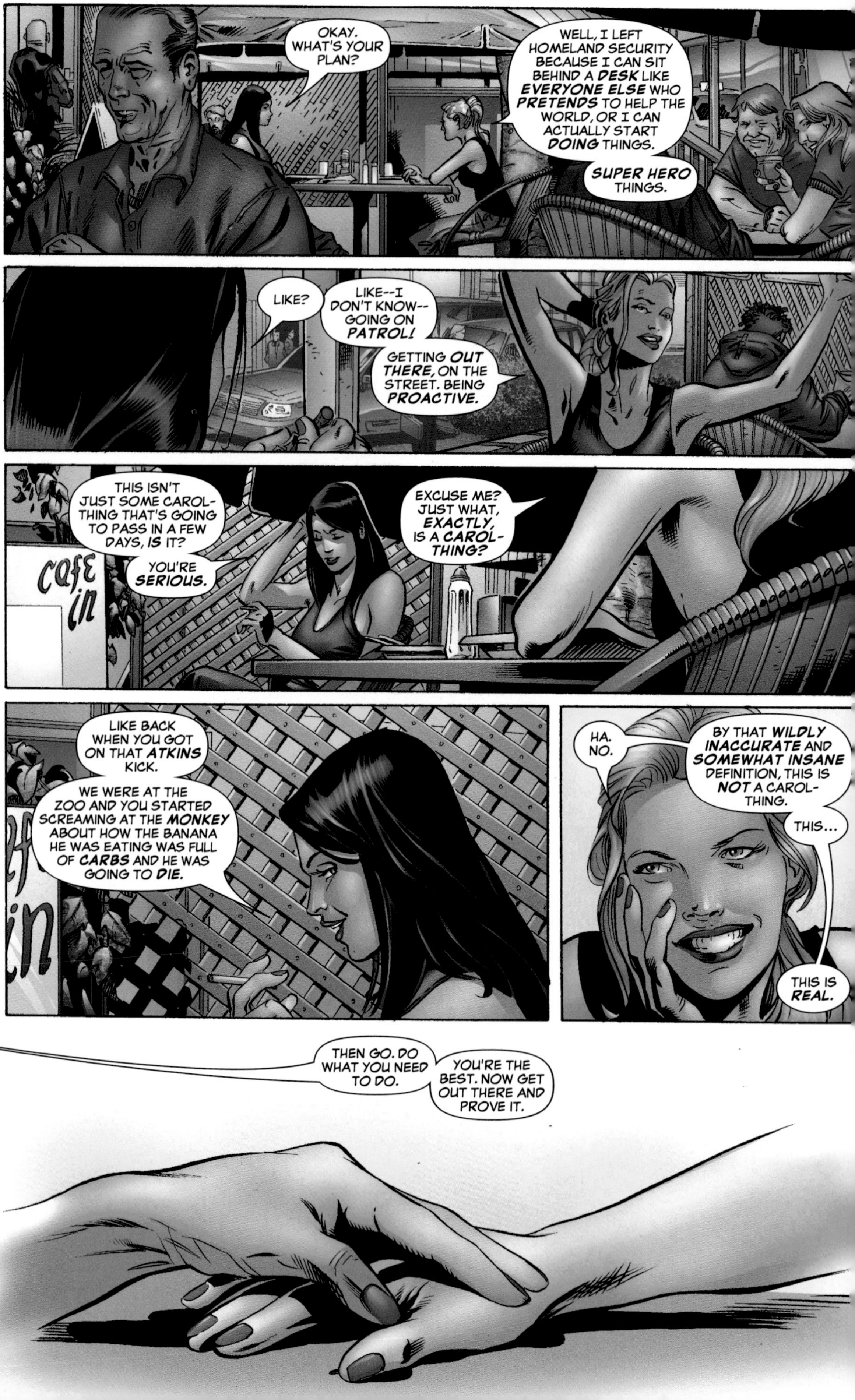
OKAY. WHAT'S YOUR PLAN?
WELL, I LEFT HOMELAND SECURITY BECAUSE I CAN SIT BEHIND A DESK LIKE EVERYONE ELSE WHO PRETENDS TO HELP THE WORLD, OR I CAN ACTUALLY START DOING THINGS.
SUPER HERO THINGS.
LIKE?
LIKE--I DON'T KNOW-- GOING ON PATROL!
GETTING OUT THERE, ON THE STREET. BEING PROACTIVE.
THIS ISN'T JUST SOME CAROL-THING THAT'S GOING TO PASS IN A FEW DAYS, IS IT?
YOU'RE SERIOUS.
EXCUSE ME? JUST WHAT, EXACTLY, IS A CAROL-THING?
CAFE IN
LIKE BACK WHEN YOU GOT ON THAT ATKINS KICK.
WE WERE AT THE ZOO AND YOU STARTED SCREAMING AT THE MONKEY ABOUT HOW THE BANANA HE WAS EATING WAS FULL OF CARBS AND HE WAS GOING TO DIE.
HA. NO.
BY THAT WILDLY INACCURATE AND SOMEWHAT INSANE DEFINITION, THIS IS NOT A CAROL-THING.
THIS...
THIS IS REAL.
THEN GO. DO WHAT YOU NEED TO DO.
YOU'RE THE BEST. NOW GET OUT THERE AND PROVE IT.

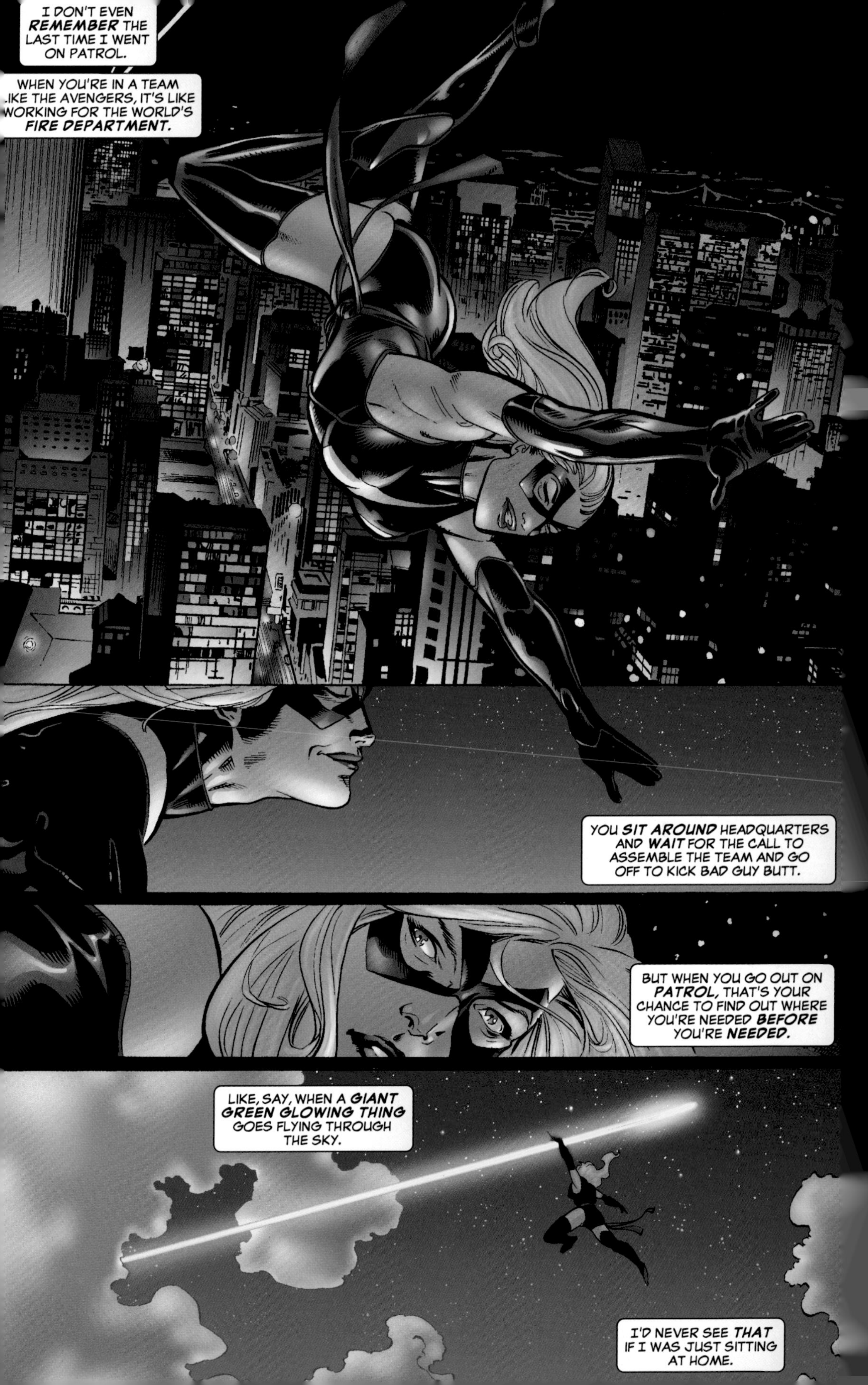
I DON'T EVEN REMEMBER THE LAST TIME I WENT ON PATROL.
WHEN YOU'RE IN A TEAM LIKE THE AVENGERS, IT'S LIKE WORKING FOR THE WORLD'S FIRE DEPARTMENT.
YOU SIT AROUND HEADQUARTERS AND WAIT FOR THE CALL TO ASSEMBLE THE TEAM AND GO OFF TO KICK BAD GUY BUTT.
BUT WHEN YOU GO OUT ON PATROL, THAT'S YOUR CHANCE TO FIND OUT WHERE YOU'RE NEEDED BEFORE YOU'RE NEEDED.
LIKE, SAY, WHEN A GIANT GREEN GLOWING THING GOES FLYING THROUGH THE SKY.
I'D NEVER SEE THAT IF I WAS JUST SITTING AT HOME.

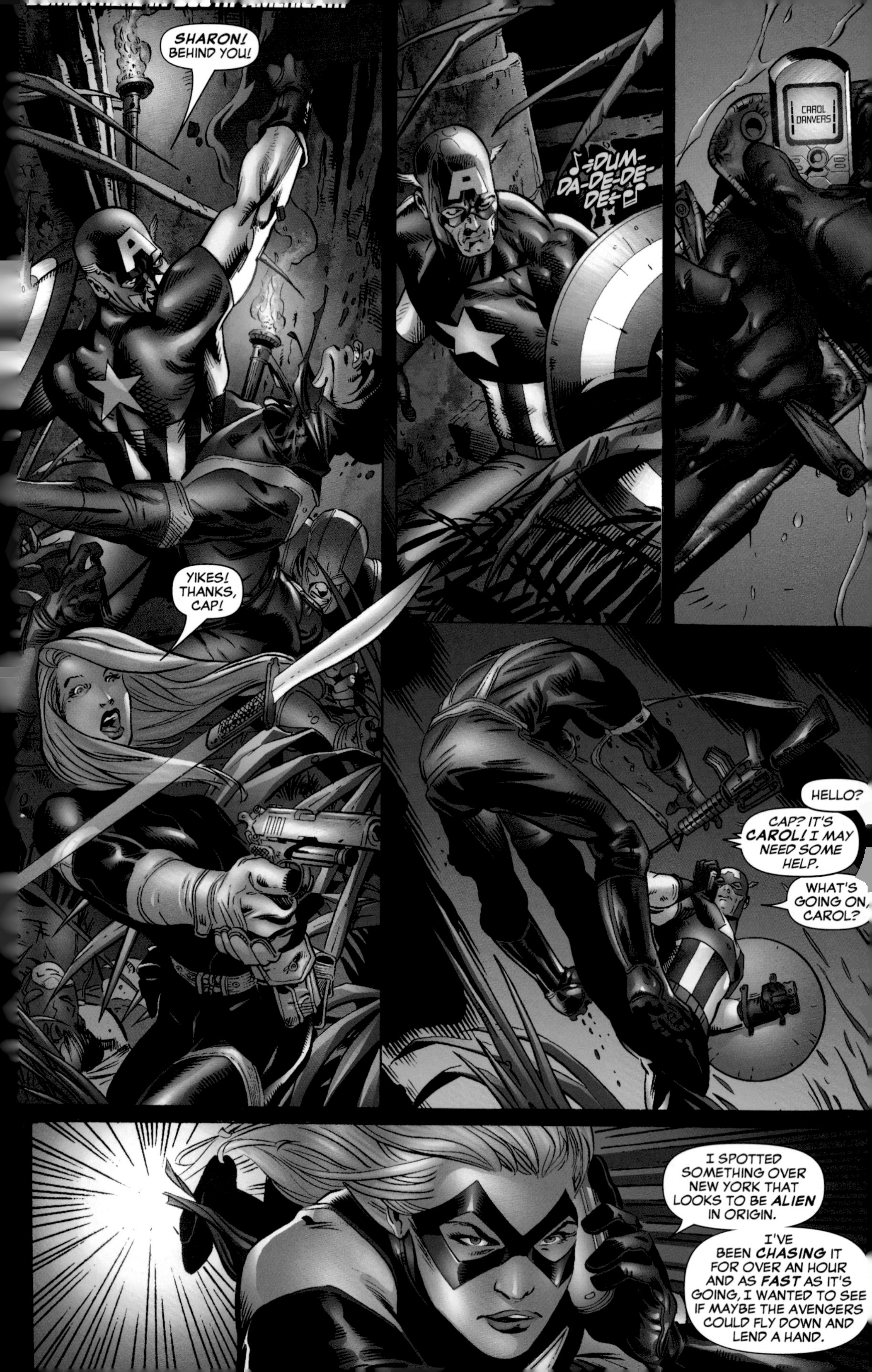

SHARON! BEHIND YOU!
DUM-DA-DE-DE-DE
CAROL DANVERS
YIKES! THANKS, CAP!
HELLO?
CAP? IT'S CAROL! I MAY NEED SOME HELP.
WHAT'S GOING ON, CAROL?
I SPOTTED SOMETHING OVER NEW YORK THAT LOOKS TO BE ALIEN IN ORIGIN.
I'VE BEEN CHASING IT FOR OVER AN HOUR AND AS FAST AS IT'S GOING, I WANTED TO SEE IF MAYBE THE AVENGERS COULD FLY DOWN AND LEND A HAND.

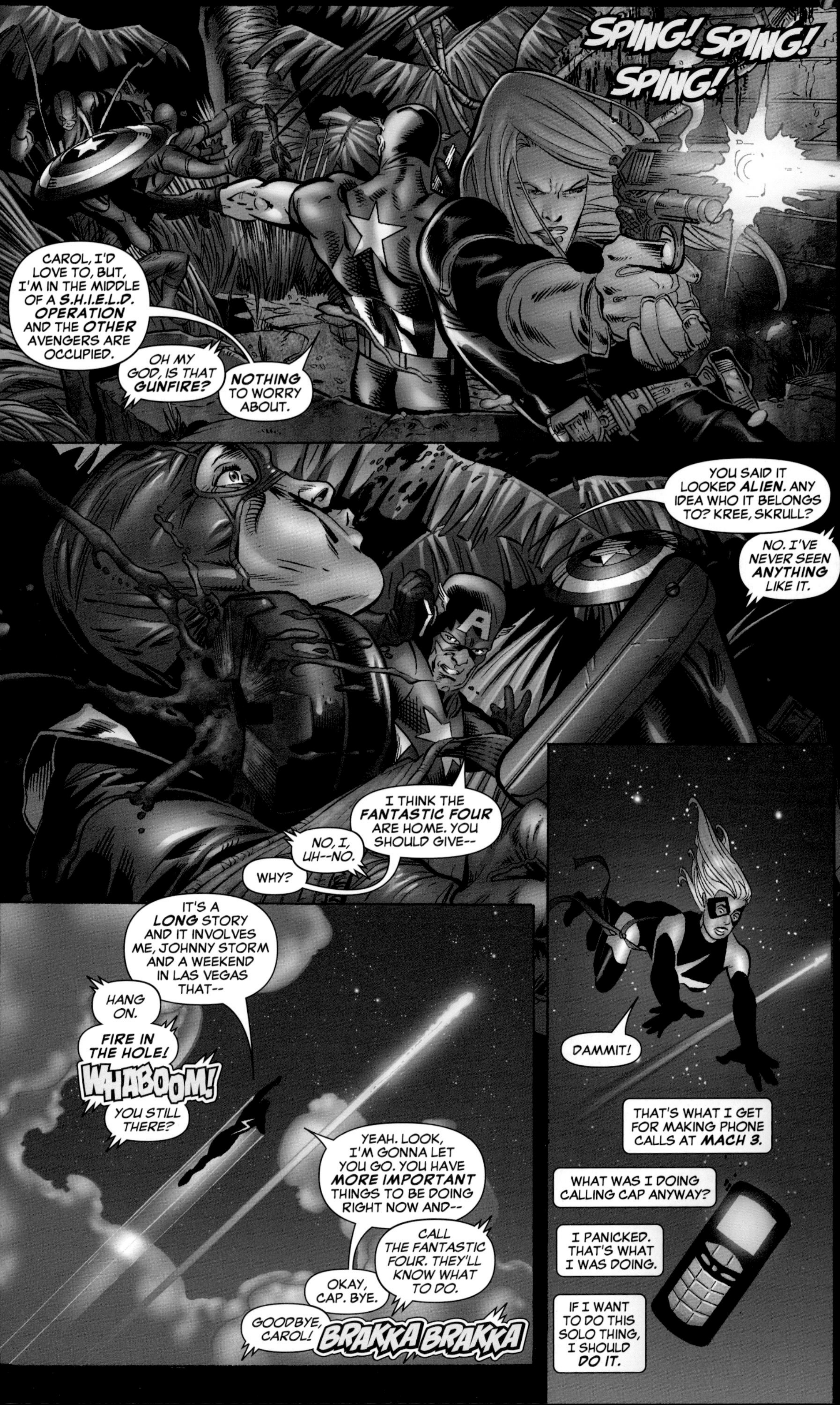
SPING! SPING! SPING!
CAROL, I'D LOVE TO, BUT, I'M IN THE MIDDLE OF A S.H.I.E.L.D. OPERATION AND THE OTHER AVENGERS ARE OCCUPIED.
OH MY GOD, IS THAT GUNFIRE?
NOTHING TO WORRY ABOUT.
YOU SAID IT LOOKED ALIEN. ANY IDEA WHO IT BELONGS TO? KREE, SKRULL?
NO. I'VE NEVER SEEN ANYTHING LIKE IT.
I THINK THE FANTASTIC FOUR ARE HOME. YOU SHOULD GIVE--
NO, I, UH--NO.
WHY?
IT'S A LONG STORY AND IT INVOLVES ME, JOHNNY STORM AND A WEEKEND IN LAS VEGAS THAT--
HANG ON.
FIRE IN THE HOLE!
WHABOOM!
YOU STILL THERE?
YEAH. LOOK, I'M GONNA LET YOU GO. YOU HAVE MORE IMPORTANT THINGS TO BE DOING RIGHT NOW AND--
CALL THE FANTASTIC FOUR. THEY'LL KNOW WHAT TO DO.
OKAY, CAP. BYE.
GOODBYE, CAROL!
BRAKKA BRAKKA
DAMMIT!
THAT'S WHAT I GET FOR MAKING PHONE CALLS AT MACH 3.
WHAT WAS I DOING CALLING CAP ANYWAY?
I PANICKED. THAT'S WHAT I WAS DOING.
IF I WANT TO DO THIS SOLO THING, I SHOULD DO IT.

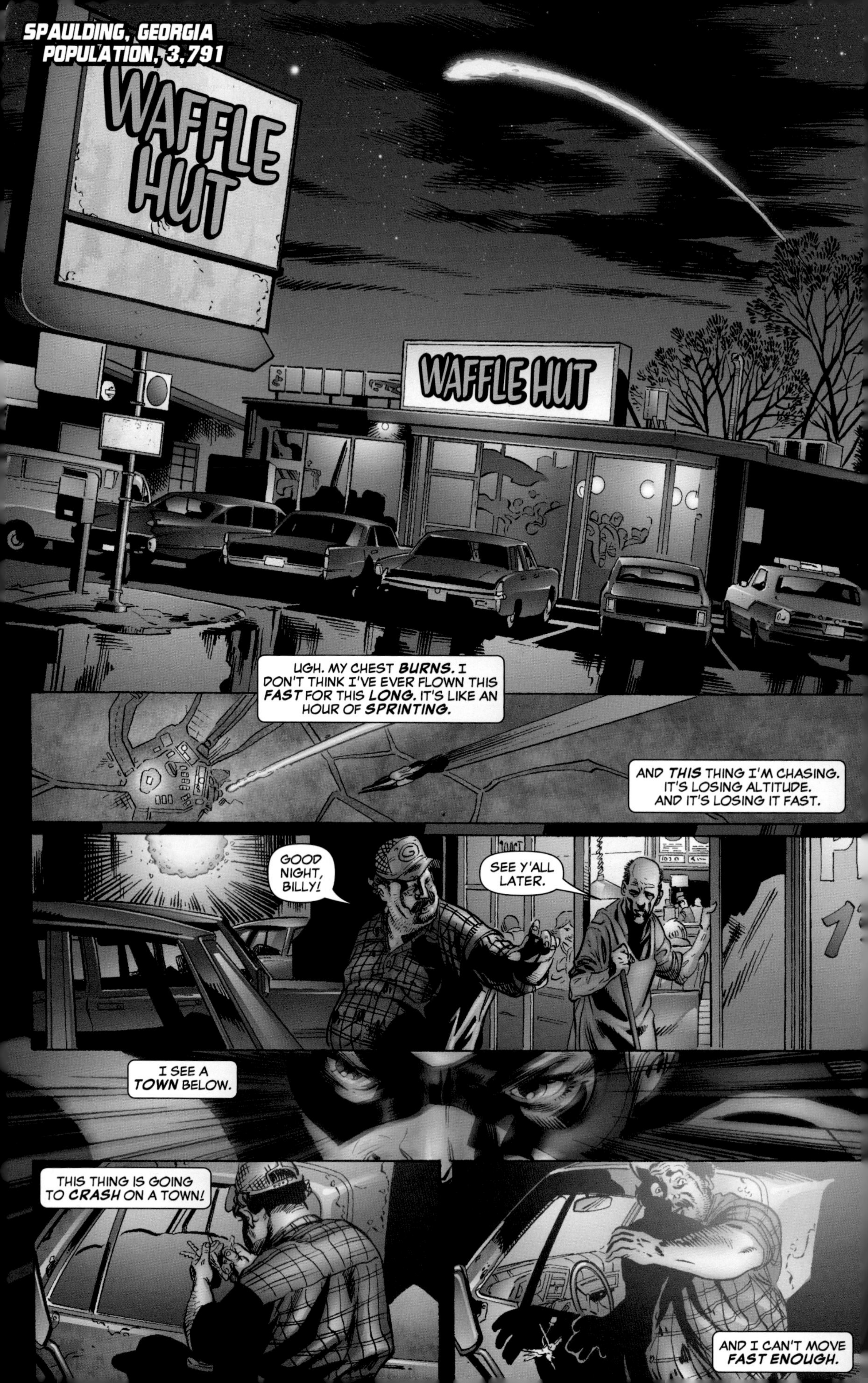
SPAULDING, GEORGIA
POPULATION, 3,791
WAFFLE HUT
WAFFLE HUT
UGH. MY CHEST BURNS. I DON'T THINK I'VE EVER FLOWN THIS FAST FOR THIS LONG. IT'S LIKE AN HOUR OF SPRINTING.
AND THIS THING I'M CHASING. IT'S LOSING ALTITUDE. AND IT'S LOSING IT FAST.
GOOD NIGHT, BILLY!
SEE Y'ALL LATER.
I SEE A TOWN BELOW.
THIS THING IS GOING TO CRASH ON A TOWN!
AND I CAN'T MOVE FAST ENOUGH.

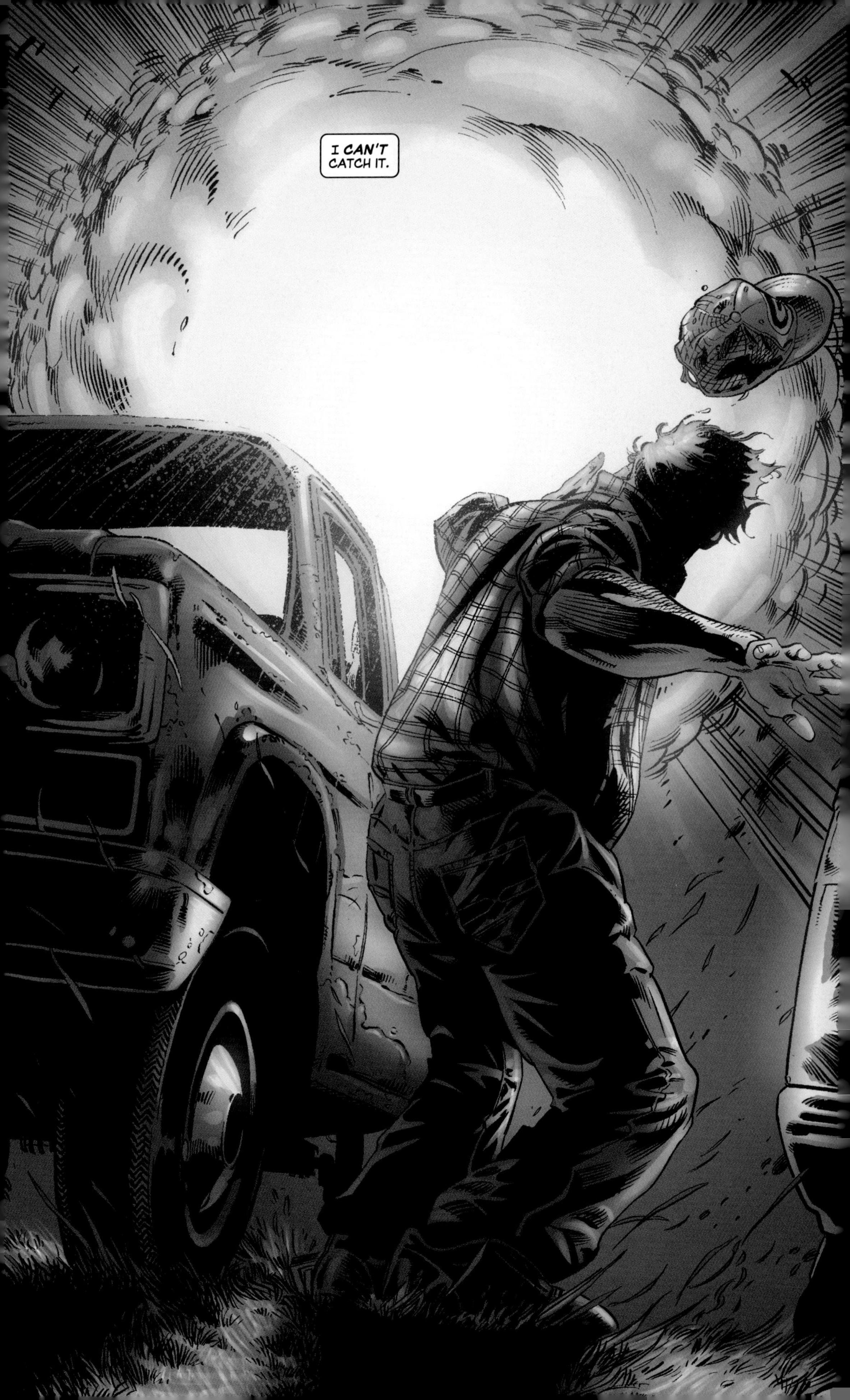
I CAN'T CATCH IT.

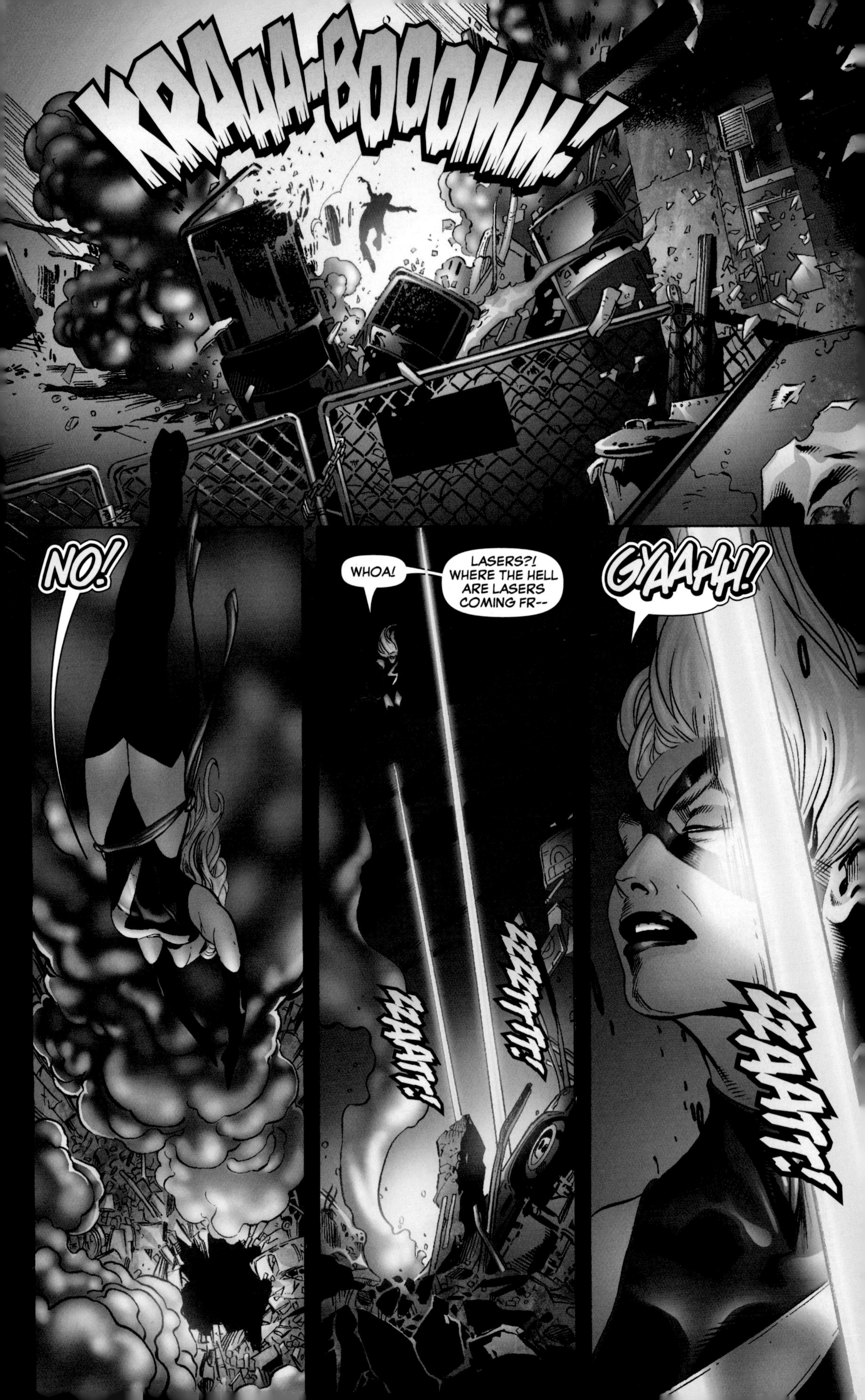
KRAAA-BOOOMM!
NO!
WHOA!
LASERS?! WHERE THE HELL ARE LASERS COMING FR--
ZZAATT!
ZZZZTTTT!
GYAAHH!
ZZAATT!

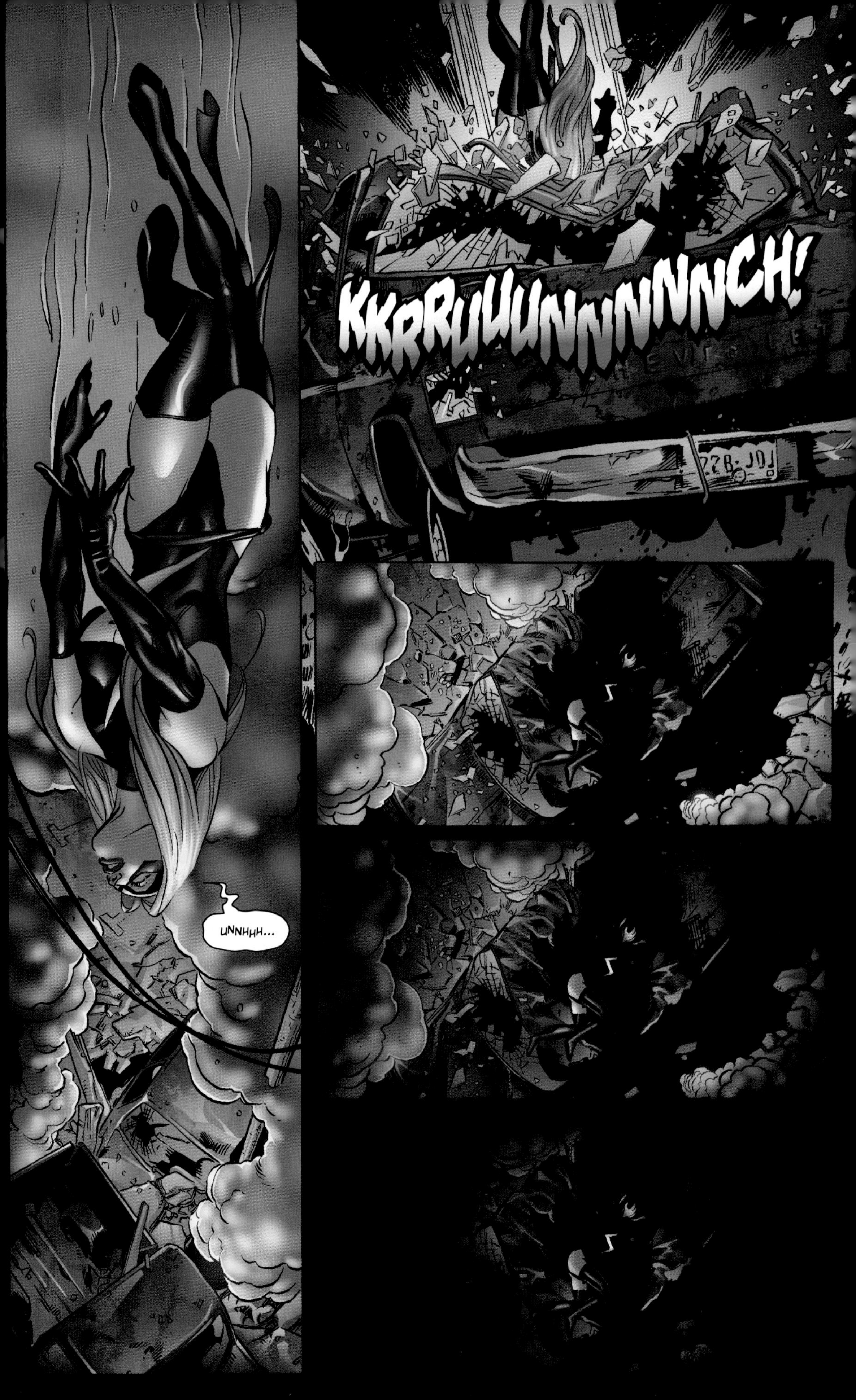
KKRRUUUNNNNNNCH!
CHEVROLET
228-JDJ
UNNHHH...

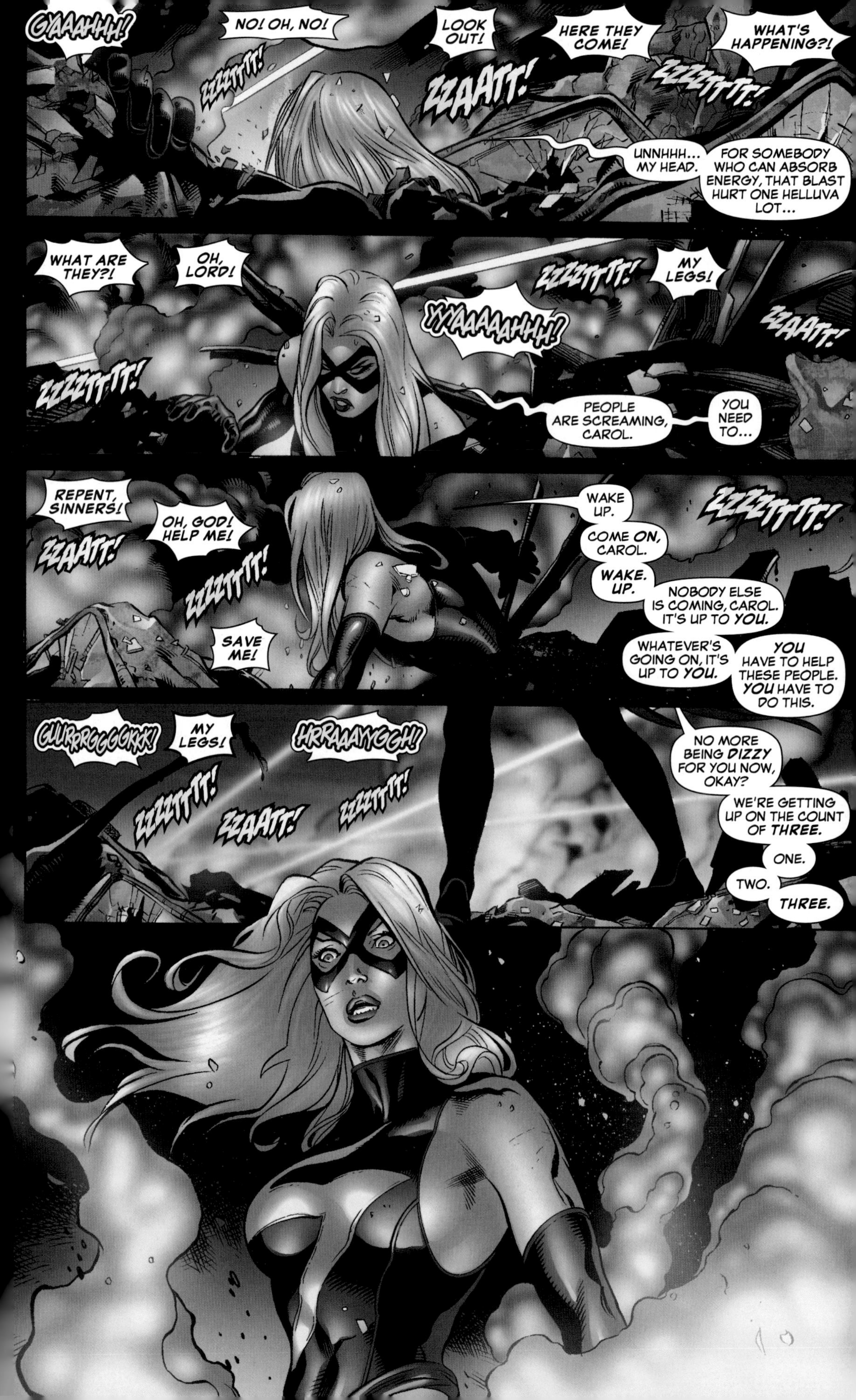
GYAAAHHH!
NO! OH, NO!
LOOK OUT!
HERE THEY COME!
WHAT'S HAPPENING?!
ZZZZTTTT!
ZZAATT!
ZZZZTTTTT!
UNNHHH... MY HEAD.
FOR SOMEBODY WHO CAN ABSORB ENERGY, THAT BLAST HURT ONE HELLUVA LOT...
WHAT ARE THEY?!
OH, LORD!
ZZZZTTTT!
MY LEGS!
YYAAAAAAHHH!
ZZAATT!
ZZZZTTTTT!
PEOPLE ARE SCREAMING, CAROL.
YOU NEED TO...
REPENT, SINNERS!
OH, GOD! HELP ME!
ZZAATT!
ZZZZTTTT!
SAVE ME!
WAKE UP.
ZZZZZTTTTT!
COME ON, CAROL.
WAKE. UP.
NOBODY ELSE IS COMING, CAROL. IT'S UP TO YOU.
WHATEVER'S GOING ON, IT'S UP TO YOU.
YOU HAVE TO HELP THESE PEOPLE. YOU HAVE TO DO THIS.
GUURRRGGGGKKK!
MY LEGS!
HRRAAAYYGGH!
ZZZZTTTT!
ZZAATT!
ZZZZTTTT!
NO MORE BEING DIZZY FOR YOU NOW, OKAY?
WE'RE GETTING UP ON THE COUNT OF THREE.
ONE.
TWO.
THREE.

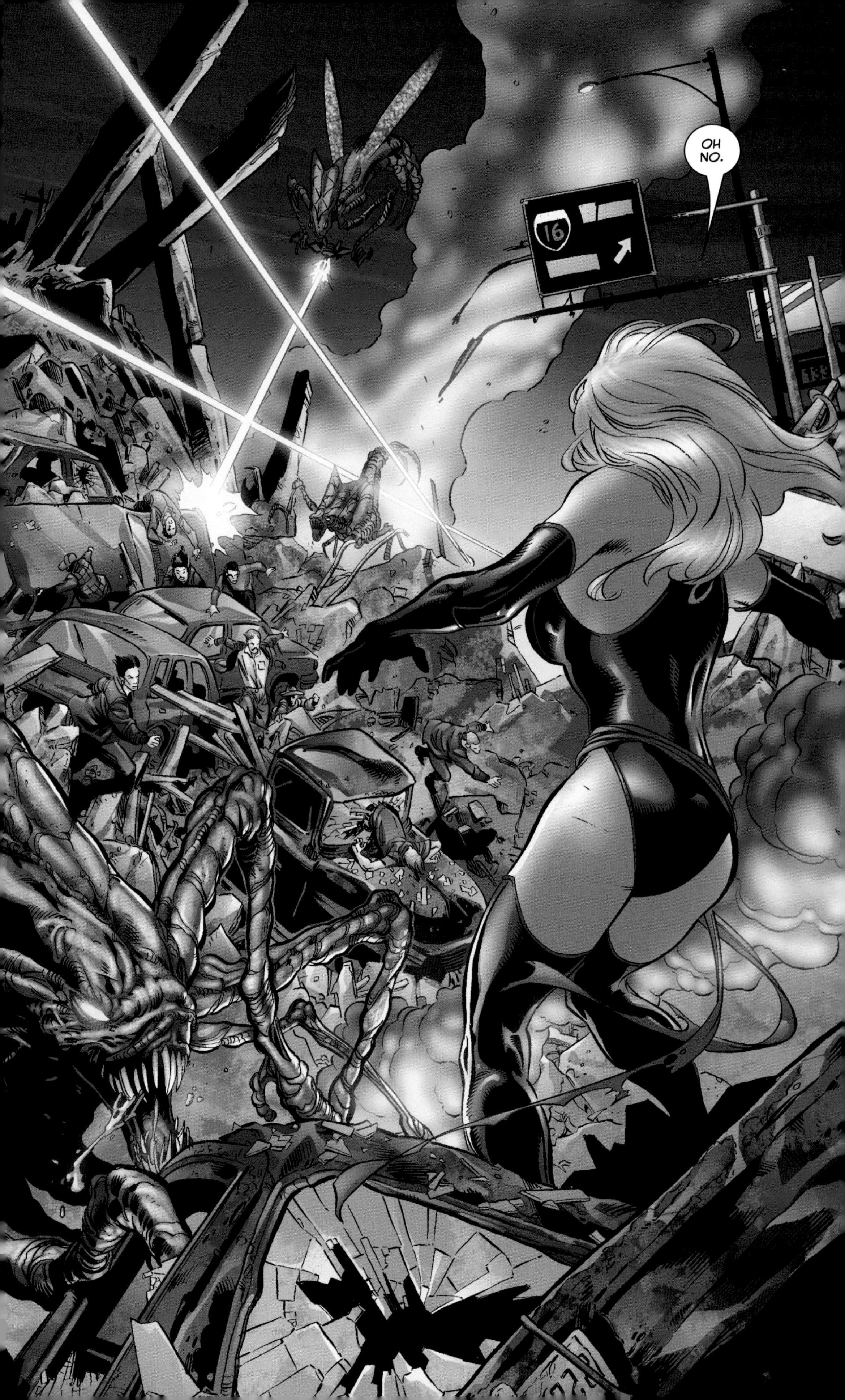
OH NO.
16

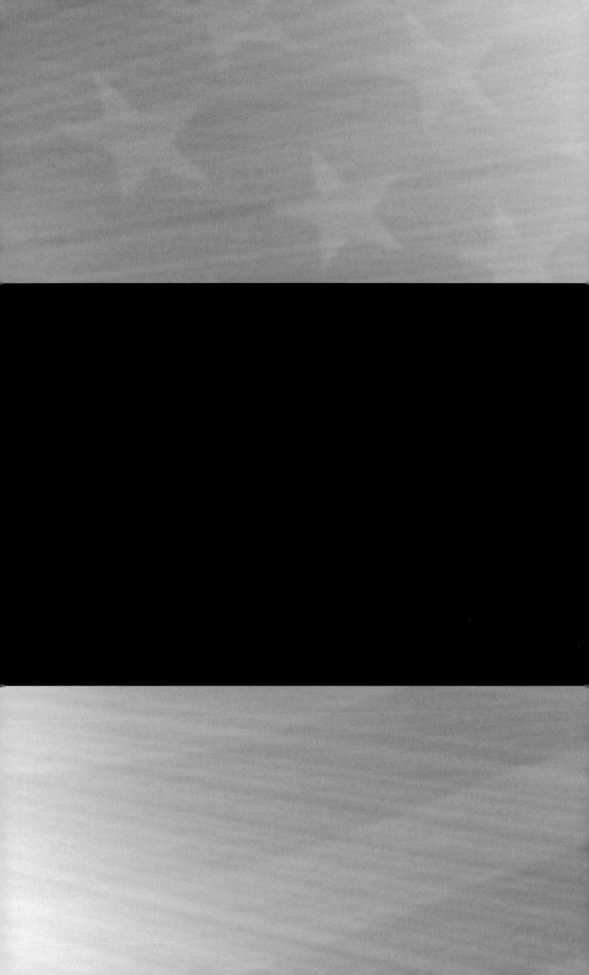

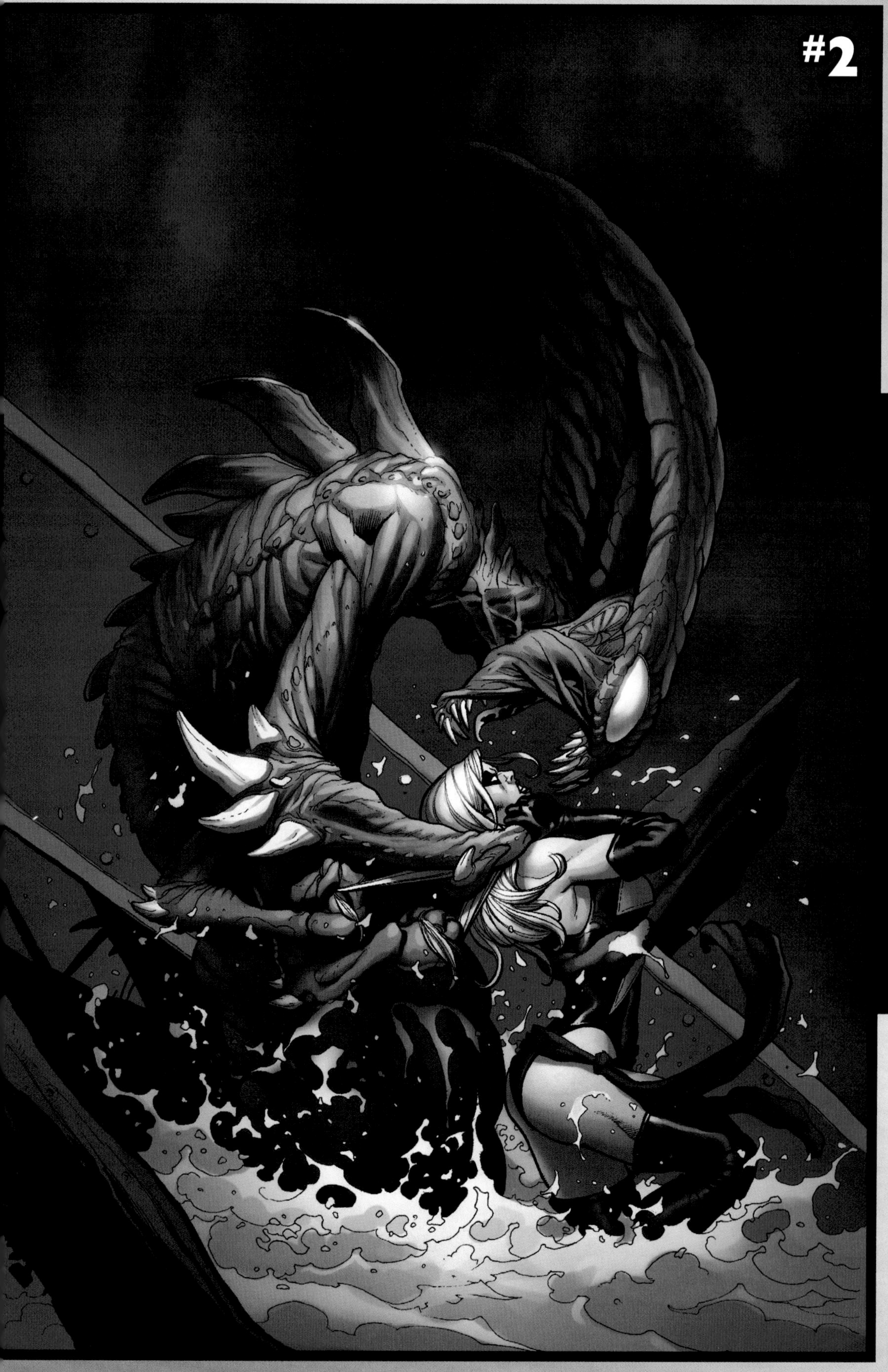
#2

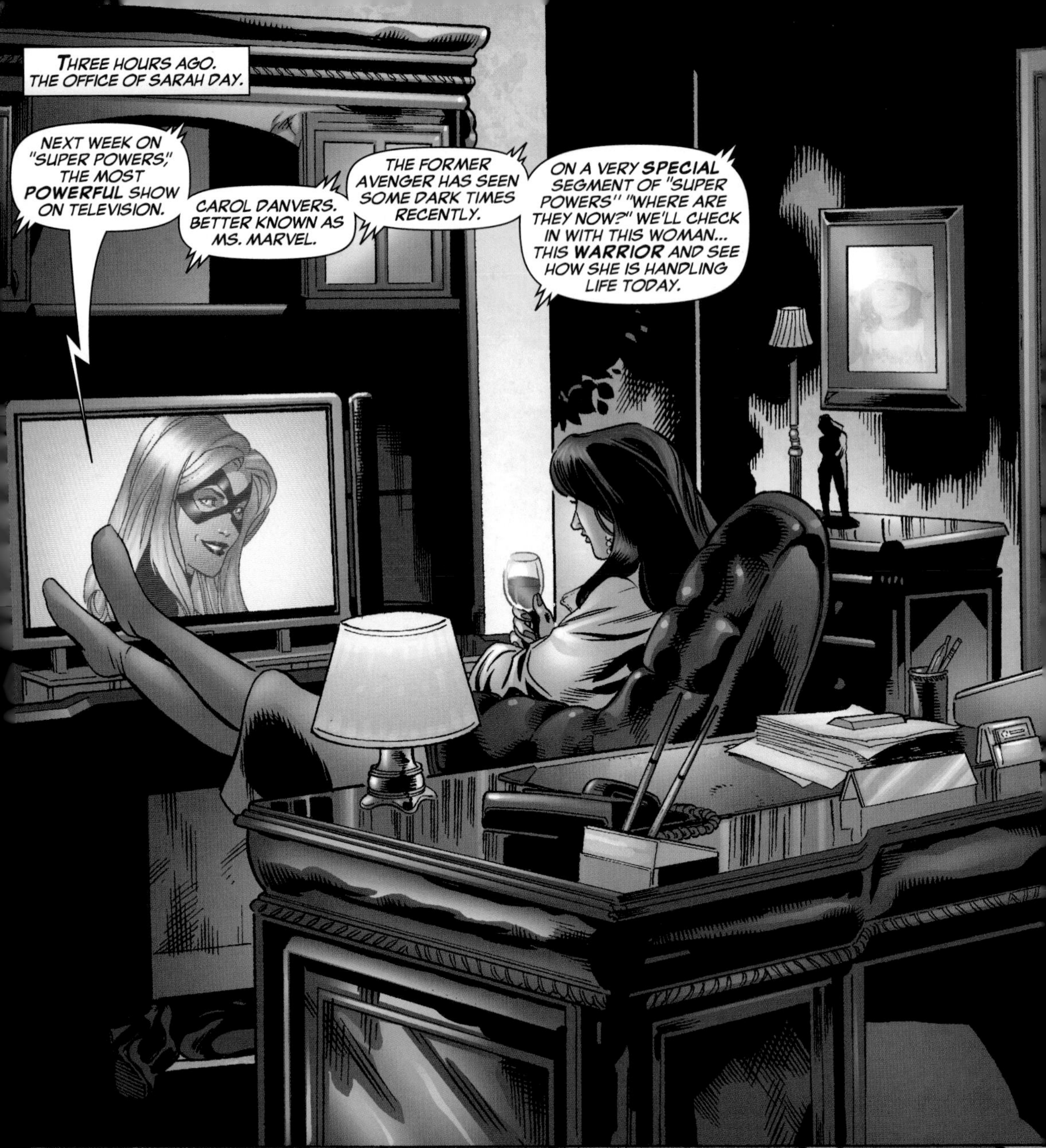
THREE HOURS AGO. THE OFFICE OF SARAH DAY.
NEXT WEEK ON "SUPER POWERS," THE MOST POWERFUL SHOW ON TELEVISION.
CAROL DANVERS. BETTER KNOWN AS MS. MARVEL.
THE FORMER AVENGER HAS SEEN SOME DARK TIMES RECENTLY.
ON A VERY SPECIAL SEGMENT OF "SUPER POWERS" "WHERE ARE THEY NOW?" WE'LL CHECK IN WITH THIS WOMAN... THIS WARRIOR AND SEE HOW SHE IS HANDLING LIFE TODAY.
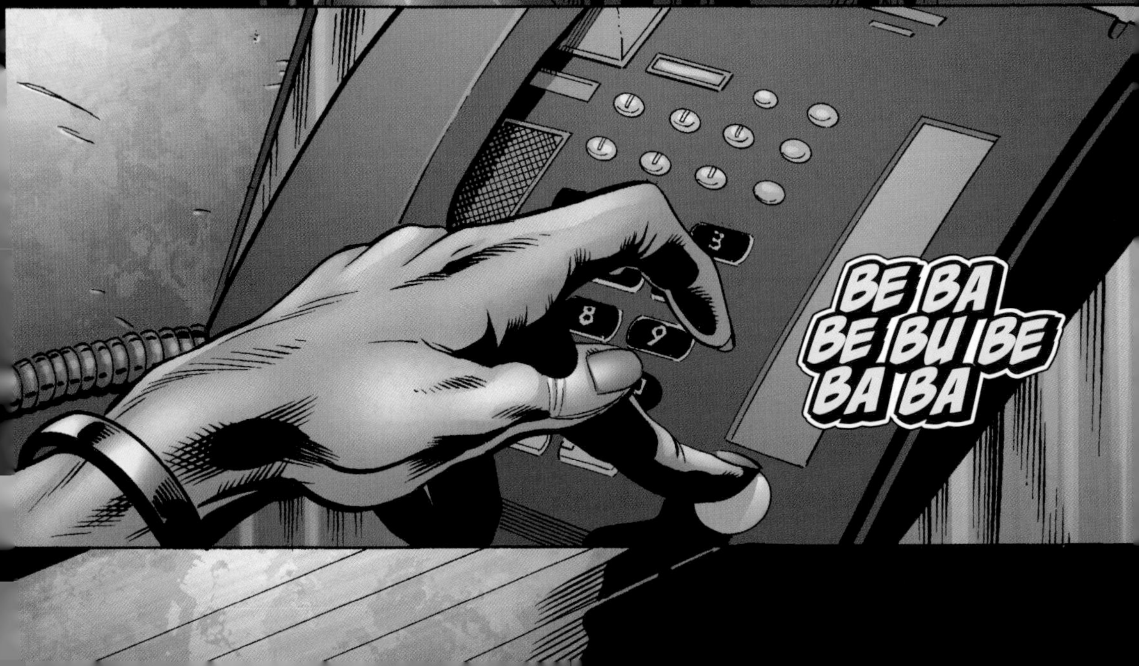
BE BA BE BU BE BA BA

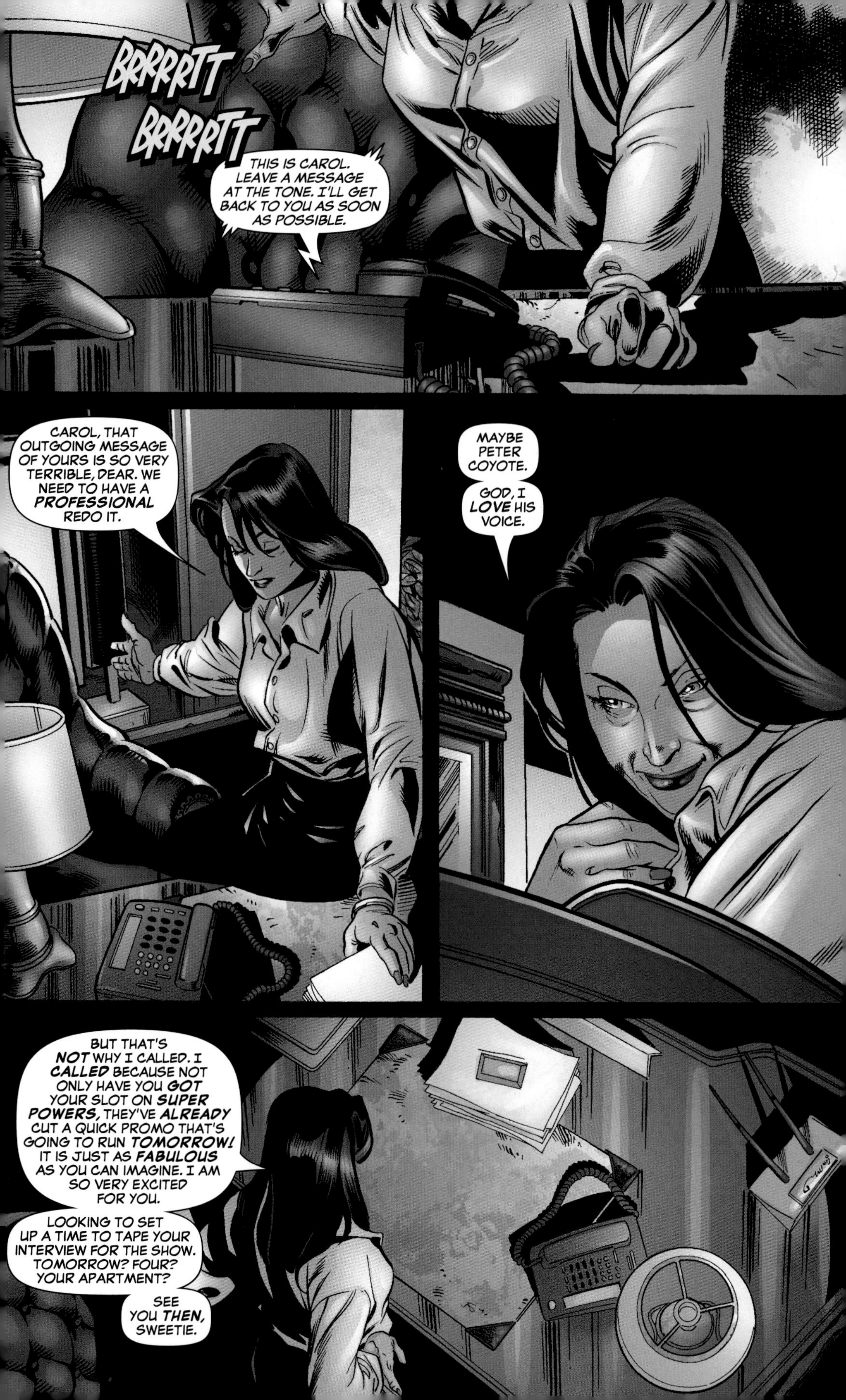
BRRRRRTT
BRRRRRTT
THIS IS CAROL. LEAVE A MESSAGE AT THE TONE. I'LL GET BACK TO YOU AS SOON AS POSSIBLE.
CAROL, THAT OUTGOING MESSAGE OF YOURS IS SO VERY TERRIBLE, DEAR. WE NEED TO HAVE A PROFESSIONAL REDO IT.
MAYBE PETER COYOTE.
GOD, I LOVE HIS VOICE.
BUT THAT'S NOT WHY I CALLED. I CALLED BECAUSE NOT ONLY HAVE YOU GOT YOUR SLOT ON SUPER POWERS, THEY'VE ALREADY CUT A QUICK PROMO THAT'S GOING TO RUN TOMORROW! IT IS JUST AS FABULOUS AS YOU CAN IMAGINE. I AM SO VERY EXCITED FOR YOU.
LOOKING TO SET UP A TIME TO TAPE YOUR INTERVIEW FOR THE SHOW. TOMORROW? FOUR? YOUR APARTMENT?
SEE YOU THEN, SWEETIE.

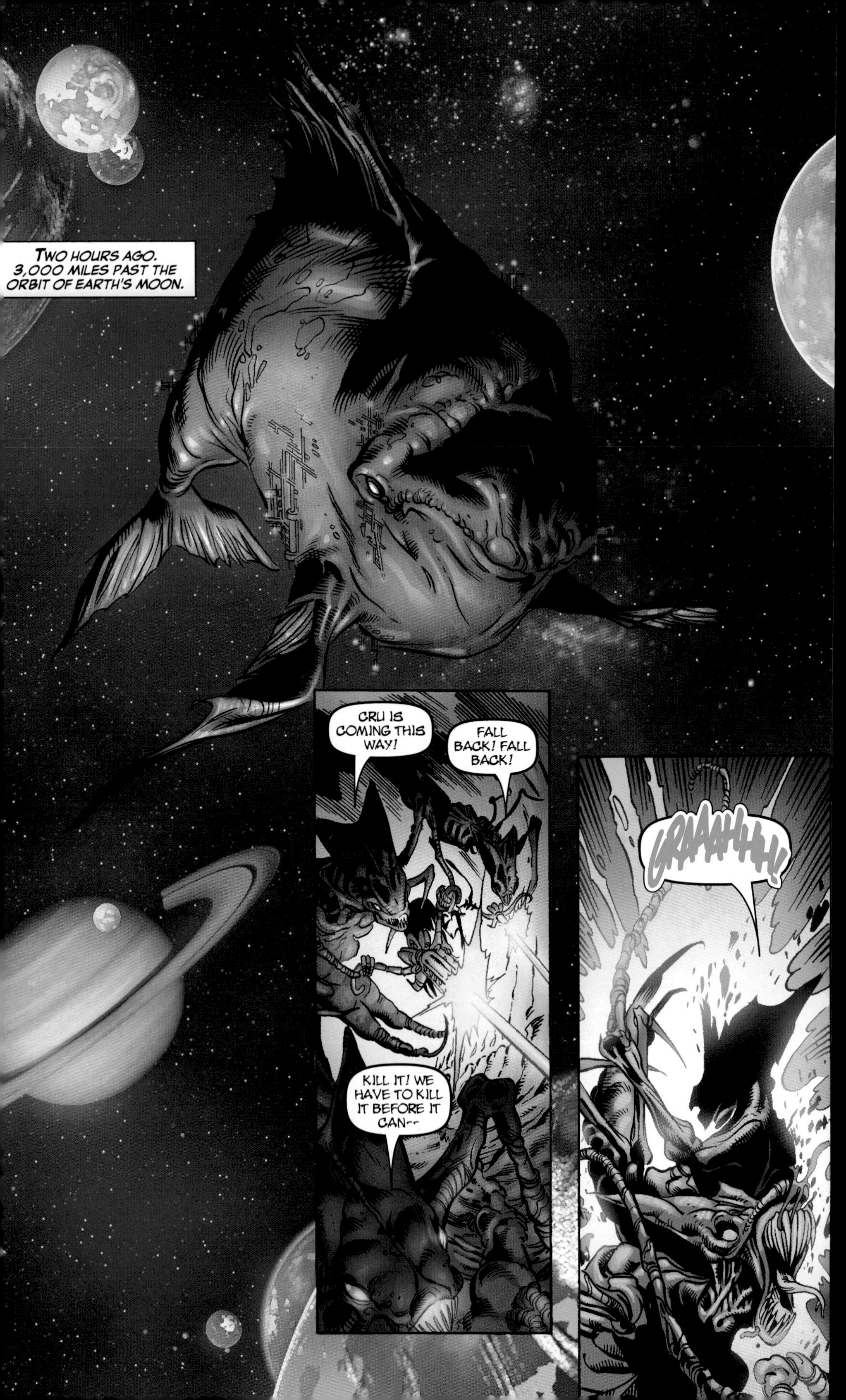
TWO HOURS AGO.
3,000 MILES PAST THE
ORBIT OF EARTH'S MOON.
CRU IS COMING THIS WAY!
FALL BACK! FALL BACK!
KILL IT! WE HAVE TO KILL IT BEFORE IT CAN--
GRAAAHHHH!

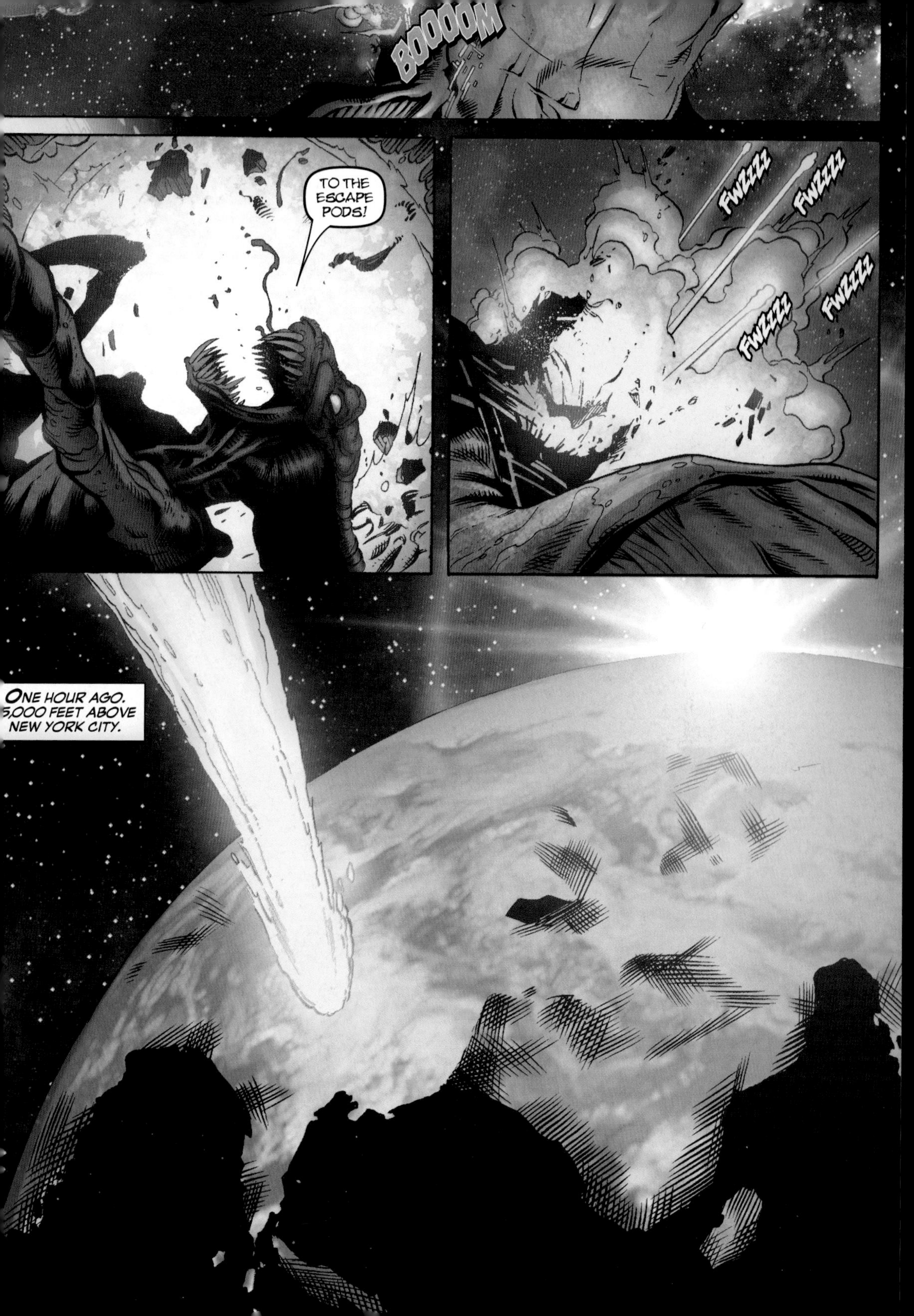
BOOOOM
TO THE ESCAPE PODS!
FWZZZZ
FWZZZZ
FWZZZZ
FWZZZZ
ONE HOUR AGO. 5,000 FEET ABOVE NEW YORK CITY.

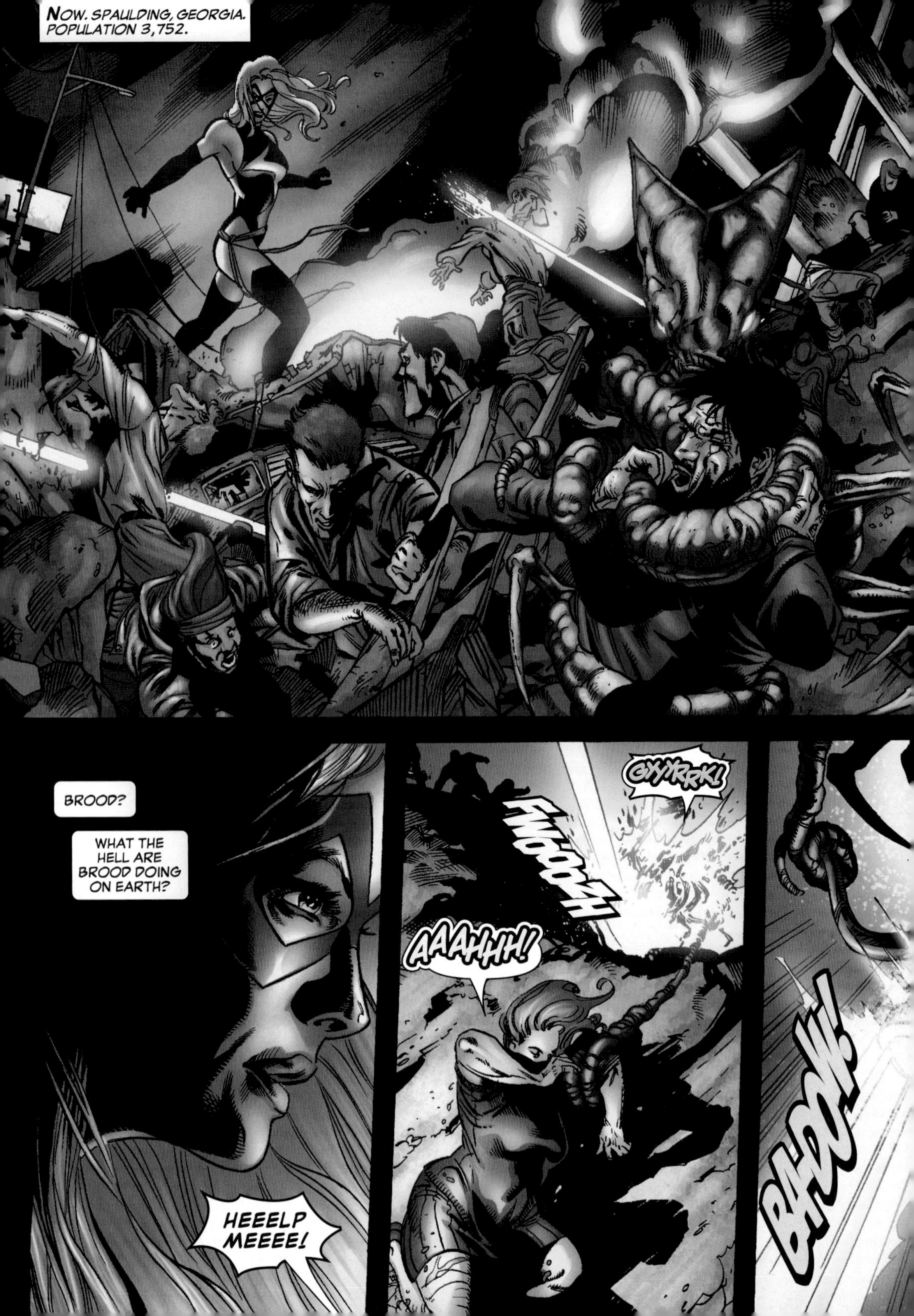
NOW. SPAULDING, GEORGIA. POPULATION 3,752.
BROOD?
WHAT THE HELL ARE BROOD DOING ON EARTH?
HEEELP MEEEE!
GYYRRK!
FWOOOSH
AAAHHH!
BHOOM!

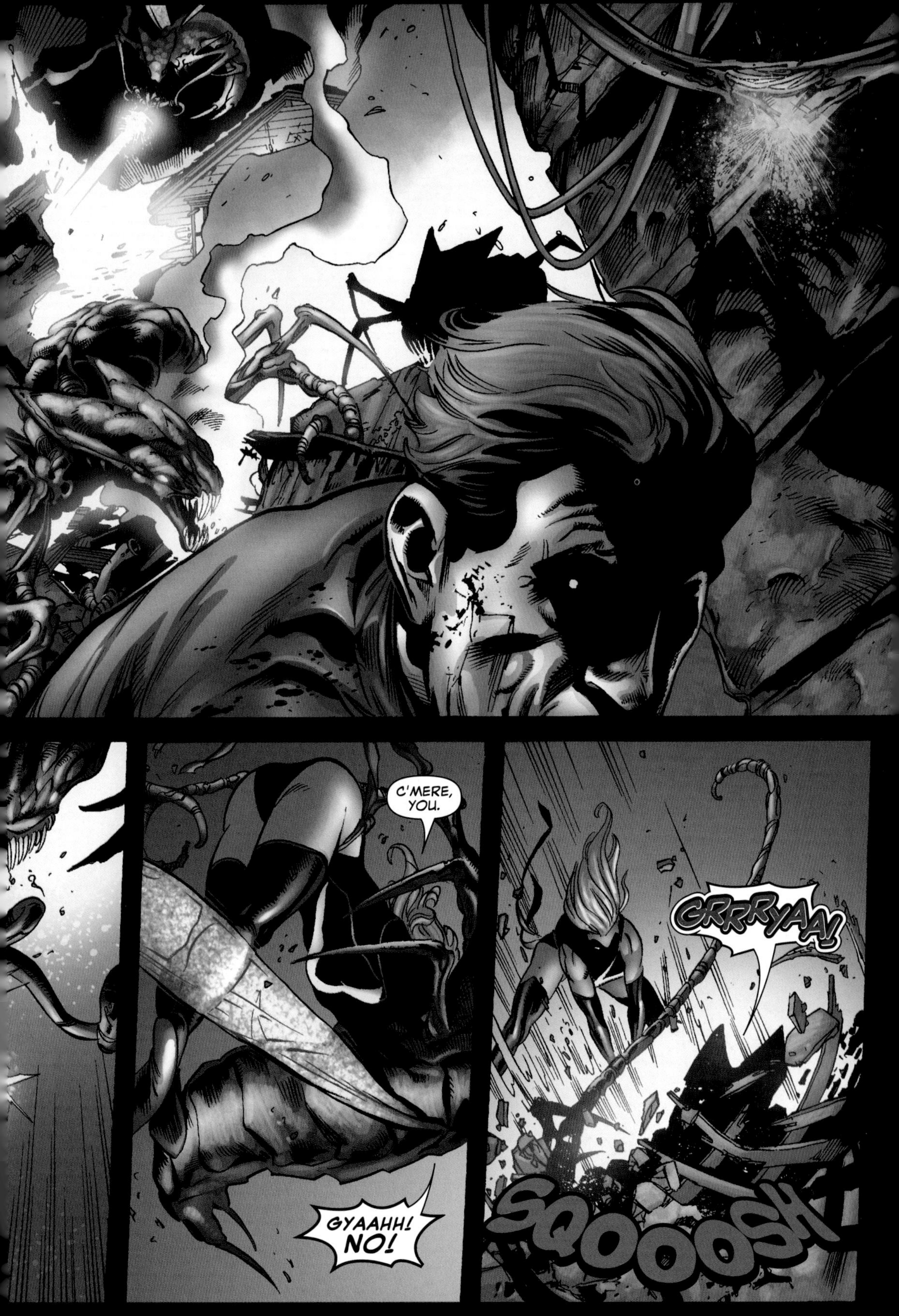
C'MERE, YOU.
GYAAHH! NO!
GRRRYAA!
SQOOOSH

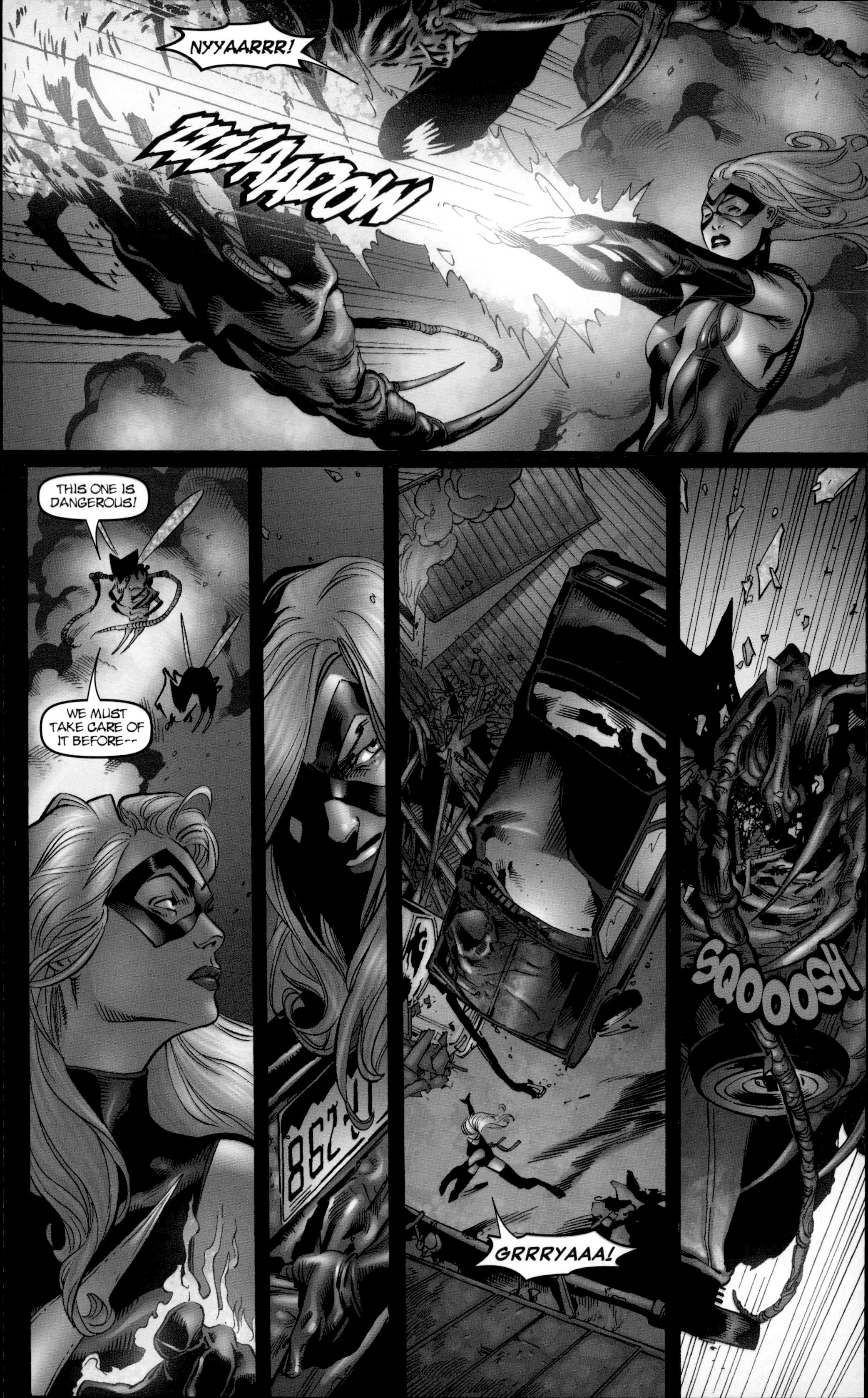

NYYAARRR!
THIS ONE IS DANGEROUS!
WE MUST TAKE CARE OF IT BEFORE--
SQOOOSH
GRRRYAAA!

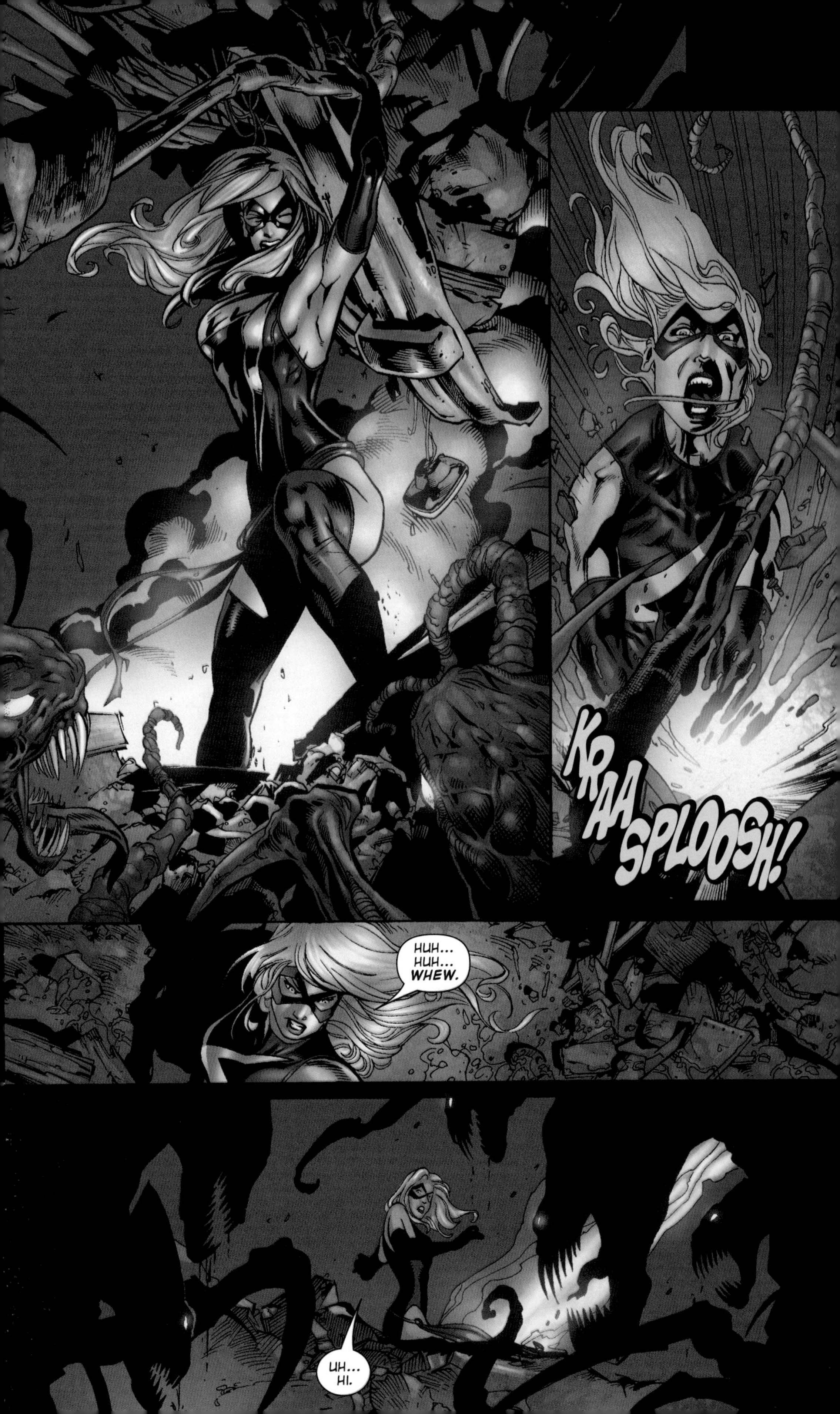
KRAASPLOOSH!
HUH... HUH... WHEW.
UH... HI.

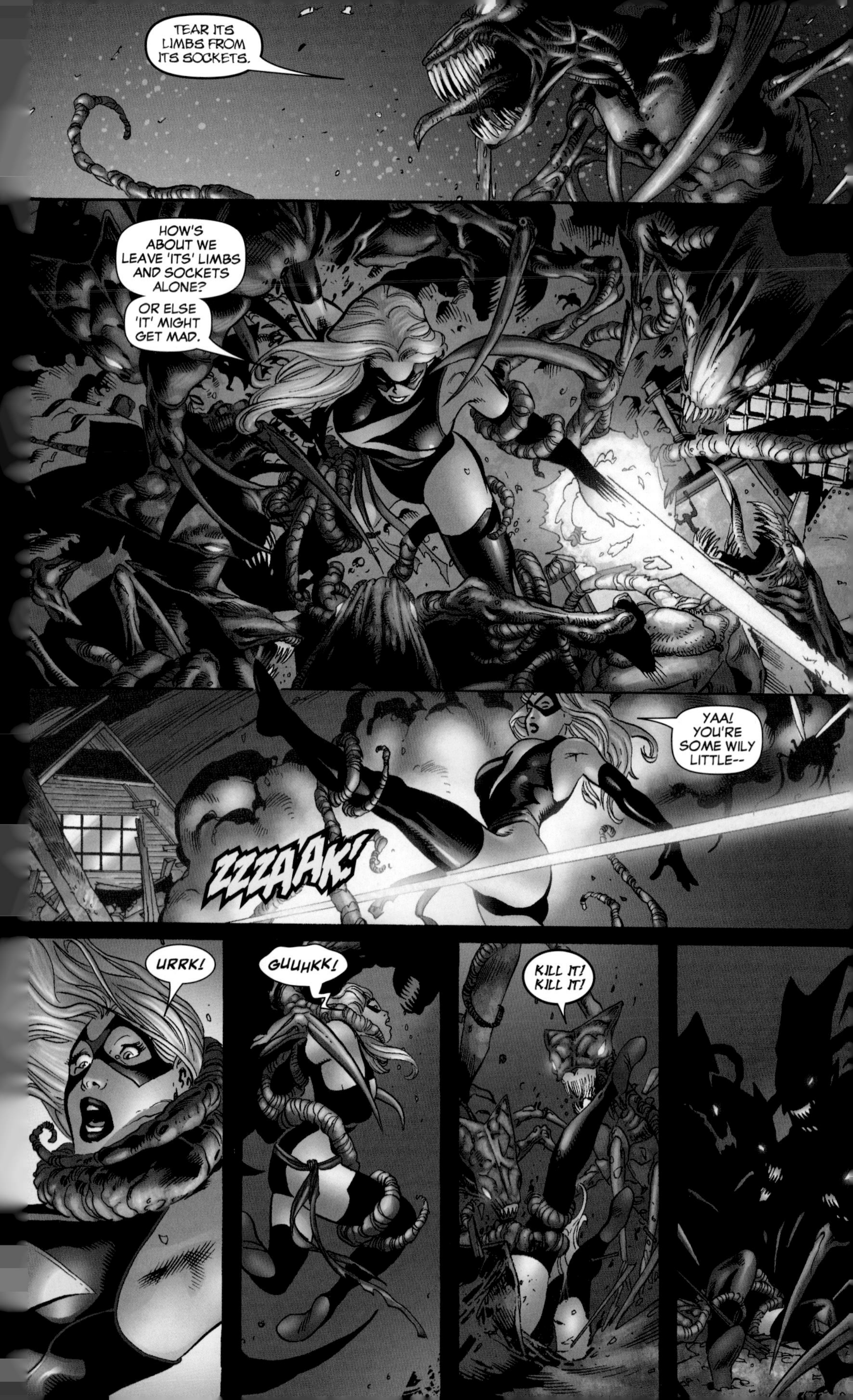
TEAR ITS LIMBS FROM ITS SOCKETS.
HOW'S ABOUT WE LEAVE 'ITS' LIMBS AND SOCKETS ALONE?
OR ELSE 'IT' MIGHT GET MAD.
YAA! YOU'RE SOME WILY LITTLE--
ZZZAAK!
URRK!
GUUHKK!
KILL IT! KILL IT!

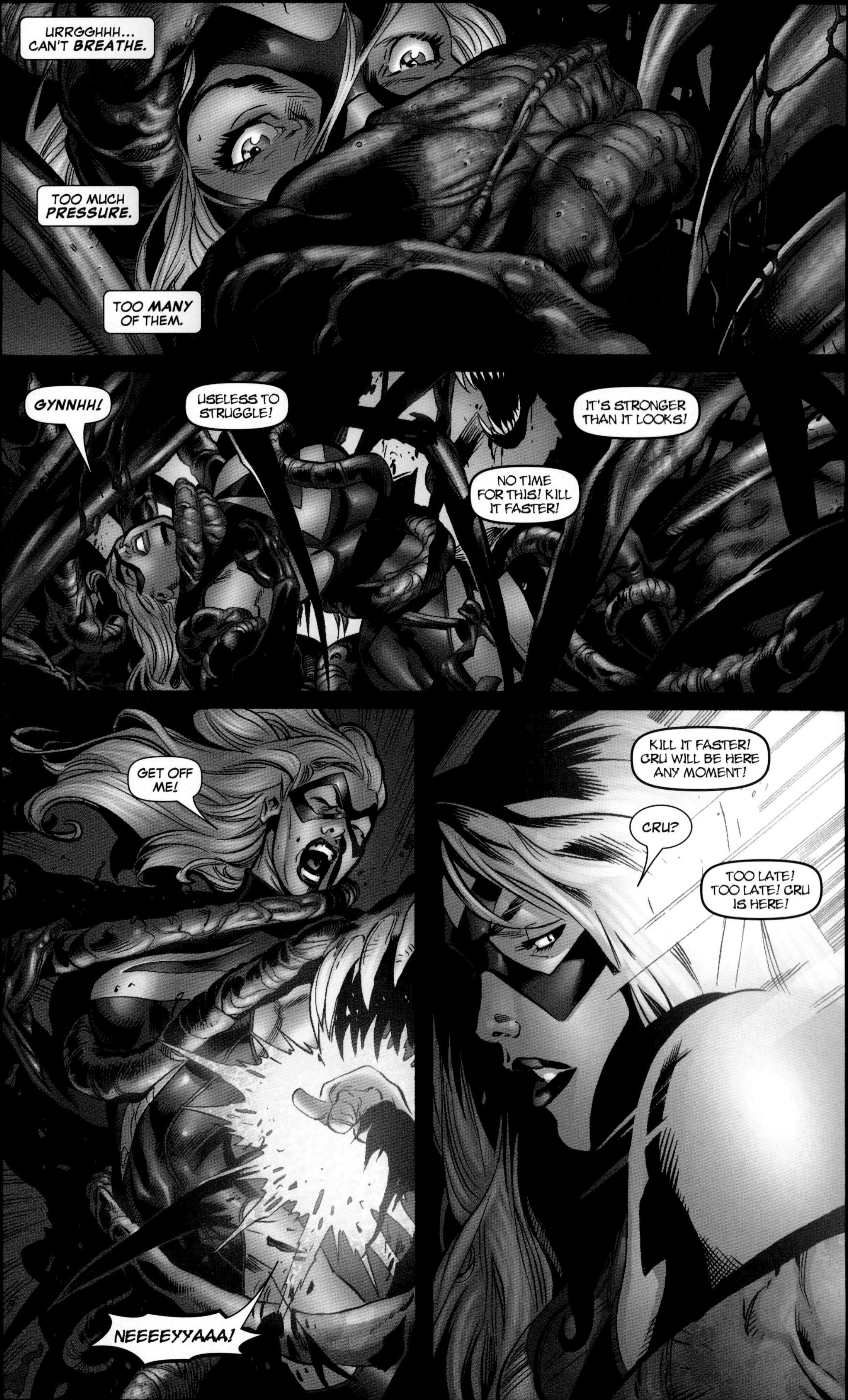
URRGGHHH... CAN'T BREATHE.
TOO MUCH PRESSURE.
TOO MANY OF THEM.
GYNNHH!
USELESS TO STRUGGLE!
IT'S STRONGER THAN IT LOOKS!
NO TIME FOR THIS! KILL IT FASTER!
GET OFF ME!
NEEEEYYAAA!
KILL IT FASTER! CRU WILL BE HERE ANY MOMENT!
CRU?
TOO LATE! TOO LATE! CRU IS HERE!

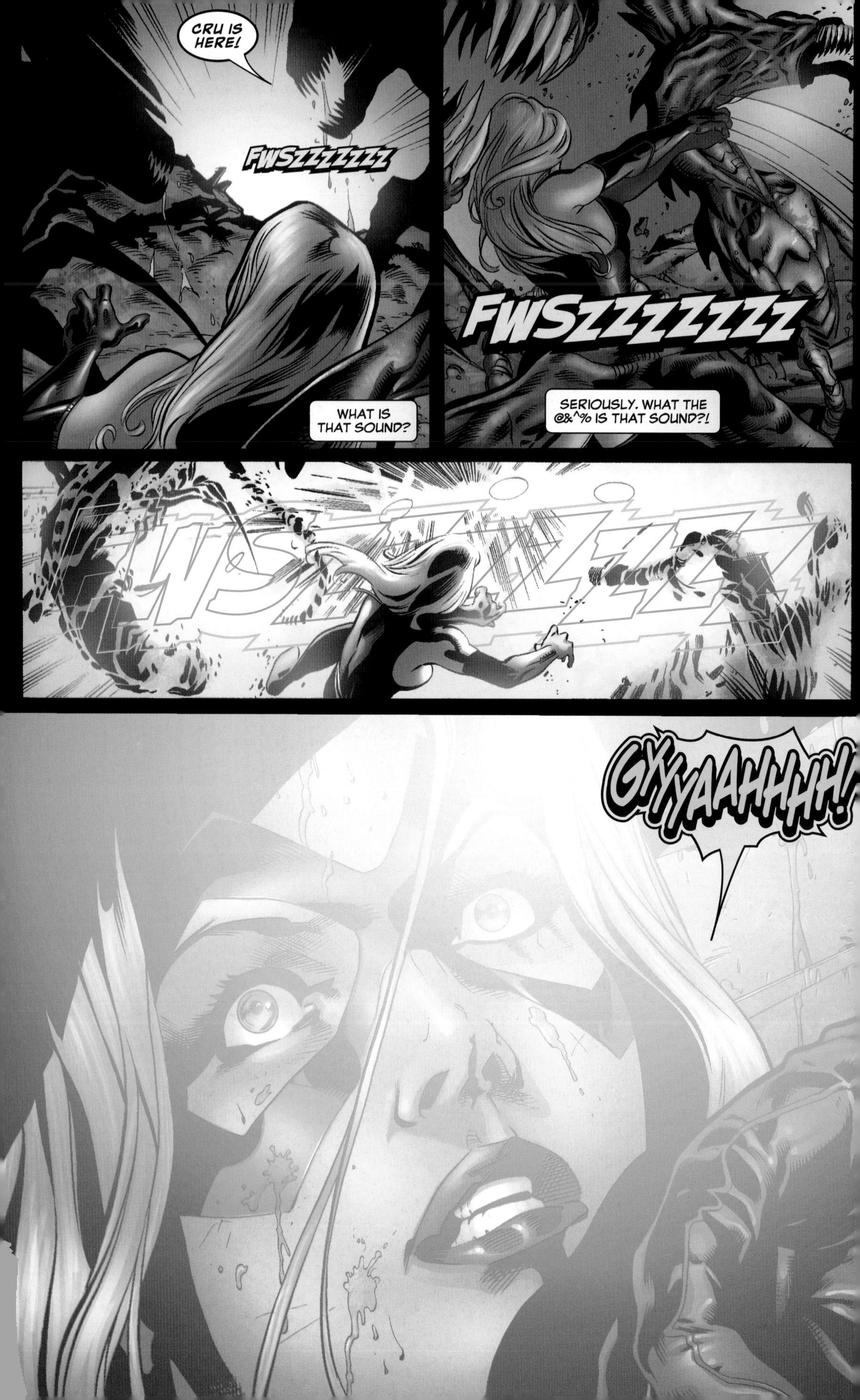
CRU IS HERE!
FWSZZZZZZZ
WHAT IS THAT SOUND?
FWSZZZZZZZ
SERIOUSLY. WHAT THE @&^% IS THAT SOUND?!
GYYYAAHHHH!

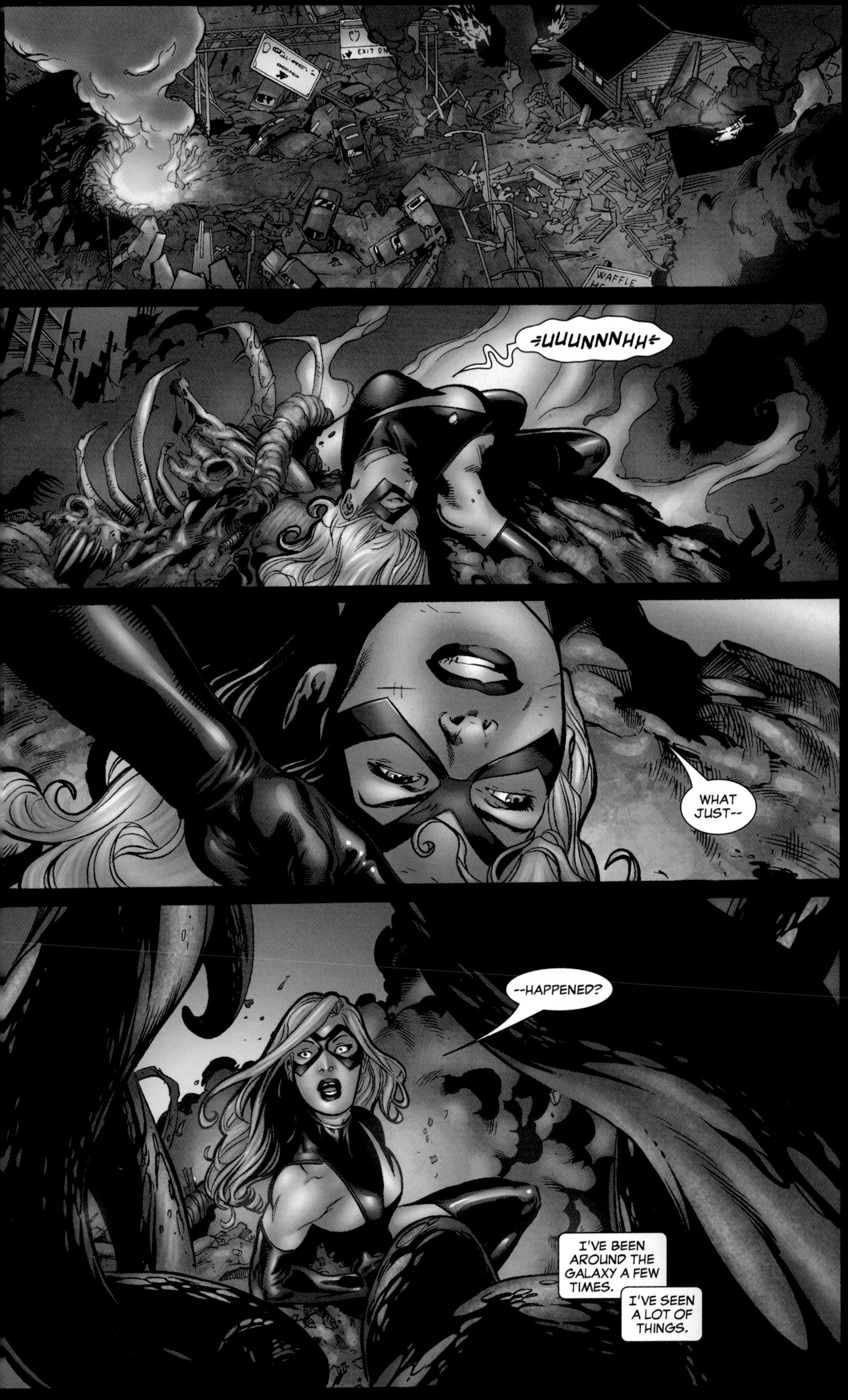
EXIT ON
WAFFLE
UUUNNNHH
WHAT JUST--
--HAPPENED?
I'VE BEEN AROUND THE GALAXY A FEW TIMES.
I'VE SEEN A LOT OF THINGS.

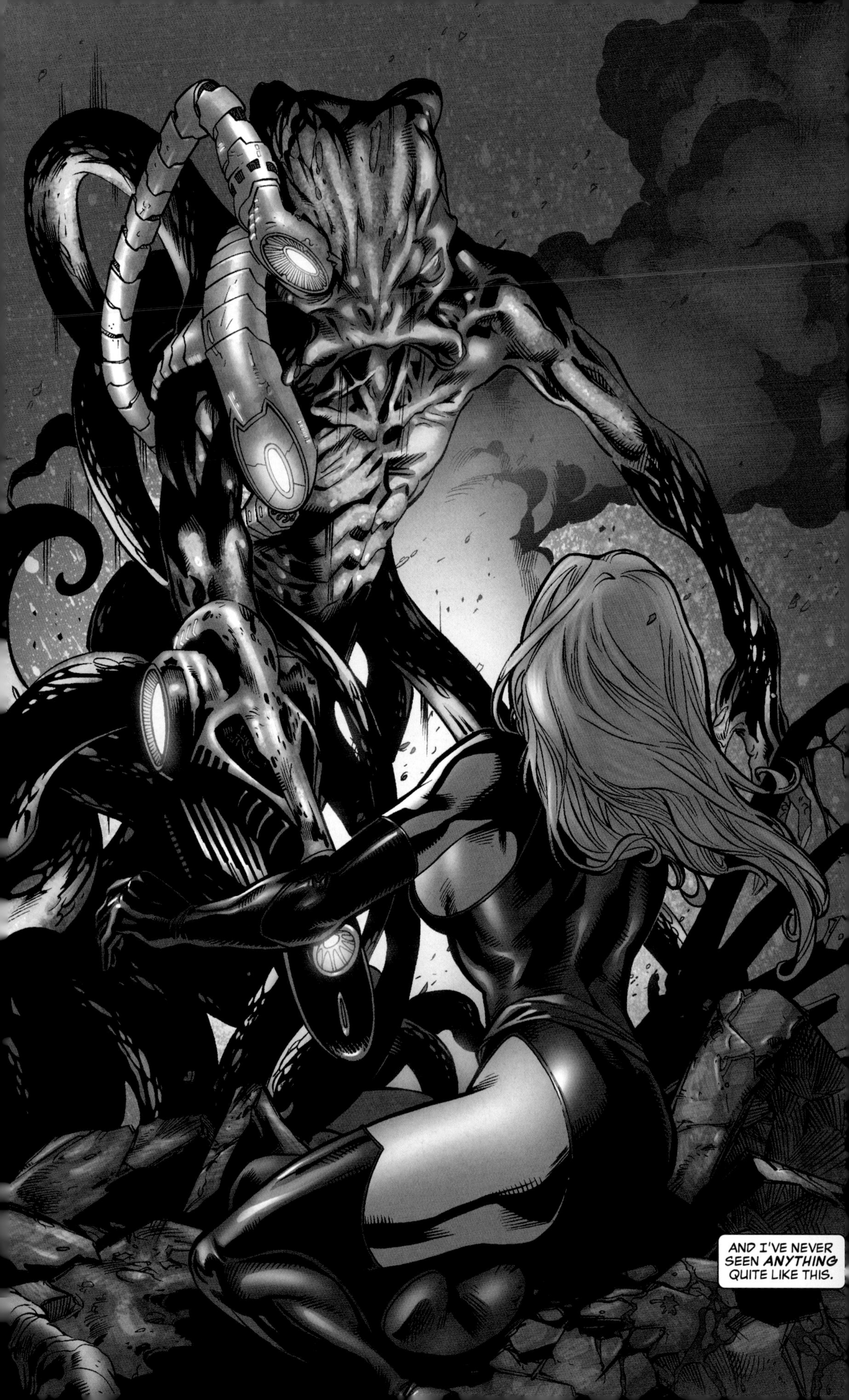
AND I'VE NEVER SEEN ANYTHING QUITE LIKE THIS.

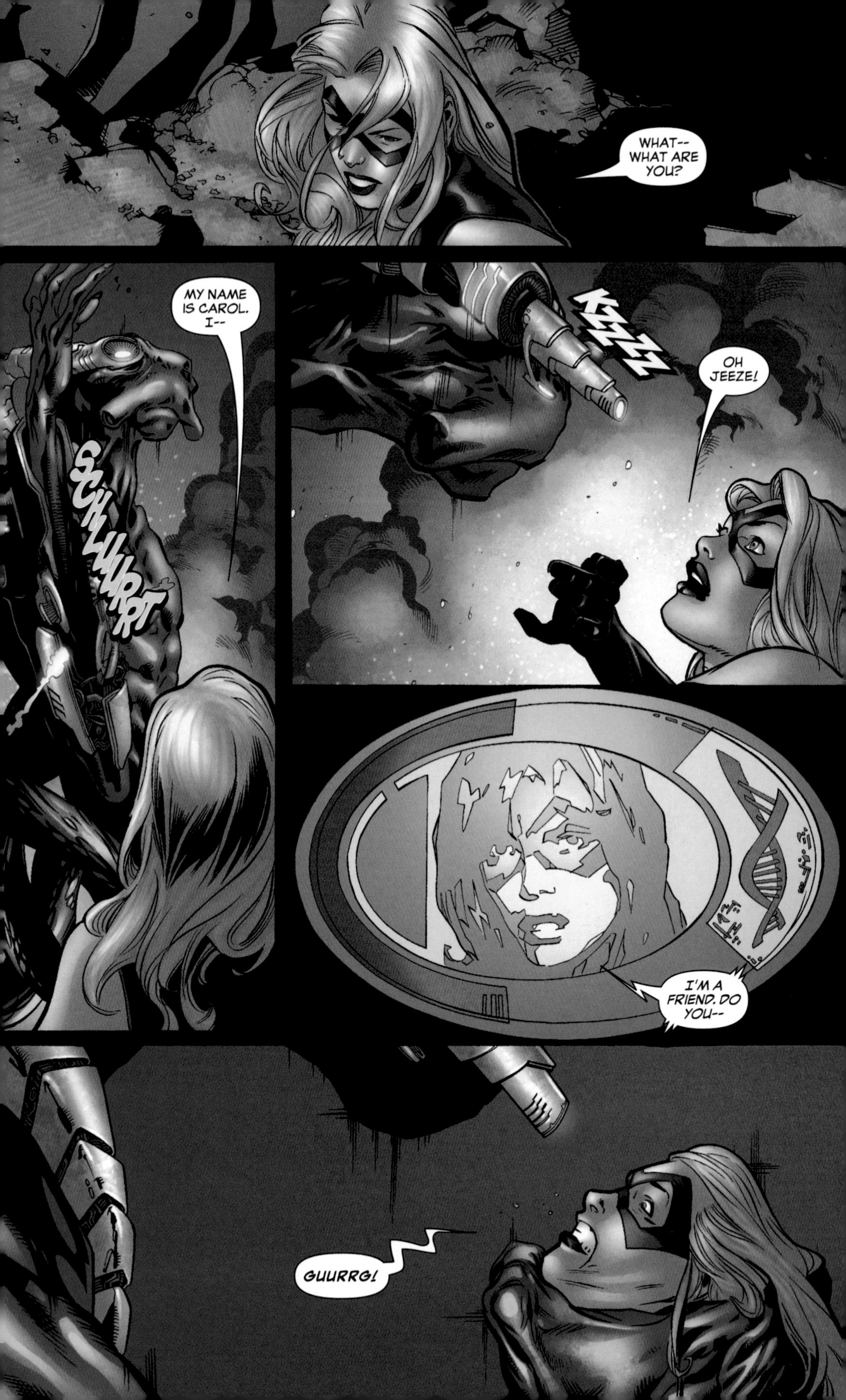
WHAT-- WHAT ARE YOU?
MY NAME IS CAROL. I--
SCHLUURRT
KZZZZ
OH JEEZE!
I'M A FRIEND. DO YOU--
GUURRG!

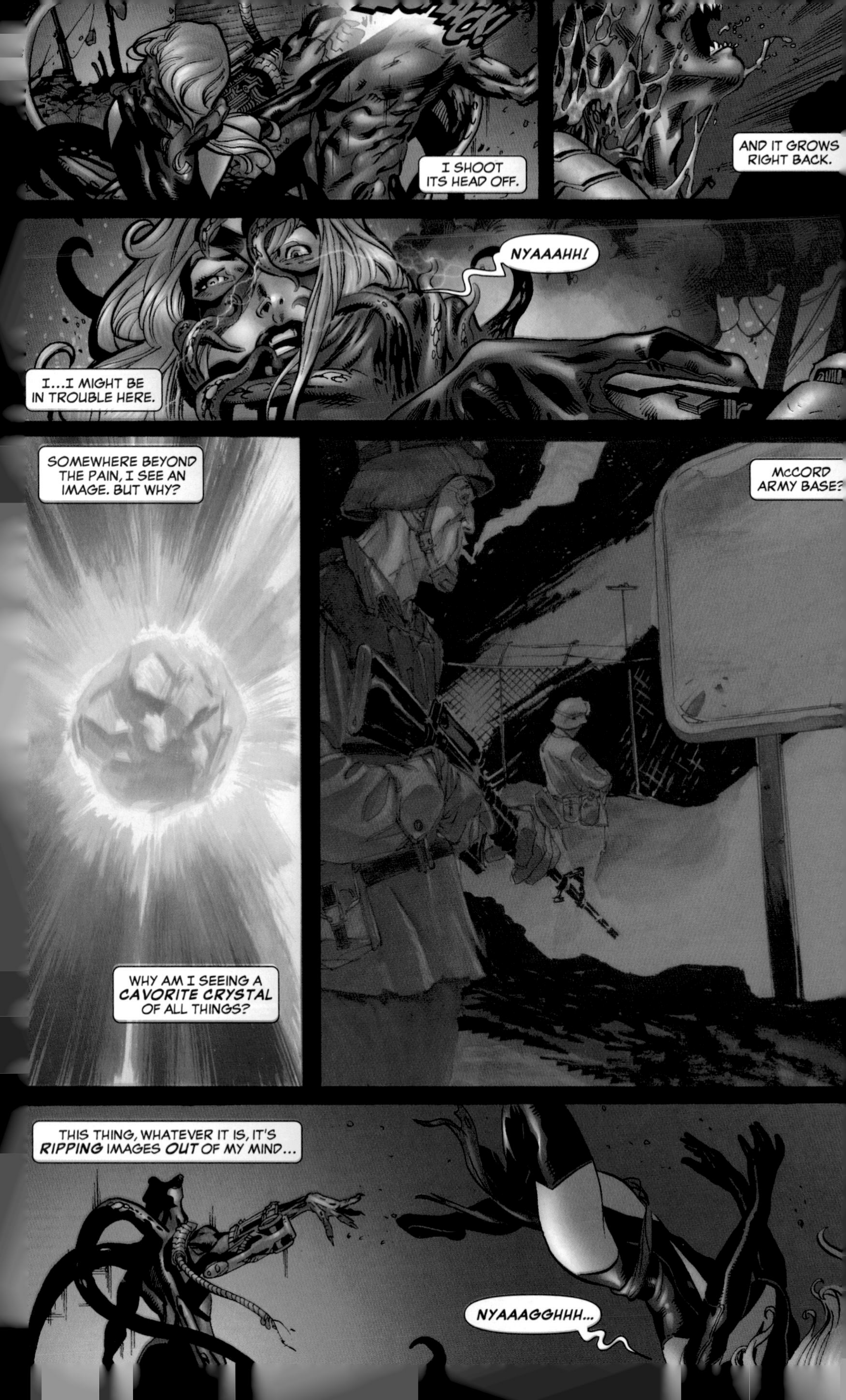
I SHOOT ITS HEAD OFF.
AND IT GROWS RIGHT BACK.
NYAAAHH!
I...I MIGHT BE IN TROUBLE HERE.
SOMEWHERE BEYOND THE PAIN, I SEE AN IMAGE. BUT WHY?
WHY AM I SEEING A CAVORITE CRYSTAL OF ALL THINGS?
McCORD ARMY BASE?
THIS THING, WHATEVER IT IS, IT'S RIPPING IMAGES OUT OF MY MIND...
NYAAAGGHHH...

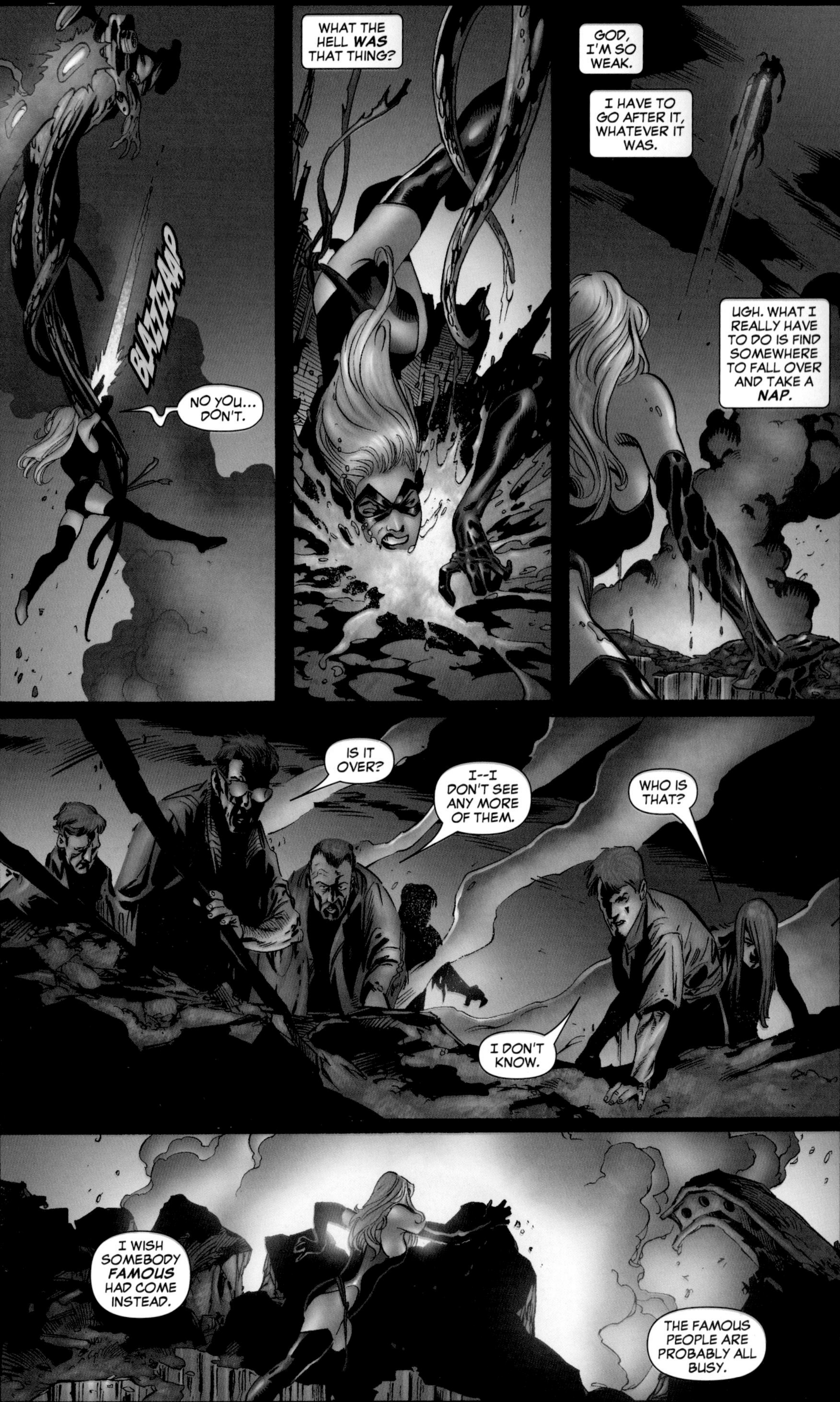
BLAZZZAP
NO YOU... DON'T.
WHAT THE HELL WAS THAT THING?
GOD, I'M SO WEAK.
I HAVE TO GO AFTER IT, WHATEVER IT WAS.
UGH. WHAT I REALLY HAVE TO DO IS FIND SOMEWHERE TO FALL OVER AND TAKE A NAP.
IS IT OVER?
I--I DON'T SEE ANY MORE OF THEM.
WHO IS THAT?
I DON'T KNOW.
I WISH SOMEBODY FAMOUS HAD COME INSTEAD.
THE FAMOUS PEOPLE ARE PROBABLY ALL BUSY.

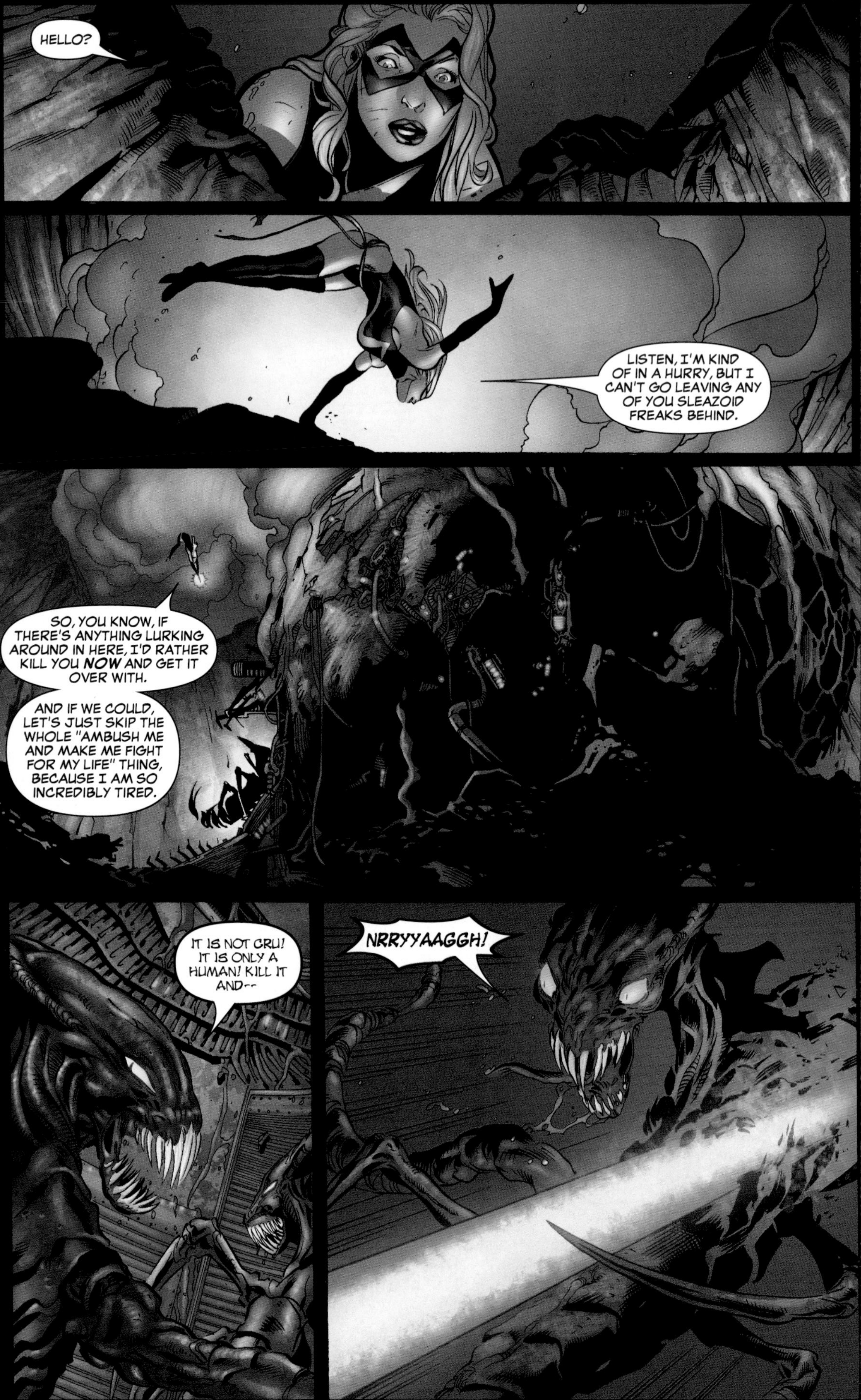
HELLO?
LISTEN, I'M KIND OF IN A HURRY, BUT I CAN'T GO LEAVING ANY OF YOU SLEAZOID FREAKS BEHIND.
SO, YOU KNOW, IF THERE'S ANYTHING LURKING AROUND IN HERE, I'D RATHER KILL YOU **NOW** AND GET IT OVER WITH.
AND IF WE COULD, LET'S JUST SKIP THE WHOLE "AMBUSH ME AND MAKE ME FIGHT FOR MY LIFE" THING, BECAUSE I AM SO INCREDIBLY TIRED.
IT IS NOT CRU! IT IS ONLY A HUMAN! KILL IT AND--
NRRYYAAGGH!

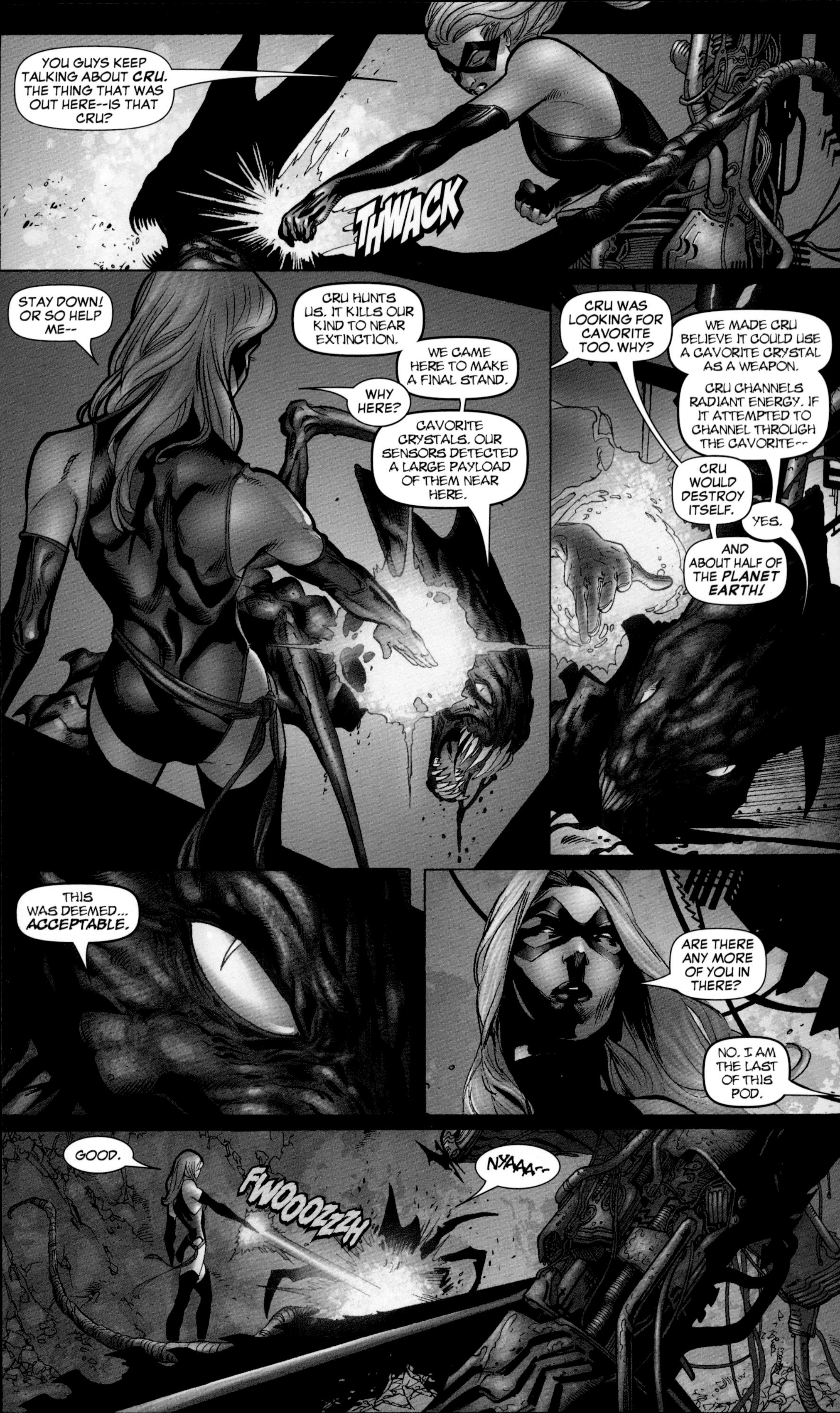

YOU GUYS KEEP TALKING ABOUT **CRU**. THE THING THAT WAS OUT HERE--IS THAT CRU?
THWACK
STAY DOWN! OR SO HELP ME--
CRU HUNTS US. IT KILLS OUR KIND TO NEAR EXTINCTION.
WE CAME HERE TO MAKE A FINAL STAND.
WHY HERE?
CAVORITE CRYSTALS. OUR SENSORS DETECTED A LARGE PAYLOAD OF THEM NEAR HERE.
CRU WAS LOOKING FOR CAVORITE TOO. WHY?
WE MADE CRU BELIEVE IT COULD USE A CAVORITE CRYSTAL AS A WEAPON.
CRU CHANNELS RADIANT ENERGY. IF IT ATTEMPTED TO CHANNEL THROUGH THE CAVORITE--
CRU WOULD DESTROY ITSELF.
YES.
AND ABOUT HALF OF THE ***PLANET EARTH!***
THIS WAS DEEMED... ***ACCEPTABLE.***
ARE THERE ANY MORE OF YOU IN THERE?
NO. I AM THE LAST OF THIS POD.
GOOD.
NYAAA--
FWOOOZZZH

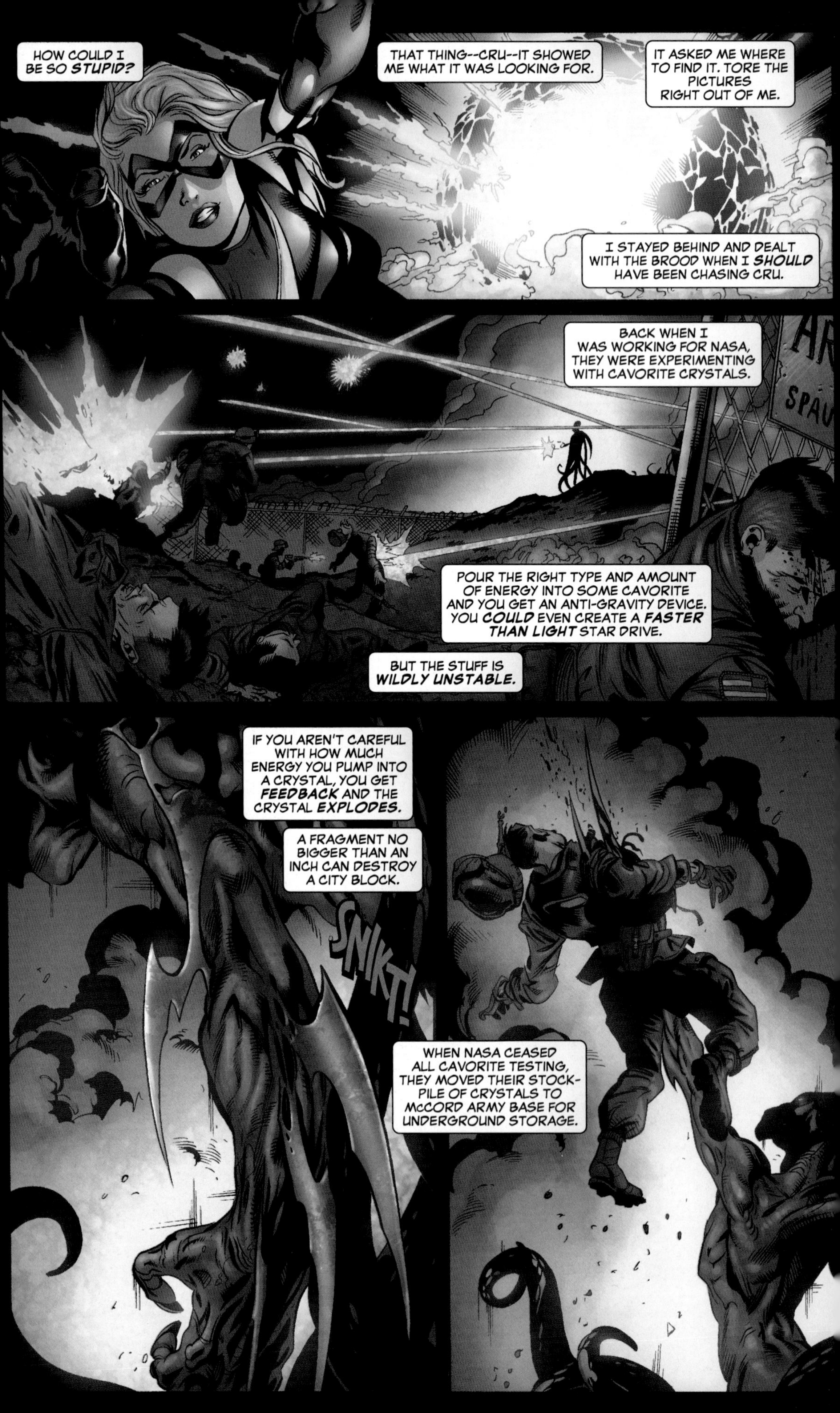
HOW COULD I BE SO STUPID?
THAT THING--CRU--IT SHOWED ME WHAT IT WAS LOOKING FOR.
IT ASKED ME WHERE TO FIND IT. TORE THE PICTURES RIGHT OUT OF ME.
I STAYED BEHIND AND DEALT WITH THE BROOD WHEN I SHOULD HAVE BEEN CHASING CRU.
BACK WHEN I WAS WORKING FOR NASA, THEY WERE EXPERIMENTING WITH CAVORITE CRYSTALS.
POUR THE RIGHT TYPE AND AMOUNT OF ENERGY INTO SOME CAVORITE AND YOU GET AN ANTI-GRAVITY DEVICE. YOU COULD EVEN CREATE A FASTER THAN LIGHT STAR DRIVE.
BUT THE STUFF IS WILDLY UNSTABLE.
IF YOU AREN'T CAREFUL WITH HOW MUCH ENERGY YOU PUMP INTO A CRYSTAL, YOU GET FEEDBACK AND THE CRYSTAL EXPLODES.
A FRAGMENT NO BIGGER THAN AN INCH CAN DESTROY A CITY BLOCK.
SNIKT!
WHEN NASA CEASED ALL CAVORITE TESTING, THEY MOVED THEIR STOCK-PILE OF CRYSTALS TO McCORD ARMY BASE FOR UNDERGROUND STORAGE.

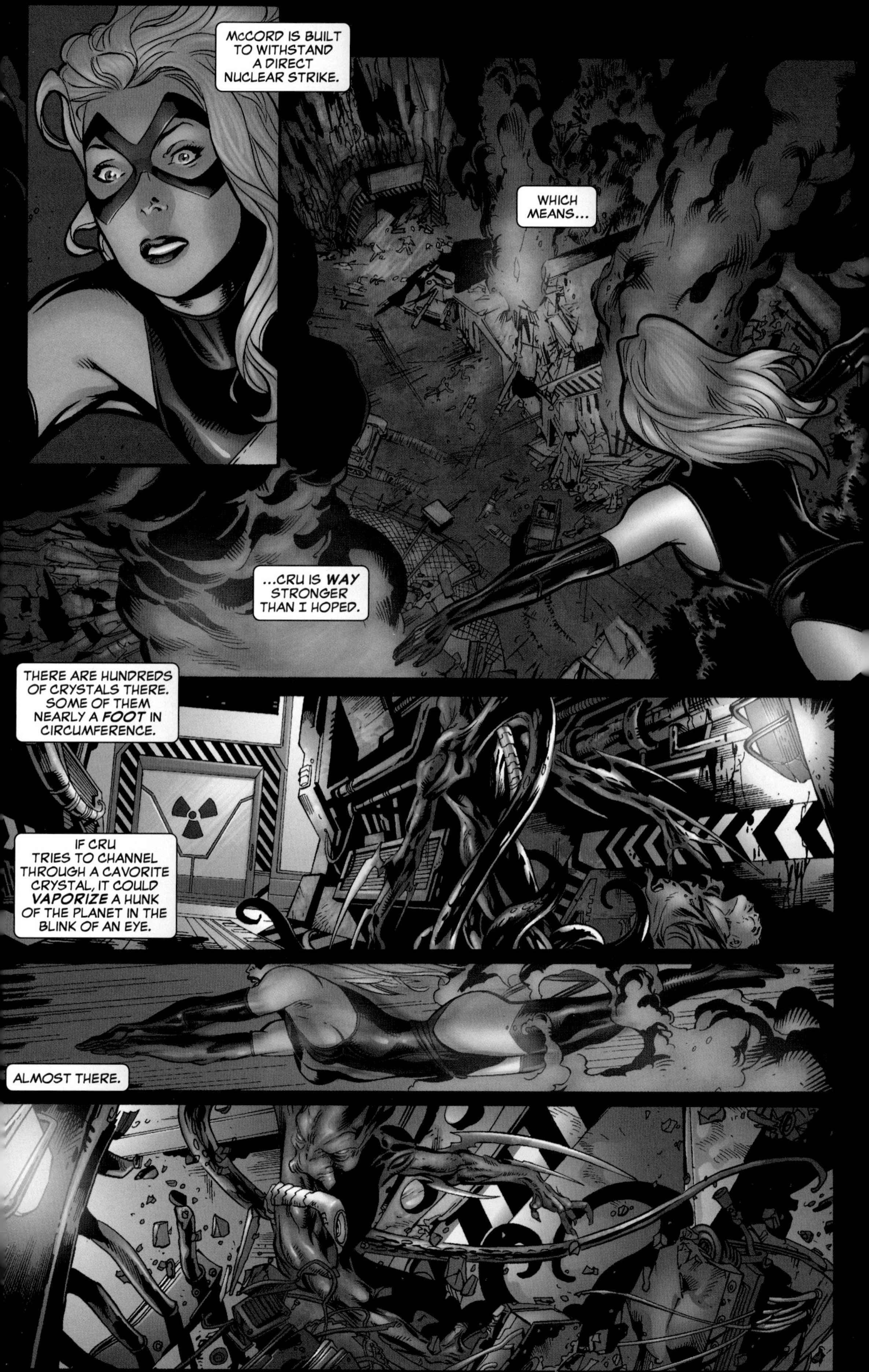
McCORD IS BUILT TO WITHSTAND A DIRECT NUCLEAR STRIKE.
WHICH MEANS...
...CRU IS WAY STRONGER THAN I HOPED.
THERE ARE HUNDREDS OF CRYSTALS THERE. SOME OF THEM NEARLY A FOOT IN CIRCUMFERENCE.
IF CRU TRIES TO CHANNEL THROUGH A CAVORITE CRYSTAL, IT COULD VAPORIZE A HUNK OF THE PLANET IN THE BLINK OF AN EYE.
ALMOST THERE.

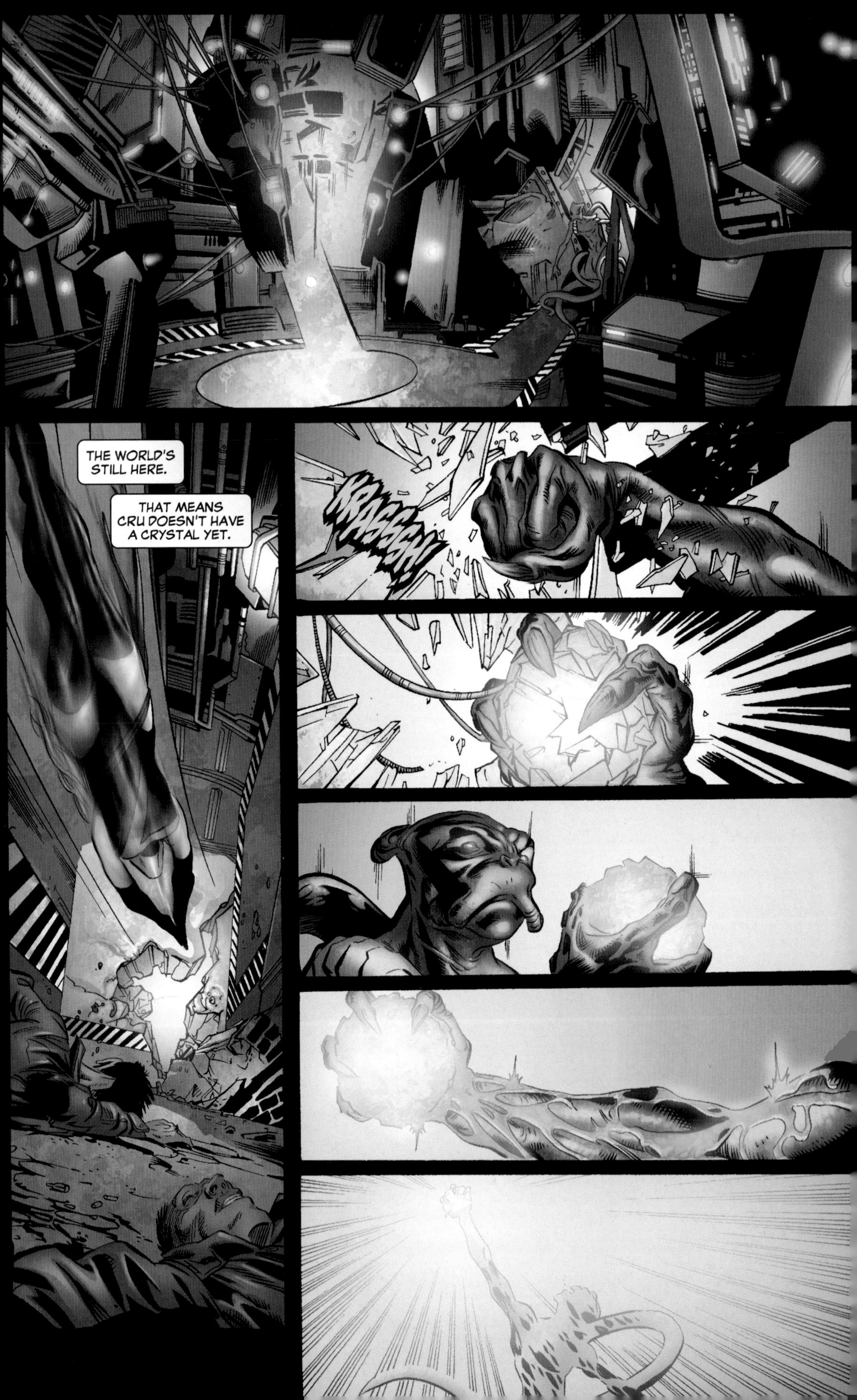
THE WORLD'S STILL HERE.
THAT MEANS CRU DOESN'T HAVE A CRYSTAL YET.
KRASSSH!

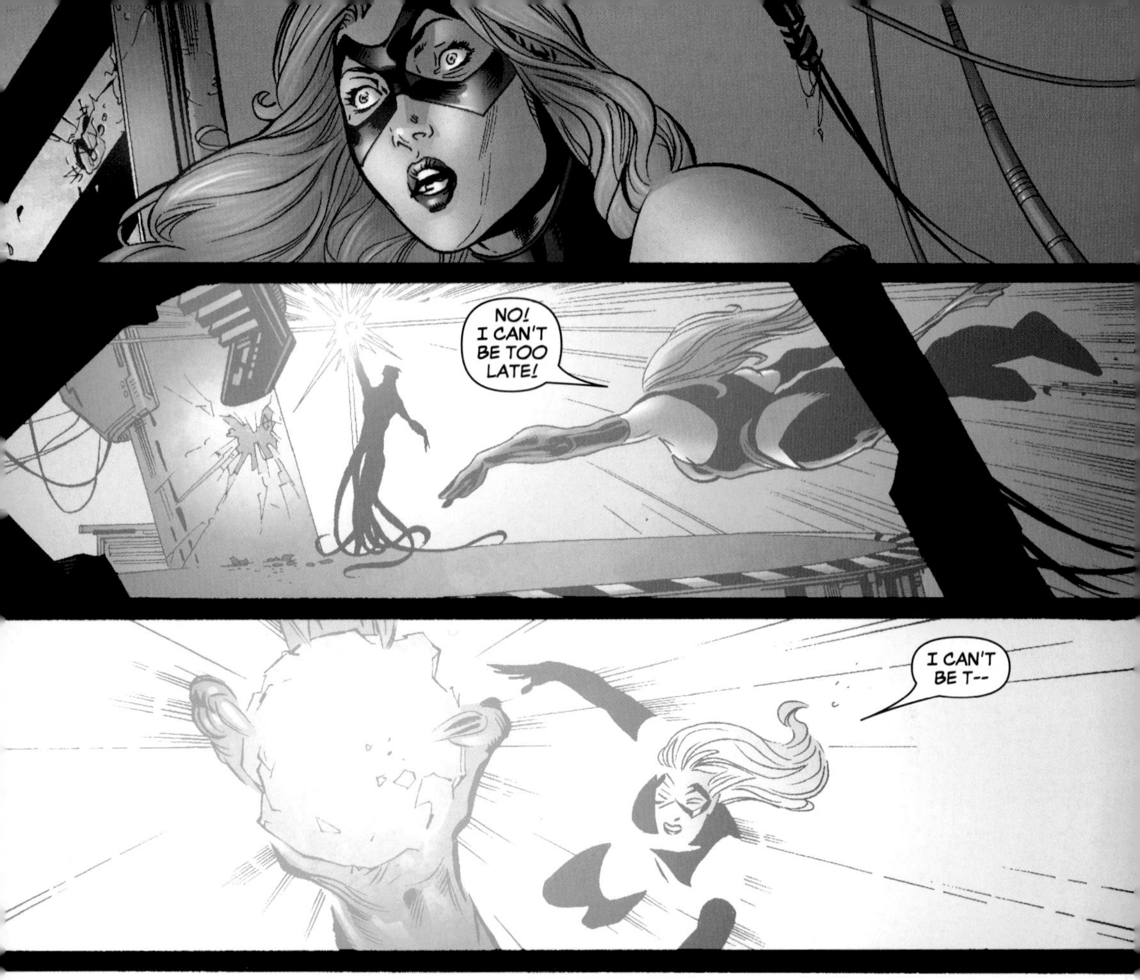
NO! I CAN'T BE TOO LATE!
I CAN'T BE T--

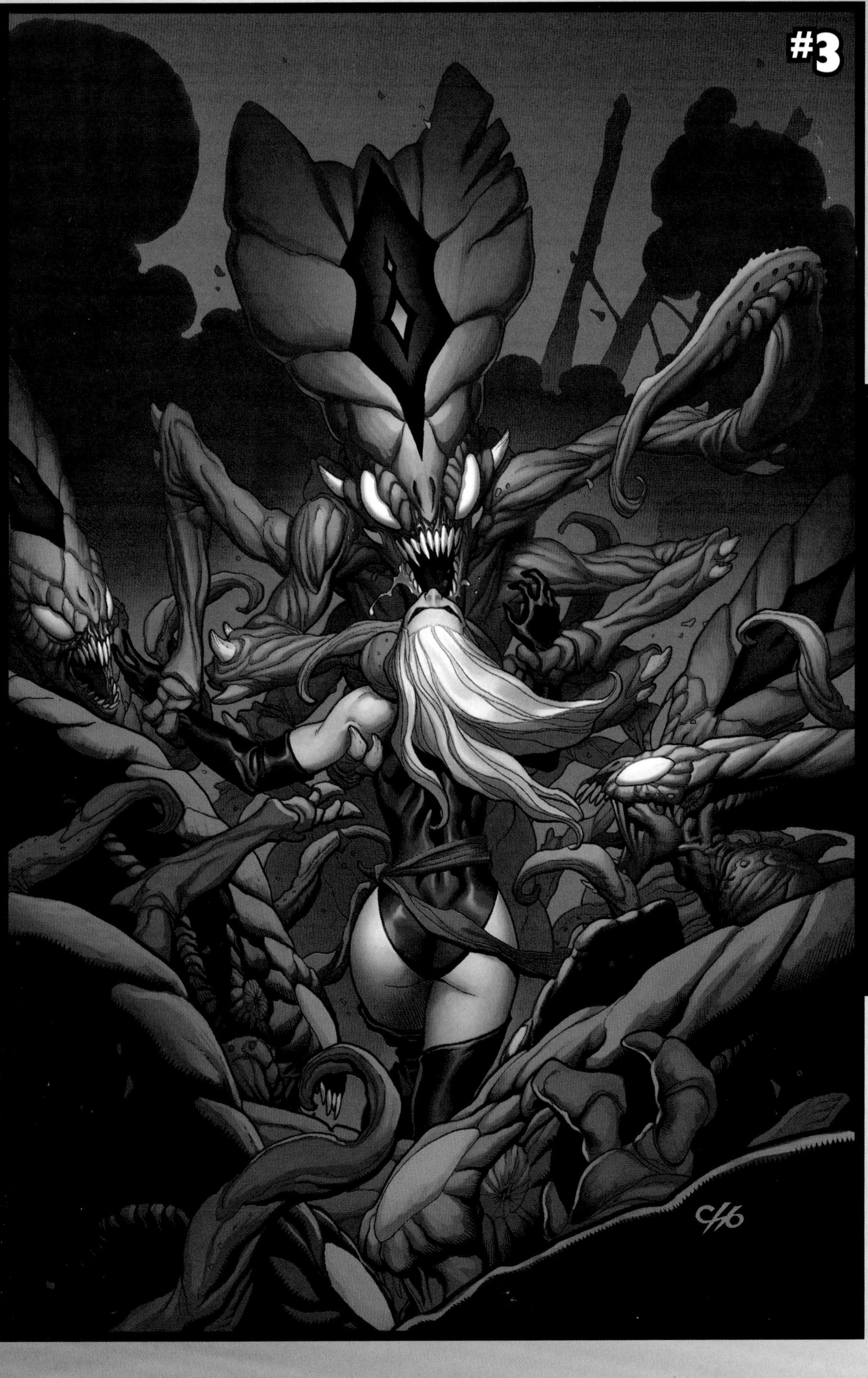
#3
CHO

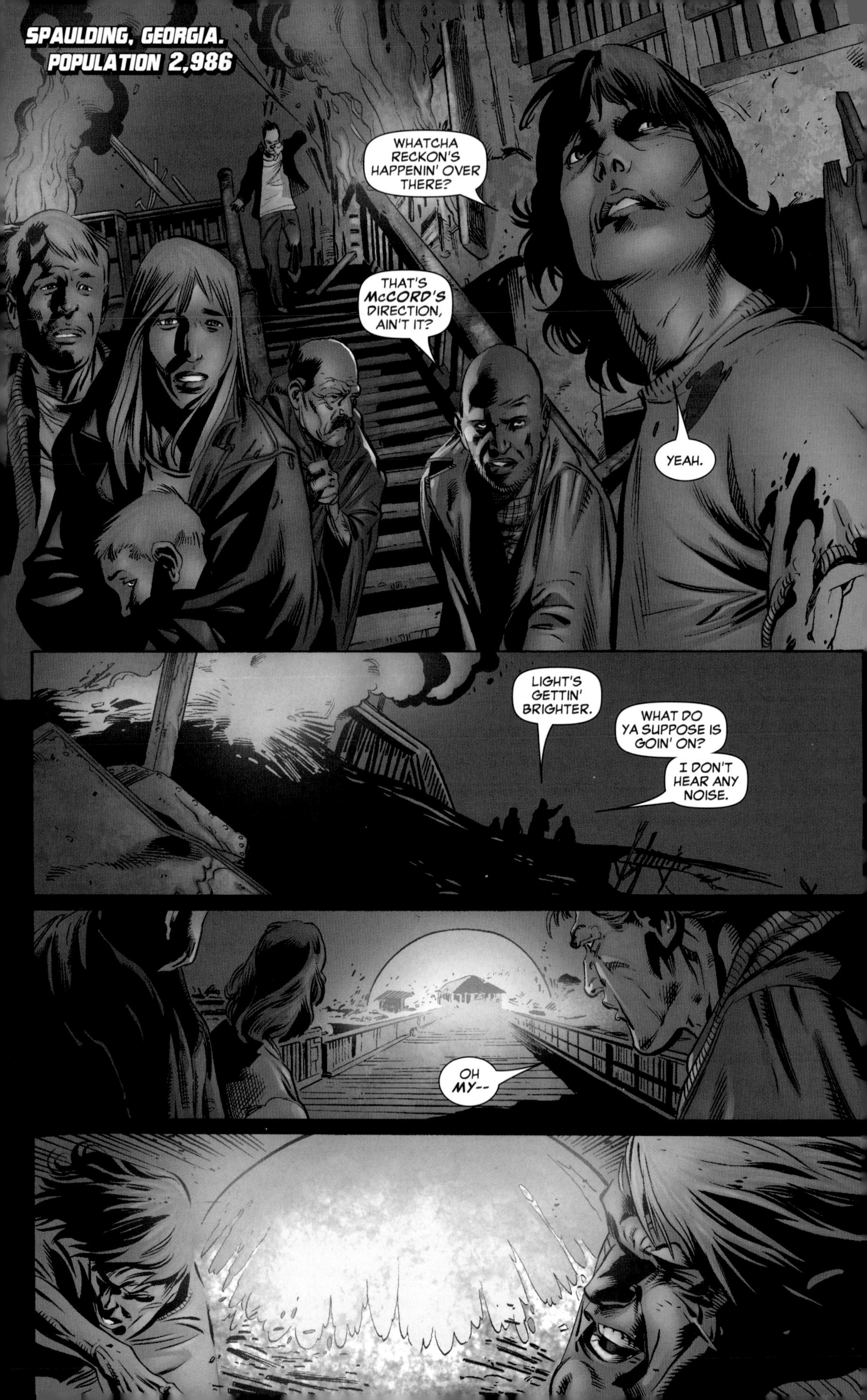
SPAULDING, GEORGIA. POPULATION 2,986
WHATCHA RECKON'S HAPPENIN' OVER THERE?
THAT'S McCORD'S DIRECTION, AIN'T IT?
YEAH.
LIGHT'S GETTIN' BRIGHTER.
WHAT DO YA SUPPOSE IS GOIN' ON?
I DON'T HEAR ANY NOISE.
OH MY--

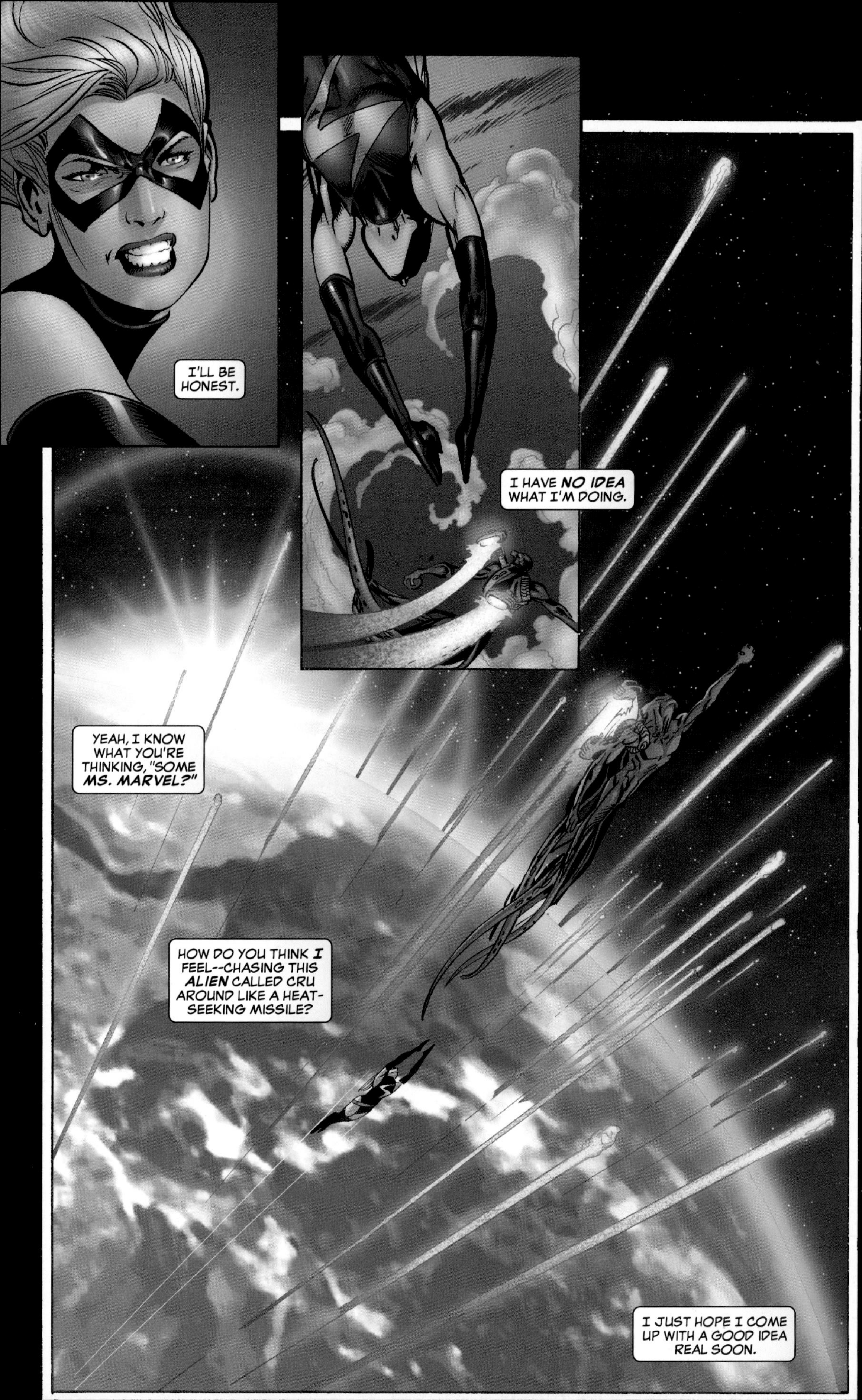
I'LL BE HONEST.
I HAVE NO IDEA WHAT I'M DOING.
YEAH, I KNOW WHAT YOU'RE THINKING, "SOME MS. MARVEL?"
HOW DO YOU THINK I FEEL--CHASING THIS ALIEN CALLED CRU AROUND LIKE A HEAT-SEEKING MISSILE?
I JUST HOPE I COME UP WITH A GOOD IDEA REAL SOON.

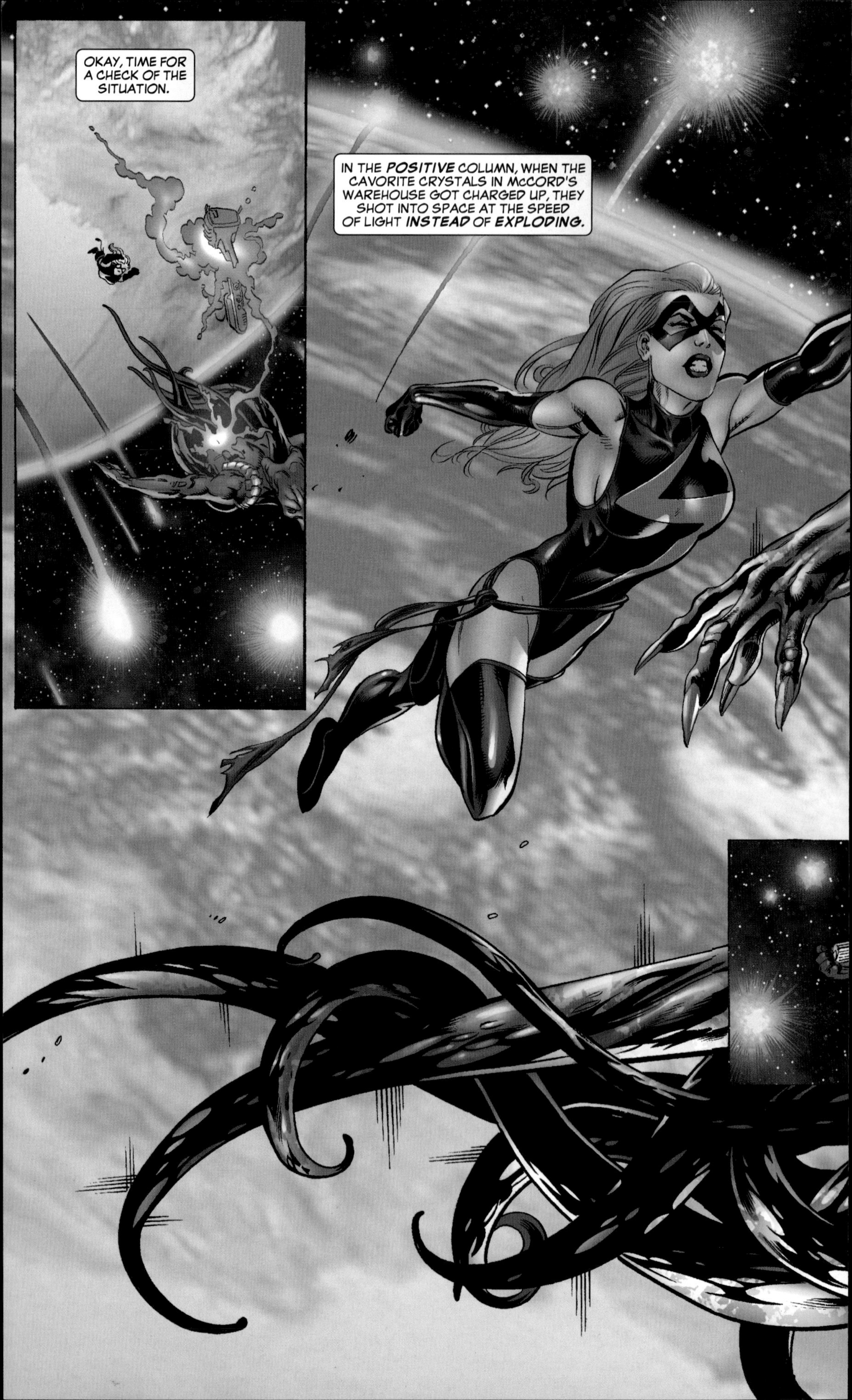
OKAY, TIME FOR A CHECK OF THE SITUATION.
IN THE POSITIVE COLUMN, WHEN THE CAVORITE CRYSTALS IN McCORD'S WAREHOUSE GOT CHARGED UP, THEY SHOT INTO SPACE AT THE SPEED OF LIGHT INSTEAD OF EXPLODING.

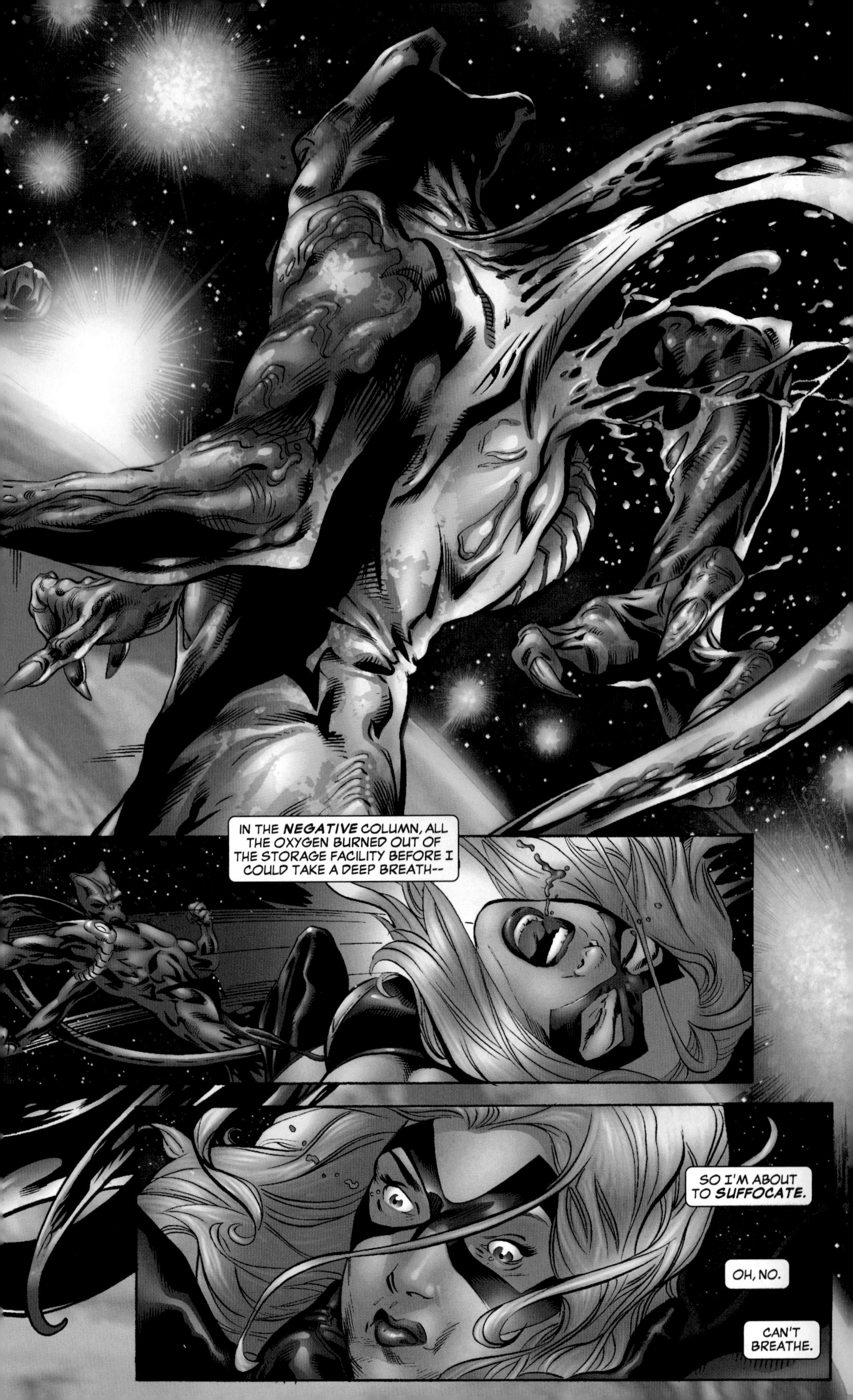
IN THE NEGATIVE COLUMN, ALL THE OXYGEN BURNED OUT OF THE STORAGE FACILITY BEFORE I COULD TAKE A DEEP BREATH--
SO I'M ABOUT TO SUFFOCATE.
OH, NO.
CAN'T BREATHE.

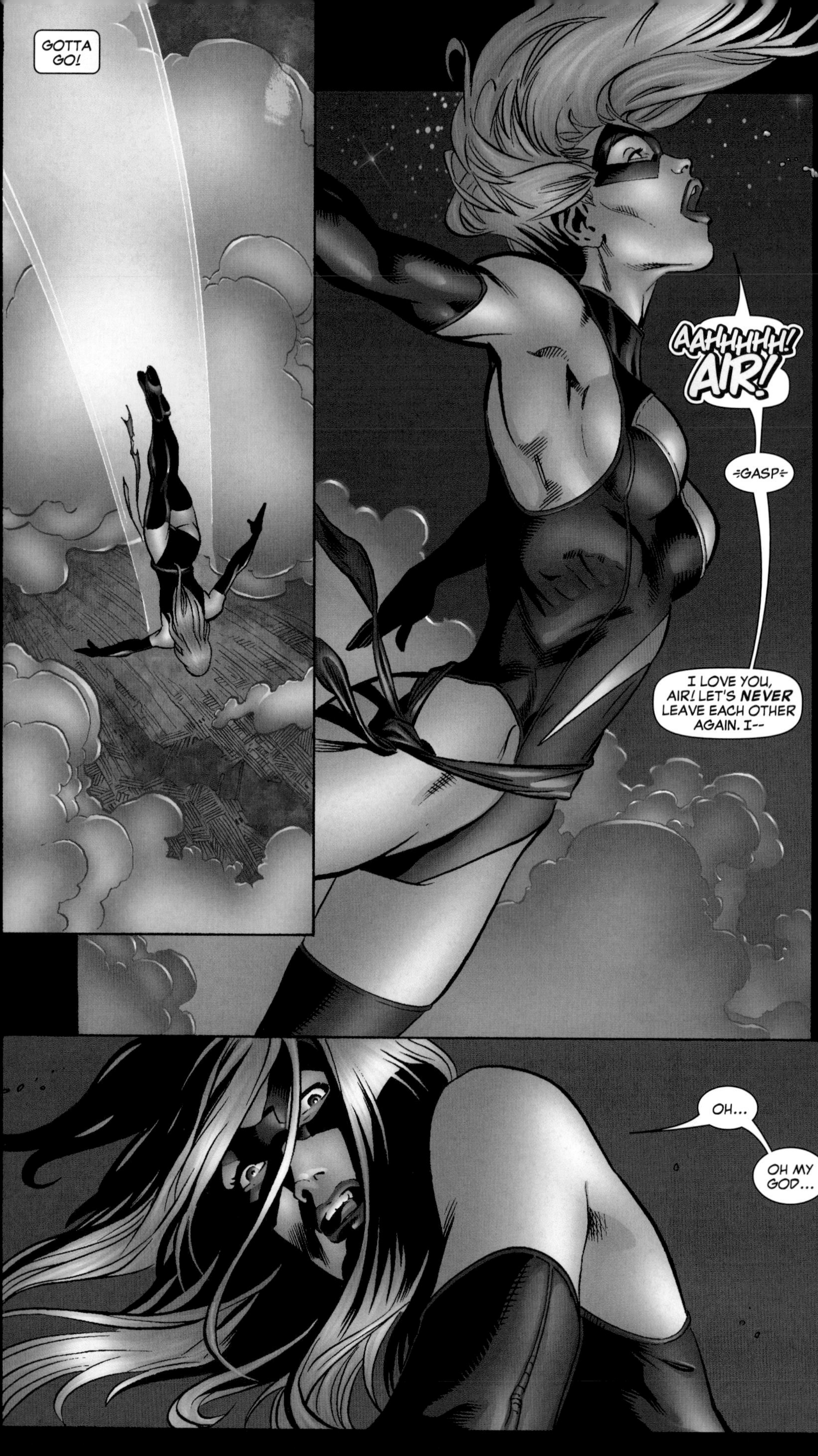
GOTTA GO!
AAHHHHH! AIR!
=GASP=
I LOVE YOU, AIR! LET'S NEVER LEAVE EACH OTHER AGAIN. I--
OH...
OH MY GOD...

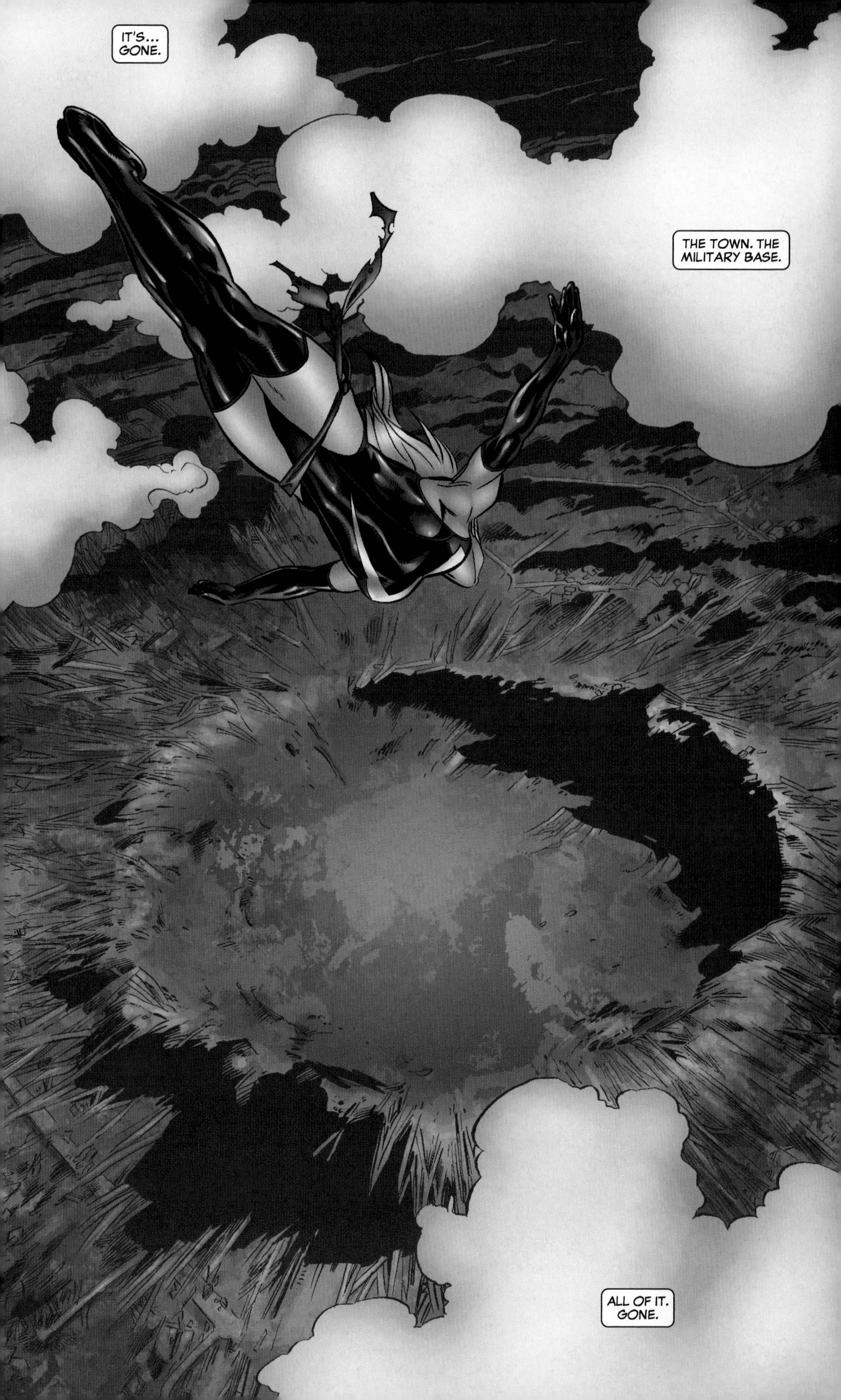
IT'S... GONE.
THE TOWN. THE MILITARY BASE.
ALL OF IT. GONE.

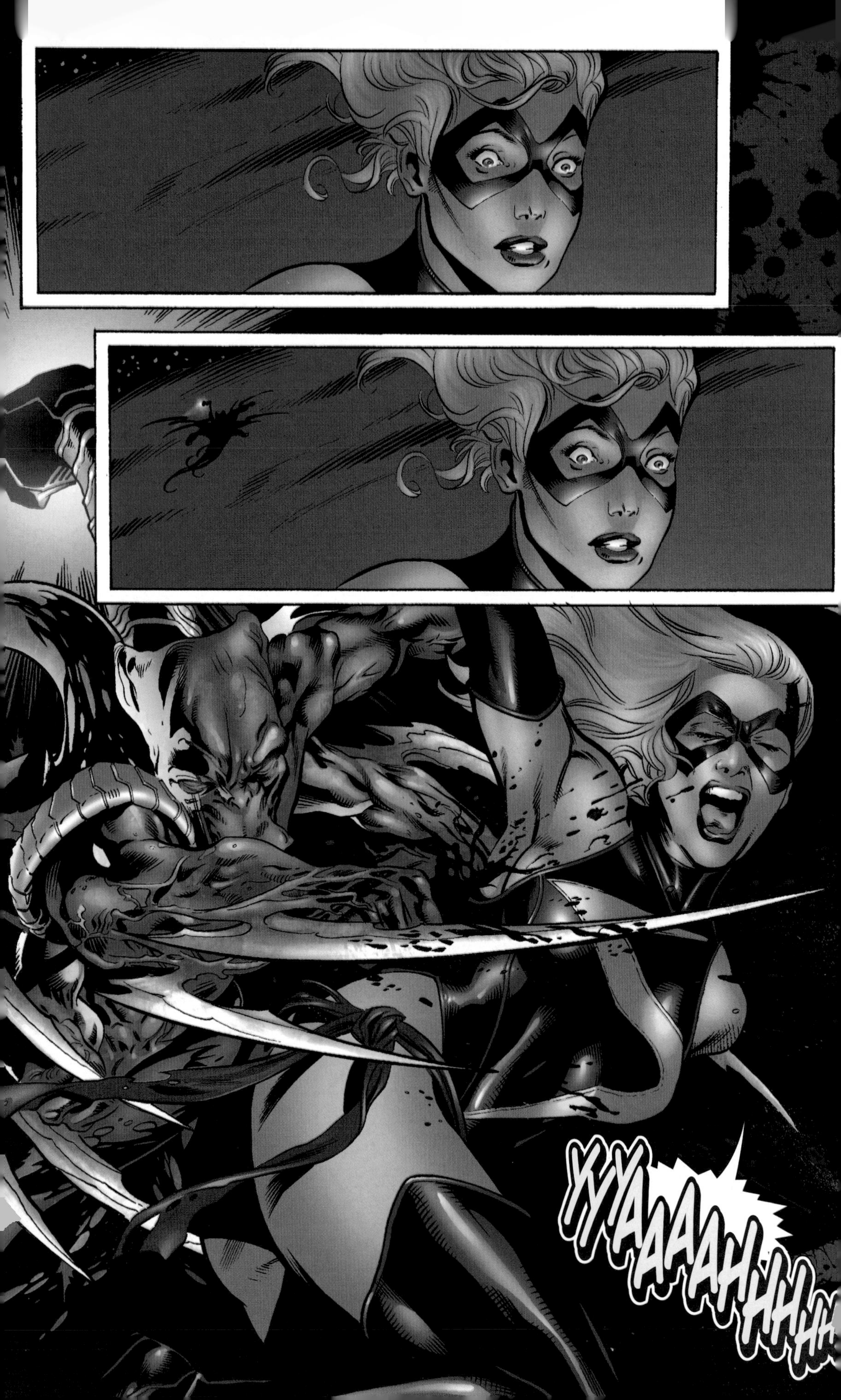
YYAAAAHHHHHH

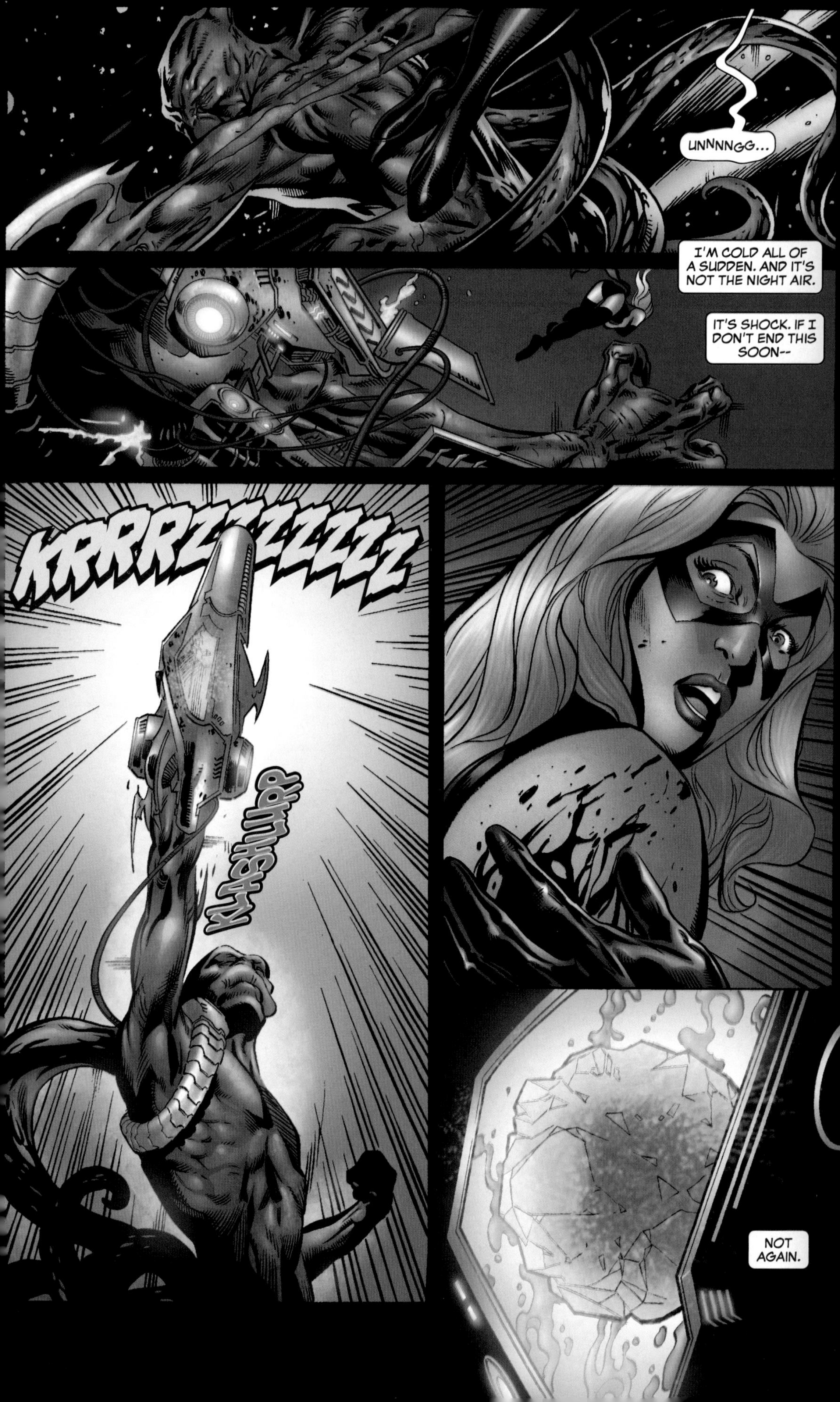
UNNNNGG...
I'M COLD ALL OF A SUDDEN. AND IT'S NOT THE NIGHT AIR.
IT'S SHOCK. IF I DON'T END THIS SOON--
KRRRZZZZZZZZ
KLASHULP
NOT AGAIN.

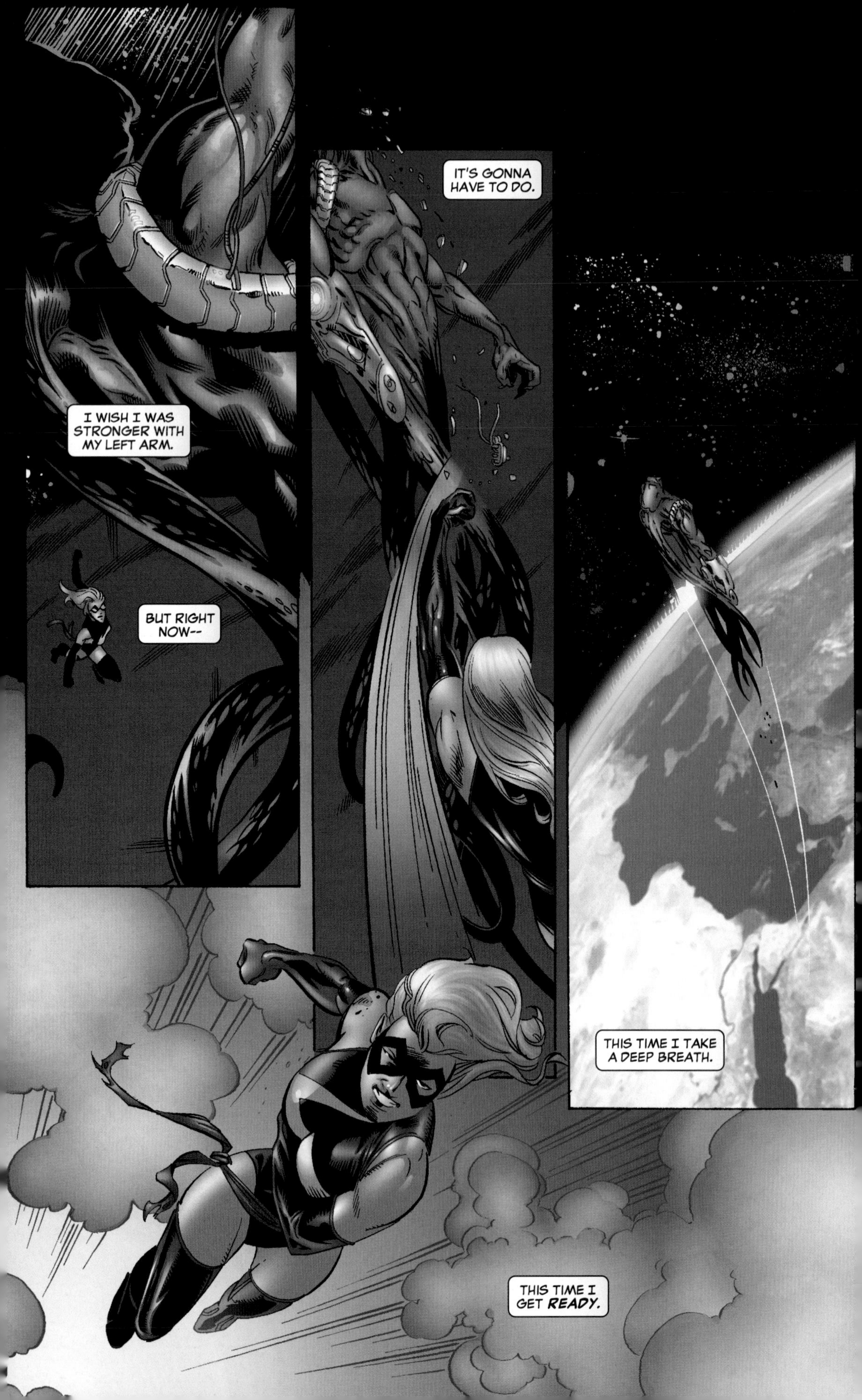
I WISH I WAS
STRONGER WITH
MY LEFT ARM.
BUT RIGHT
NOW--
IT'S GONNA
HAVE TO DO.
THIS TIME I TAKE
A DEEP BREATH.
THIS TIME I
GET *READY.*

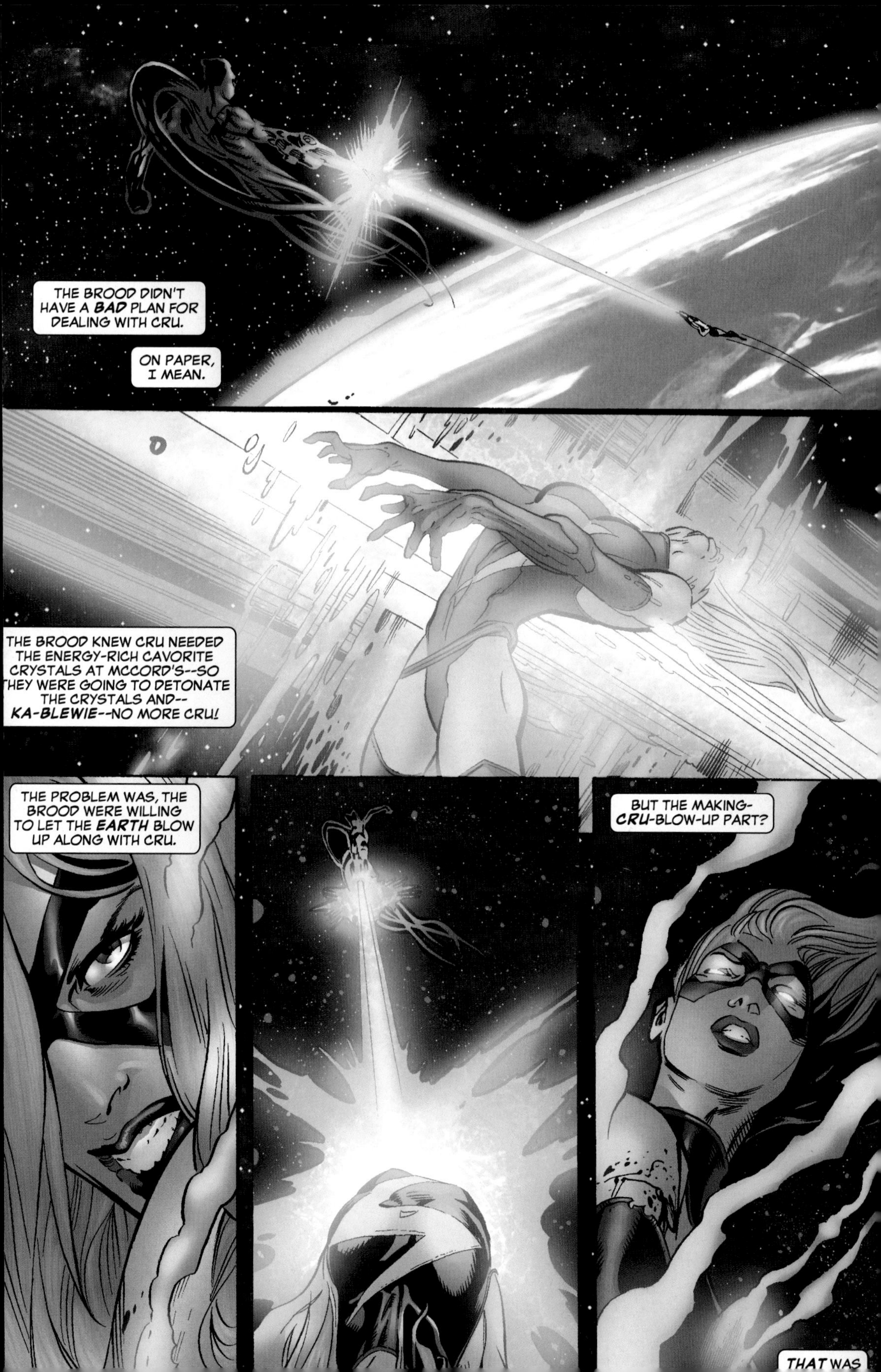
THE BROOD DIDN'T HAVE A BAD PLAN FOR DEALING WITH CRU.
ON PAPER, I MEAN.
THE BROOD KNEW CRU NEEDED THE ENERGY-RICH CAVORITE CRYSTALS AT MCCORD'S--SO THEY WERE GOING TO DETONATE THE CRYSTALS AND-- KA-BLEWIE--NO MORE CRU!
THE PROBLEM WAS, THE BROOD WERE WILLING TO LET THE EARTH BLOW UP ALONG WITH CRU.
BUT THE MAKING-CRU-BLOW-UP PART?
THAT WAS

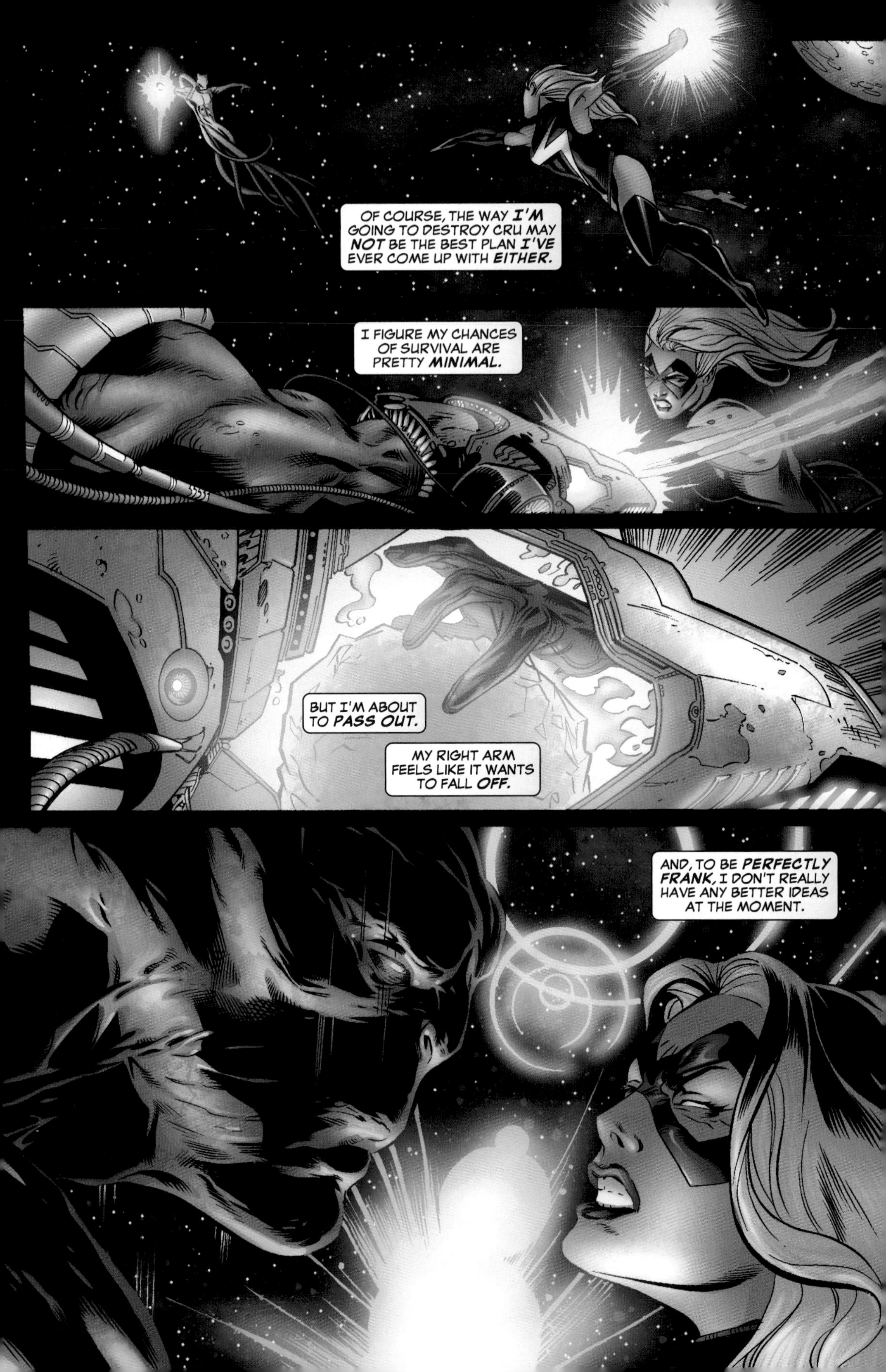
OF COURSE, THE WAY I'M GOING TO DESTROY CRU MAY NOT BE THE BEST PLAN I'VE EVER COME UP WITH EITHER.
I FIGURE MY CHANCES OF SURVIVAL ARE PRETTY MINIMAL.
BUT I'M ABOUT TO PASS OUT.
MY RIGHT ARM FEELS LIKE IT WANTS TO FALL OFF.
AND, TO BE PERFECTLY FRANK, I DON'T REALLY HAVE ANY BETTER IDEAS AT THE MOMENT.

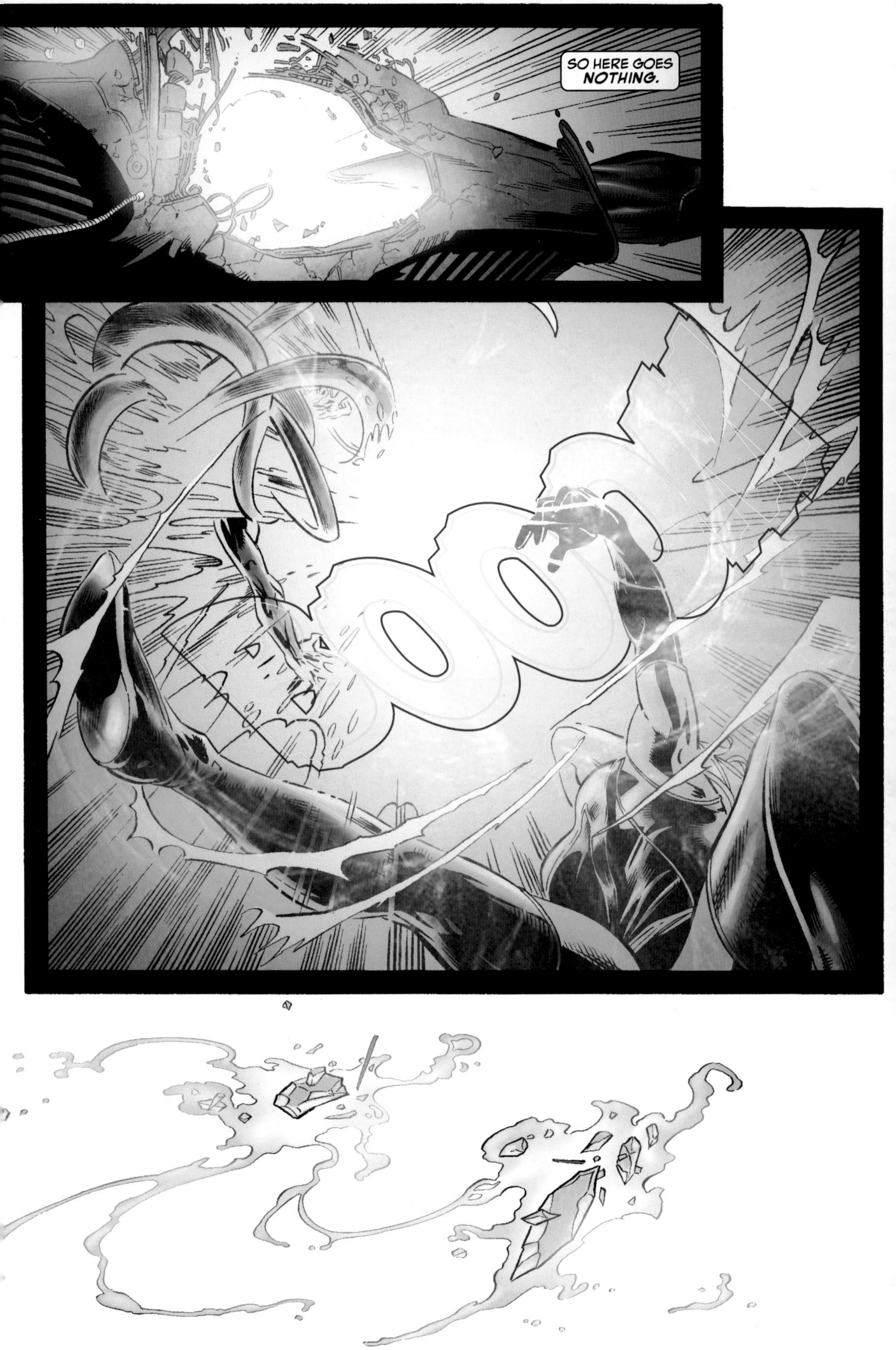
SO HERE GOES NOTHING.

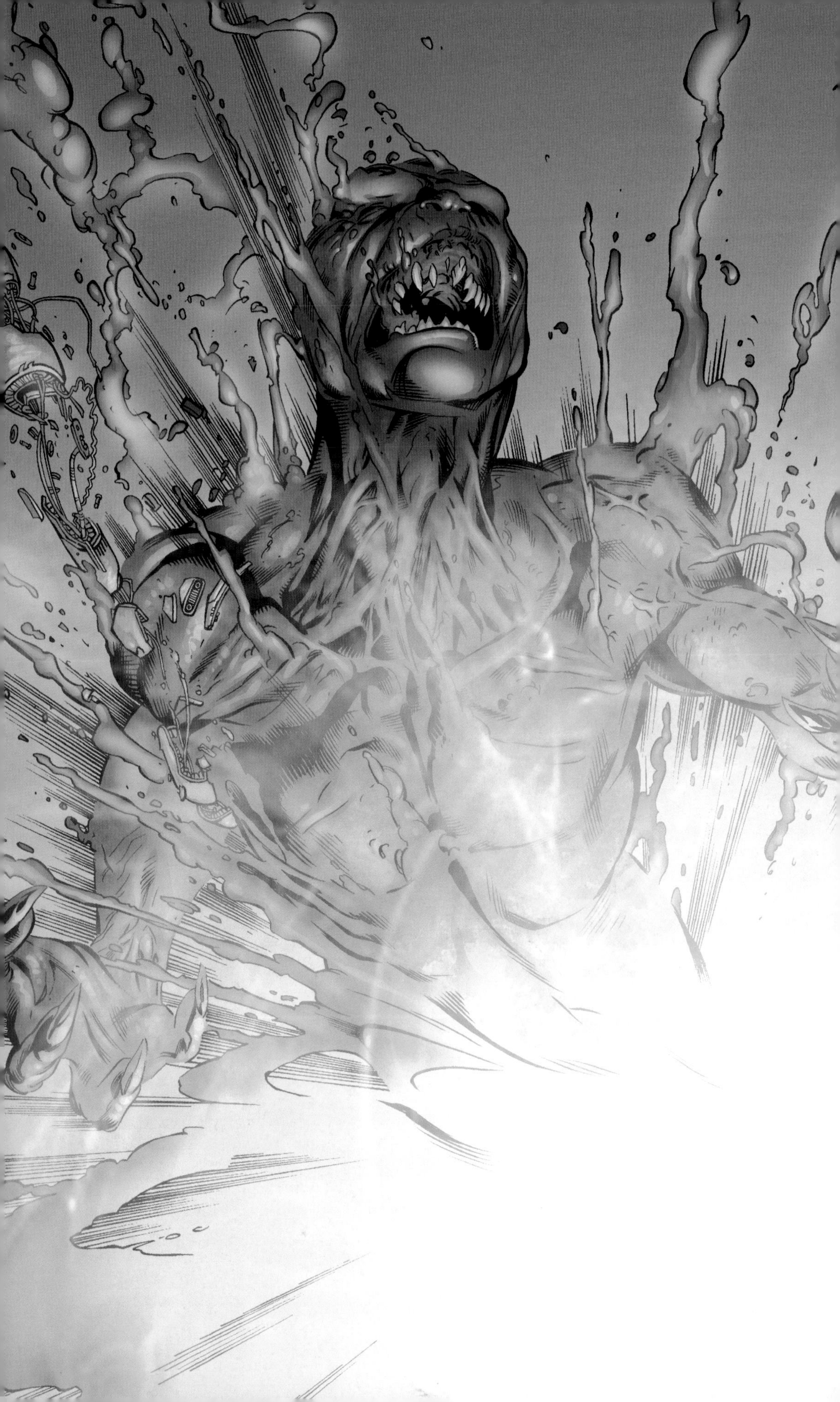

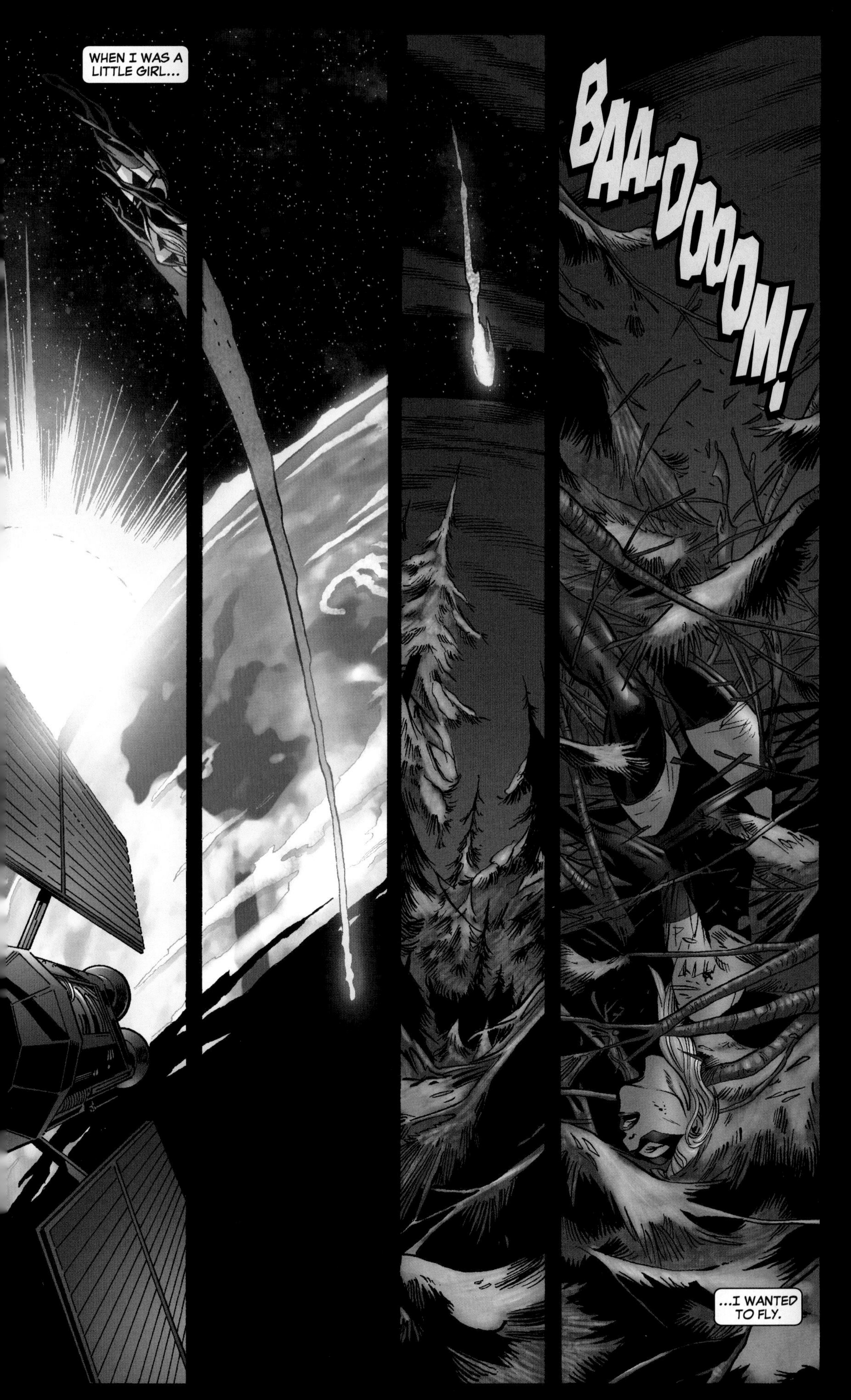
WHEN I WAS A LITTLE GIRL...
BAA-DOOOM!
...I WANTED TO FLY.

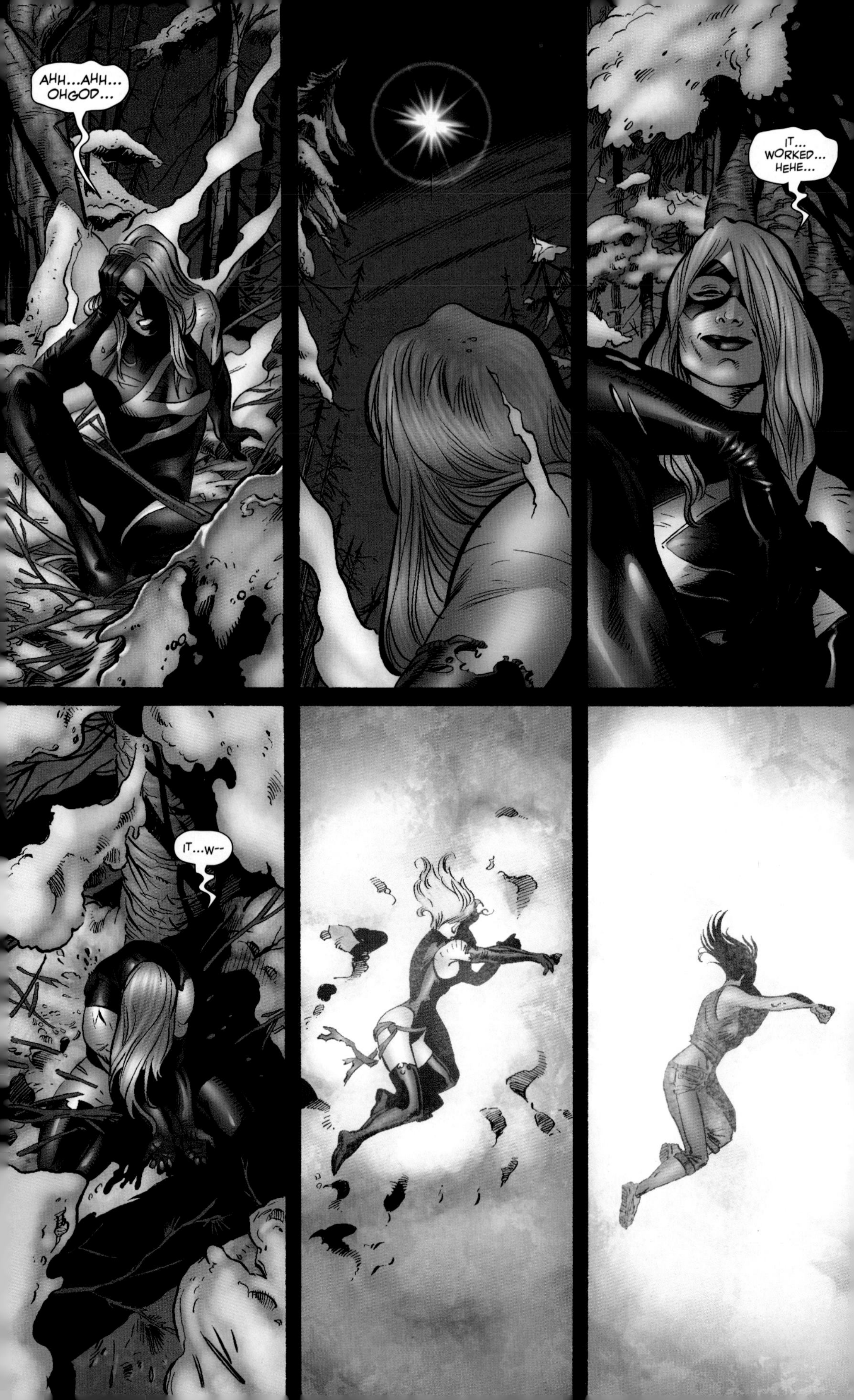
AHH...AHH... OHGOD...
IT... WORKED... HEHE...
IT...W--

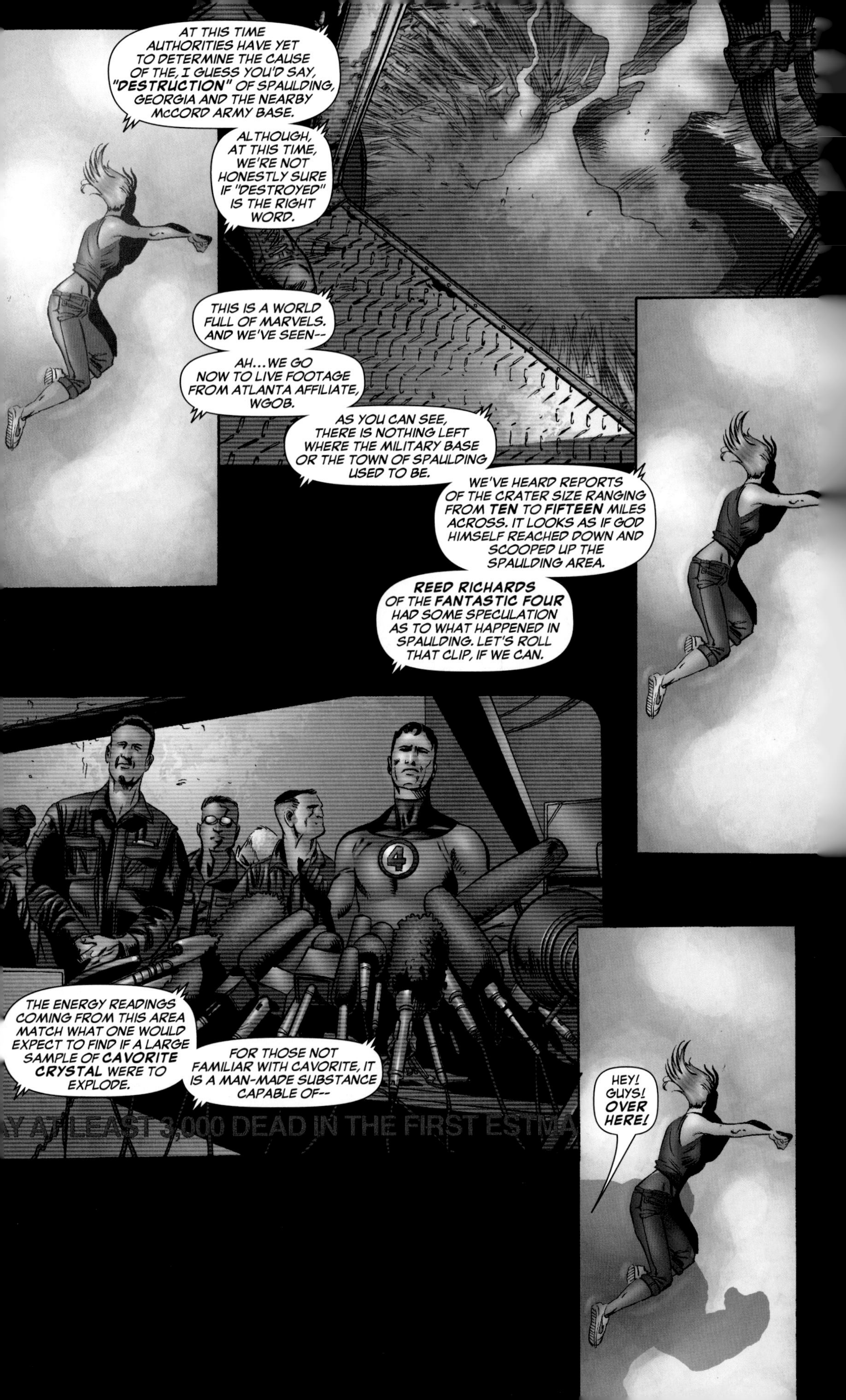
AT THIS TIME AUTHORITIES HAVE YET TO DETERMINE THE CAUSE OF THE, I GUESS YOU'D SAY, "DESTRUCTION" OF SPAULDING, GEORGIA AND THE NEARBY McCORD ARMY BASE.
ALTHOUGH, AT THIS TIME, WE'RE NOT HONESTLY SURE IF "DESTROYED" IS THE RIGHT WORD.
THIS IS A WORLD FULL OF MARVELS. AND WE'VE SEEN--
AH...WE GO NOW TO LIVE FOOTAGE FROM ATLANTA AFFILIATE, WGOB.
AS YOU CAN SEE, THERE IS NOTHING LEFT WHERE THE MILITARY BASE OR THE TOWN OF SPAULDING USED TO BE.
WE'VE HEARD REPORTS OF THE CRATER SIZE RANGING FROM TEN TO FIFTEEN MILES ACROSS. IT LOOKS AS IF GOD HIMSELF REACHED DOWN AND SCOOPED UP THE SPAULDING AREA.
REED RICHARDS OF THE FANTASTIC FOUR HAD SOME SPECULATION AS TO WHAT HAPPENED IN SPAULDING. LET'S ROLL THAT CLIP, IF WE CAN.
THE ENERGY READINGS COMING FROM THIS AREA MATCH WHAT ONE WOULD EXPECT TO FIND IF A LARGE SAMPLE OF CAVORITE CRYSTAL WERE TO EXPLODE.
FOR THOSE NOT FAMILIAR WITH CAVORITE, IT IS A MAN-MADE SUBSTANCE CAPABLE OF--
AY AT LEAST 3,000 DEAD IN THE FIRST ESTIMA
HEY! GUYS! OVER HERE!

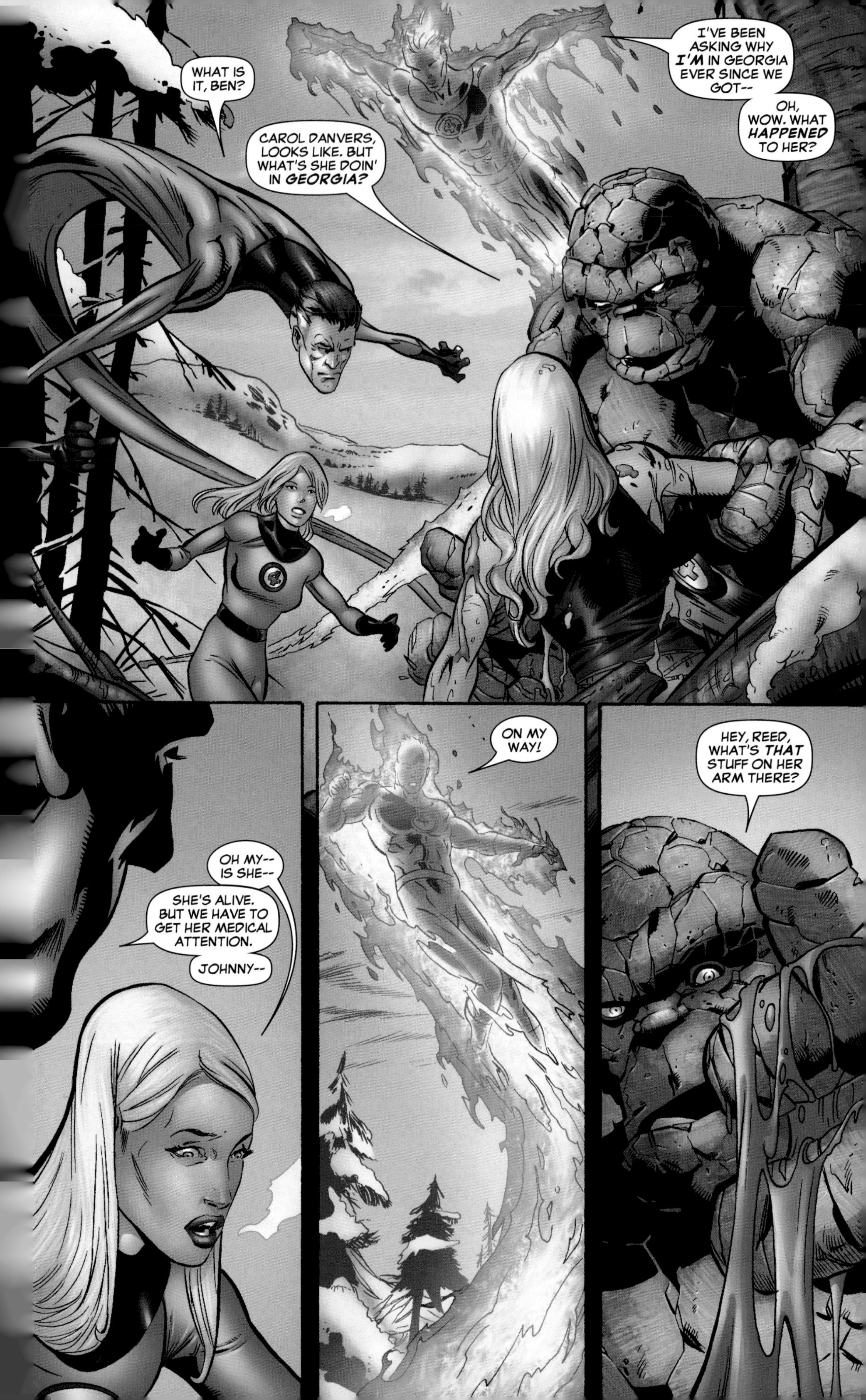

WHAT IS IT, BEN?
CAROL DANVERS, LOOKS LIKE. BUT WHAT'S SHE DOIN' IN GEORGIA?
I'VE BEEN ASKING WHY I'M IN GEORGIA EVER SINCE WE GOT--
OH, WOW. WHAT HAPPENED TO HER?
OH MY-- IS SHE--
SHE'S ALIVE. BUT WE HAVE TO GET HER MEDICAL ATTENTION.
JOHNNY--
ON MY WAY!
HEY, REED, WHAT'S THAT STUFF ON HER ARM THERE?

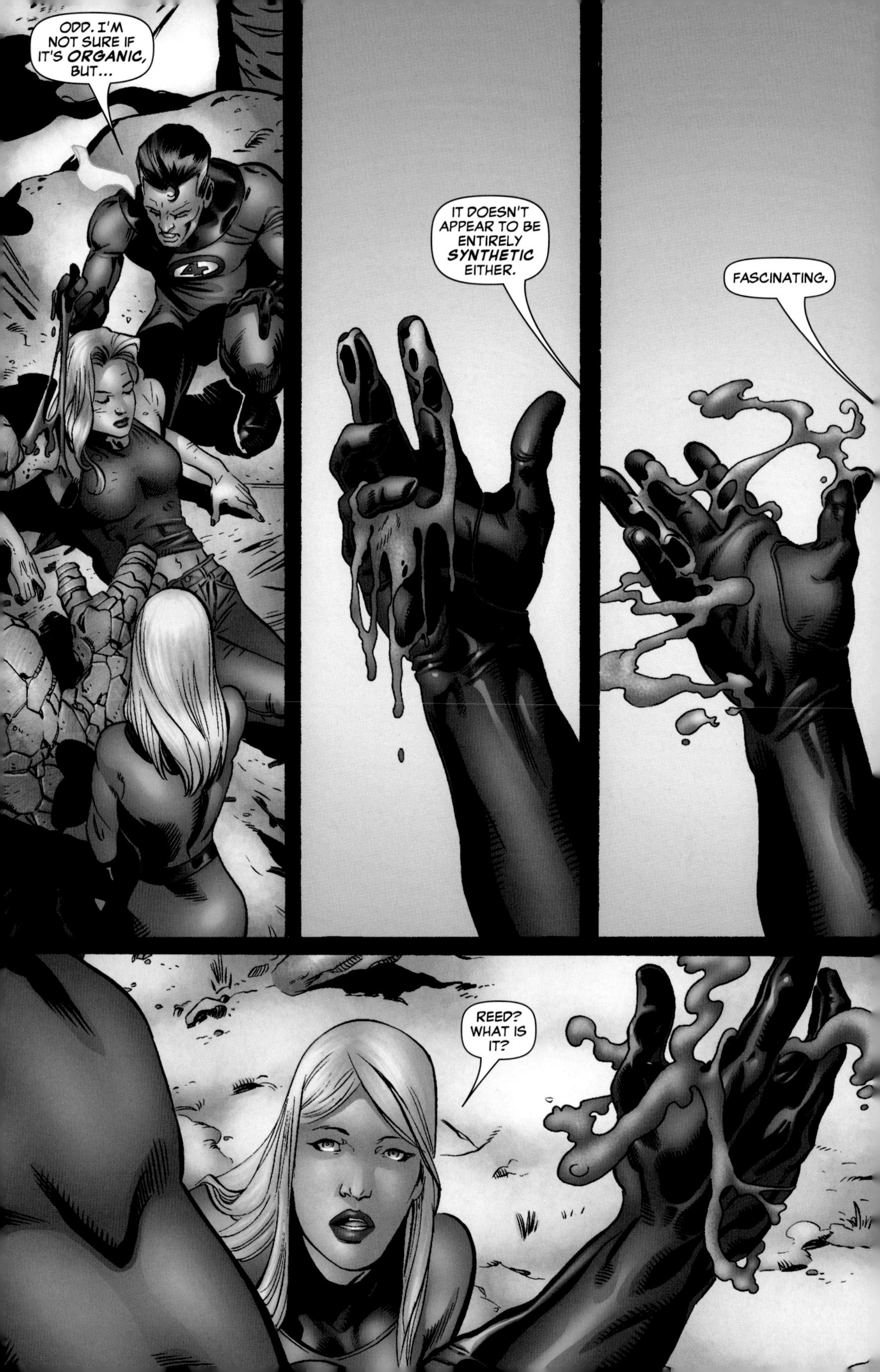
ODD. I'M NOT SURE IF IT'S ORGANIC, BUT...
IT DOESN'T APPEAR TO BE ENTIRELY SYNTHETIC EITHER.
FASCINATING.
REED? WHAT IS IT?

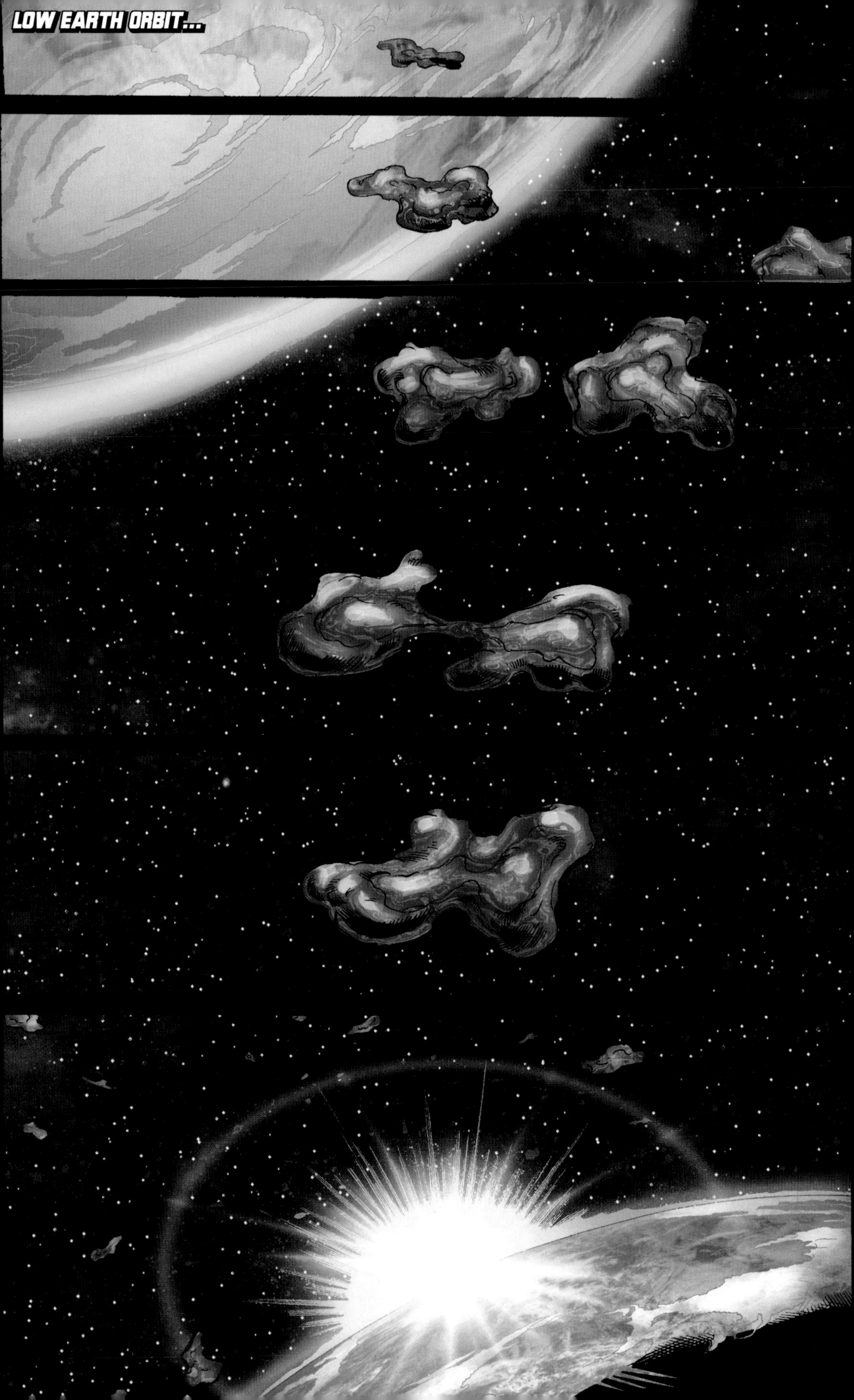
LOW EARTH ORBIT...

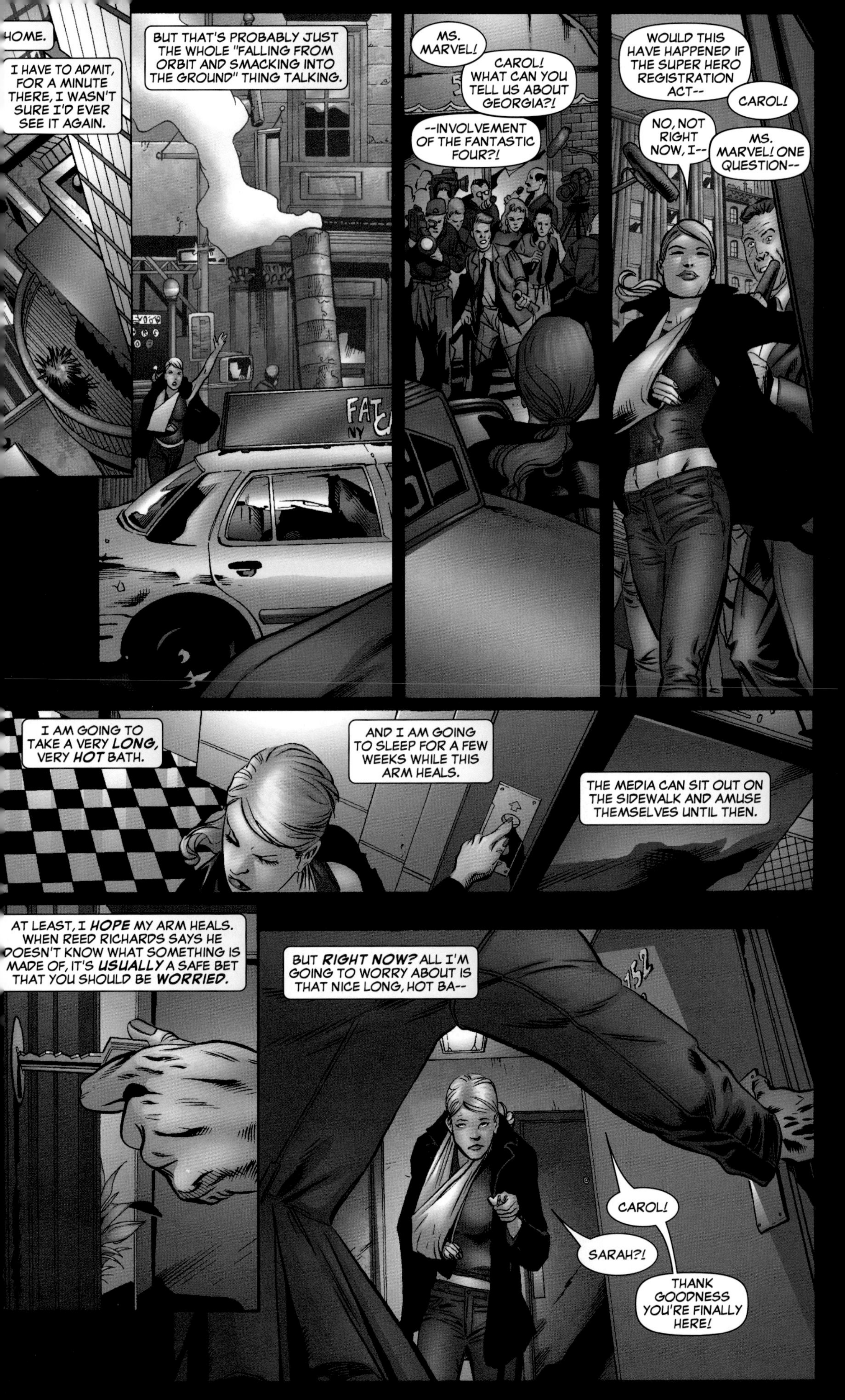
HOME.
I HAVE TO ADMIT, FOR A MINUTE THERE, I WASN'T SURE I'D EVER SEE IT AGAIN.
BUT THAT'S PROBABLY JUST THE WHOLE "FALLING FROM ORBIT AND SMACKING INTO THE GROUND" THING TALKING.
MS. MARVEL!
CAROL! WHAT CAN YOU TELL US ABOUT GEORGIA?!
--INVOLVEMENT OF THE FANTASTIC FOUR?!
WOULD THIS HAVE HAPPENED IF THE SUPER HERO REGISTRATION ACT--
CAROL!
NO, NOT RIGHT NOW, I--
MS. MARVEL! ONE QUESTION--
I AM GOING TO TAKE A VERY LONG, VERY HOT BATH.
AND I AM GOING TO SLEEP FOR A FEW WEEKS WHILE THIS ARM HEALS.
THE MEDIA CAN SIT OUT ON THE SIDEWALK AND AMUSE THEMSELVES UNTIL THEN.
AT LEAST, I HOPE MY ARM HEALS. WHEN REED RICHARDS SAYS HE DOESN'T KNOW WHAT SOMETHING IS MADE OF, IT'S USUALLY A SAFE BET THAT YOU SHOULD BE WORRIED.
BUT RIGHT NOW? ALL I'M GOING TO WORRY ABOUT IS THAT NICE LONG, HOT BA--
CAROL!
SARAH?!
THANK GOODNESS YOU'RE FINALLY HERE!

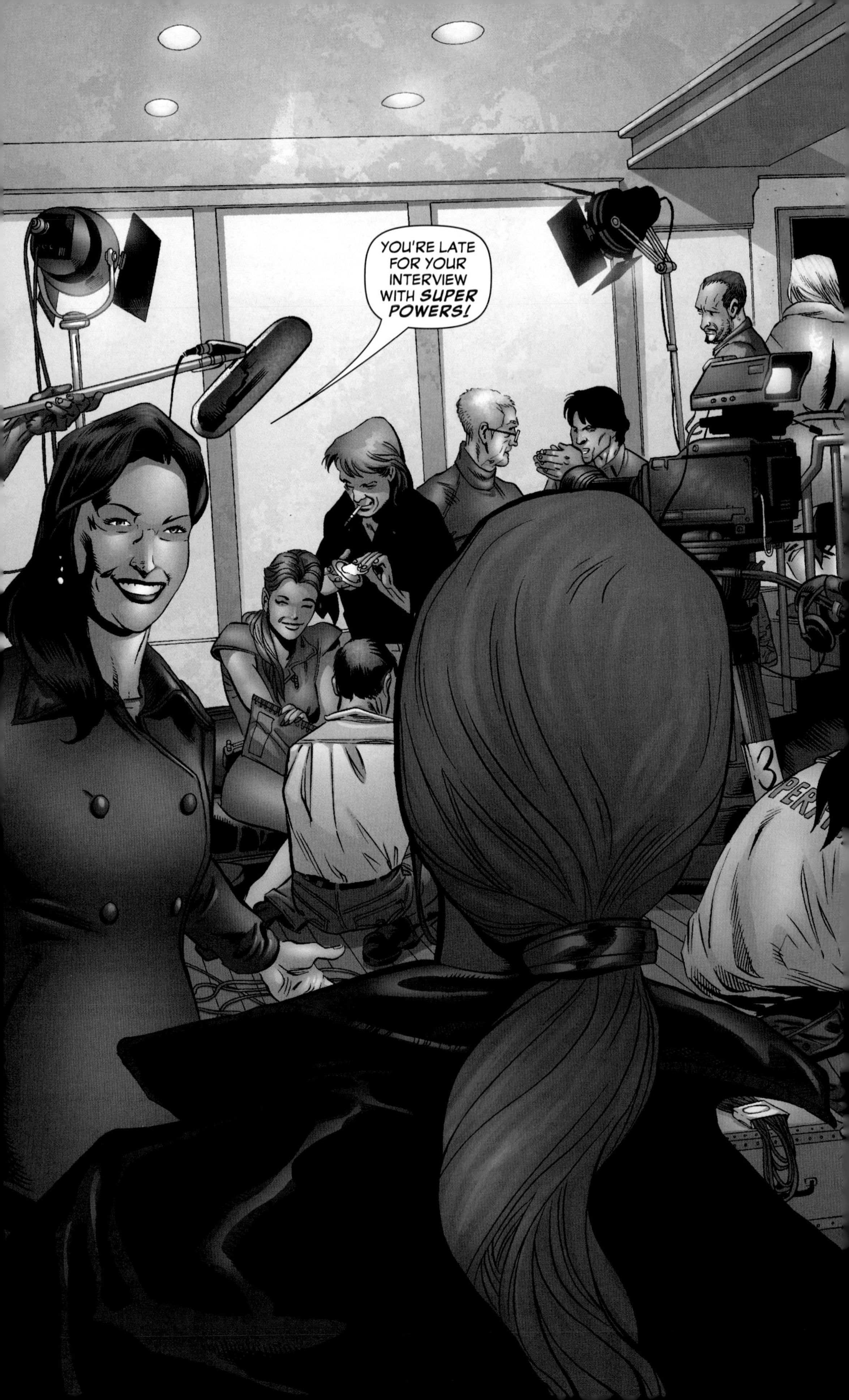
YOU'RE LATE FOR YOUR INTERVIEW WITH SUPER POWERS!

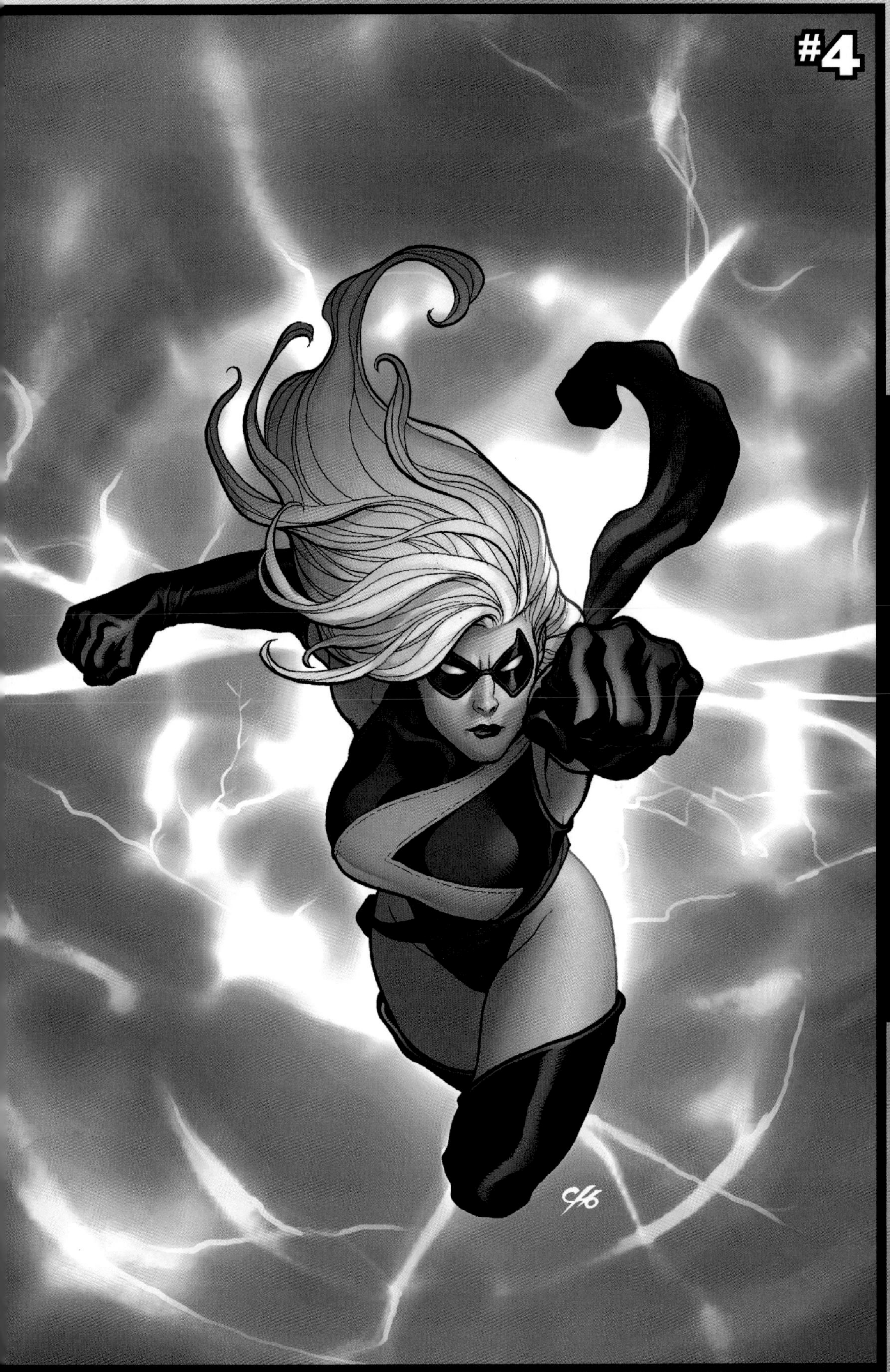
#4

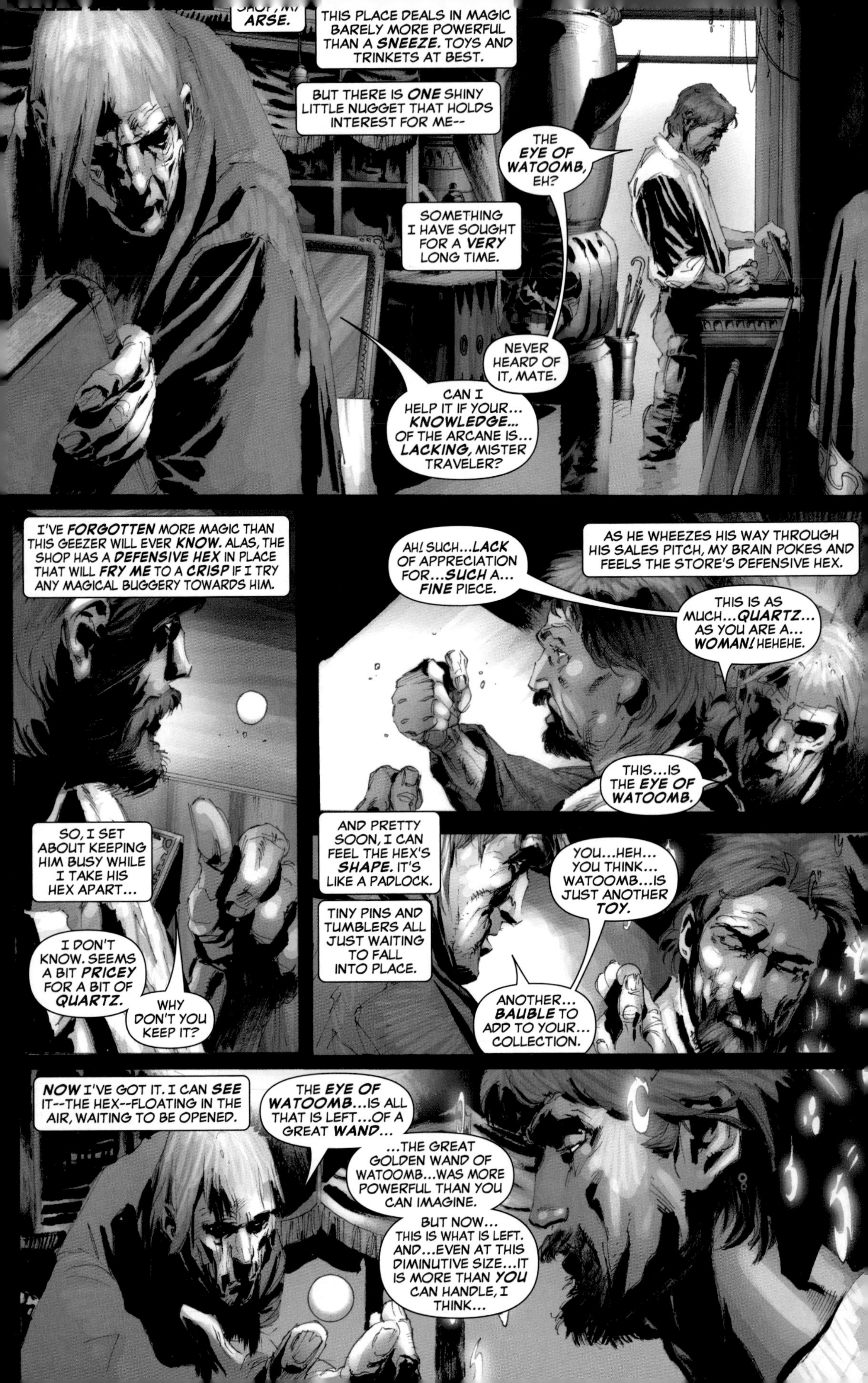

ARSE.
THIS PLACE DEALS IN MAGIC BARELY MORE POWERFUL THAN A SNEEZE. TOYS AND TRINKETS AT BEST.
BUT THERE IS ONE SHINY LITTLE NUGGET THAT HOLDS INTEREST FOR ME--
THE EYE OF WATOOMB, EH?
SOMETHING I HAVE SOUGHT FOR A VERY LONG TIME.
NEVER HEARD OF IT, MATE.
CAN I HELP IT IF YOUR... KNOWLEDGE... OF THE ARCANE IS... LACKING, MISTER TRAVELER?
I'VE FORGOTTEN MORE MAGIC THAN THIS GEEZER WILL EVER KNOW. ALAS, THE SHOP HAS A DEFENSIVE HEX IN PLACE THAT WILL FRY ME TO A CRISP IF I TRY ANY MAGICAL BUGGERY TOWARDS HIM.
SO, I SET ABOUT KEEPING HIM BUSY WHILE I TAKE HIS HEX APART...
I DON'T KNOW. SEEMS A BIT PRICEY FOR A BIT OF QUARTZ.
WHY DON'T YOU KEEP IT?
AS HE WHEEZES HIS WAY THROUGH HIS SALES PITCH, MY BRAIN POKES AND FEELS THE STORE'S DEFENSIVE HEX.
AH! SUCH...LACK OF APPRECIATION FOR...SUCH A... FINE PIECE.
THIS IS AS MUCH...QUARTZ... AS YOU ARE A... WOMAN! HEHEHE.
THIS...IS THE EYE OF WATOOMB.
AND PRETTY SOON, I CAN FEEL THE HEX'S SHAPE. IT'S LIKE A PADLOCK.
TINY PINS AND TUMBLERS ALL JUST WAITING TO FALL INTO PLACE.
YOU...HEH... YOU THINK... WATOOMB...IS JUST ANOTHER TOY.
ANOTHER... BAUBLE TO ADD TO YOUR... COLLECTION.
NOW I'VE GOT IT. I CAN SEE IT--THE HEX--FLOATING IN THE AIR, WAITING TO BE OPENED.
THE EYE OF WATOOMB...IS ALL THAT IS LEFT...OF A GREAT WAND...
...THE GREAT GOLDEN WAND OF WATOOMB...WAS MORE POWERFUL THAN YOU CAN IMAGINE.
BUT NOW... THIS IS WHAT IS LEFT. AND...EVEN AT THIS DIMINUTIVE SIZE...IT IS MORE THAN YOU CAN HANDLE, I THINK...

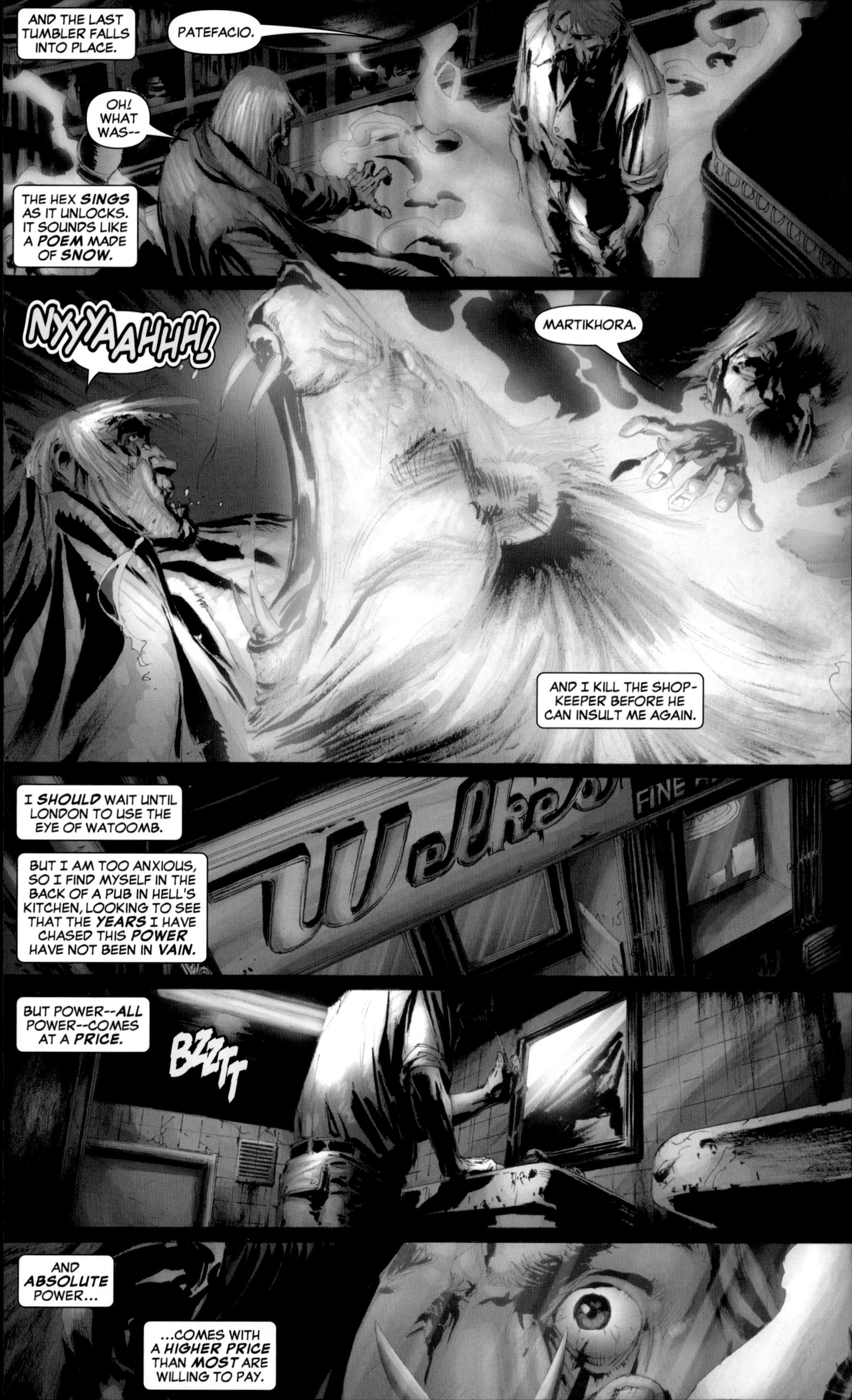
AND THE LAST TUMBLER FALLS INTO PLACE.
PATEFACIO.
OH! WHAT WAS--
THE HEX SINGS AS IT UNLOCKS. IT SOUNDS LIKE A POEM MADE OF SNOW.
NYYAAHHH!
MARTIKHORA.
AND I KILL THE SHOP-KEEPER BEFORE HE CAN INSULT ME AGAIN.
I SHOULD WAIT UNTIL LONDON TO USE THE EYE OF WATOOMB.
BUT I AM TOO ANXIOUS, SO I FIND MYSELF IN THE BACK OF A PUB IN HELL'S KITCHEN, LOOKING TO SEE THAT THE YEARS I HAVE CHASED THIS POWER HAVE NOT BEEN IN VAIN.
Welke's
FINE
BUT POWER--ALL POWER--COMES AT A PRICE.
BZZTT
AND ABSOLUTE POWER...
...COMES WITH A HIGHER PRICE THAN MOST ARE WILLING TO PAY.

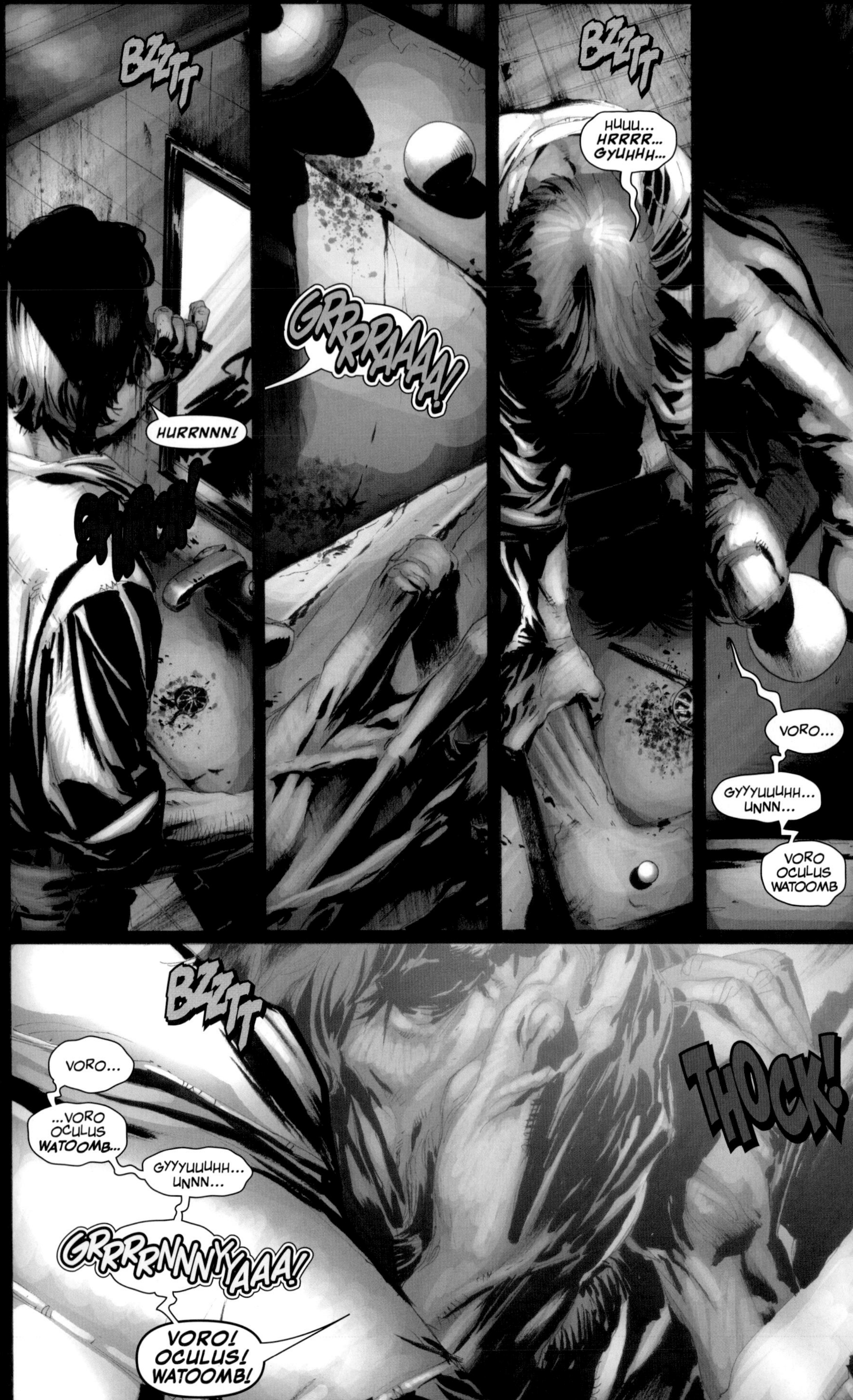
BZZTT
HURRNNN!
GRRRRAAAAA!
BZZTT
HUUU... HRRRR... GYUHHH...
VORO...
GYYYUUUHH... UNNN...
VORO OCULUS WATOOMB
BZZTT
VORO...
...VORO OCULUS WATOOMB...
GYYYUUUHH... UNNN...
GRRRRNNNYAAA!
VORO! OCULUS! WATOOMB!
THOCK!

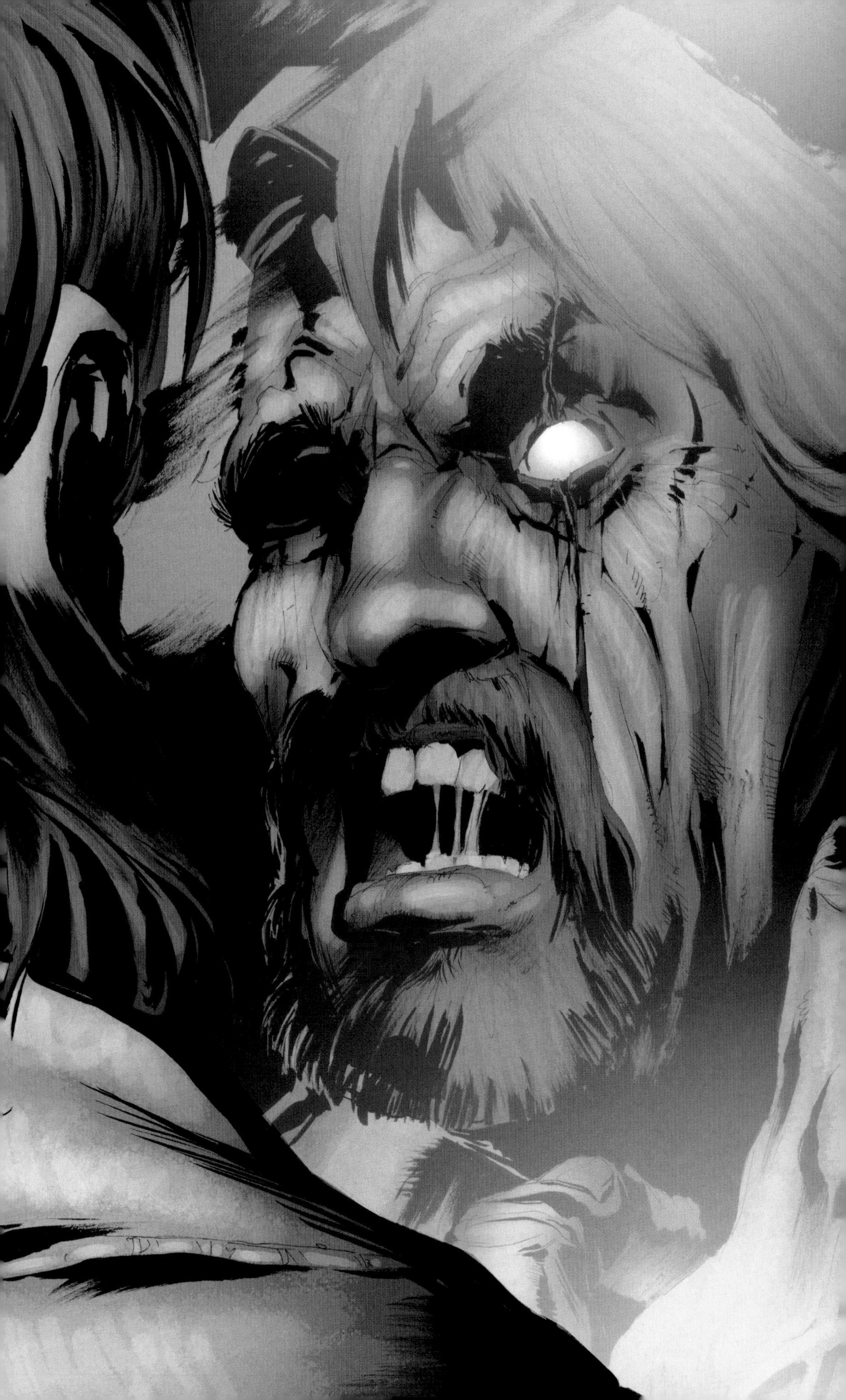

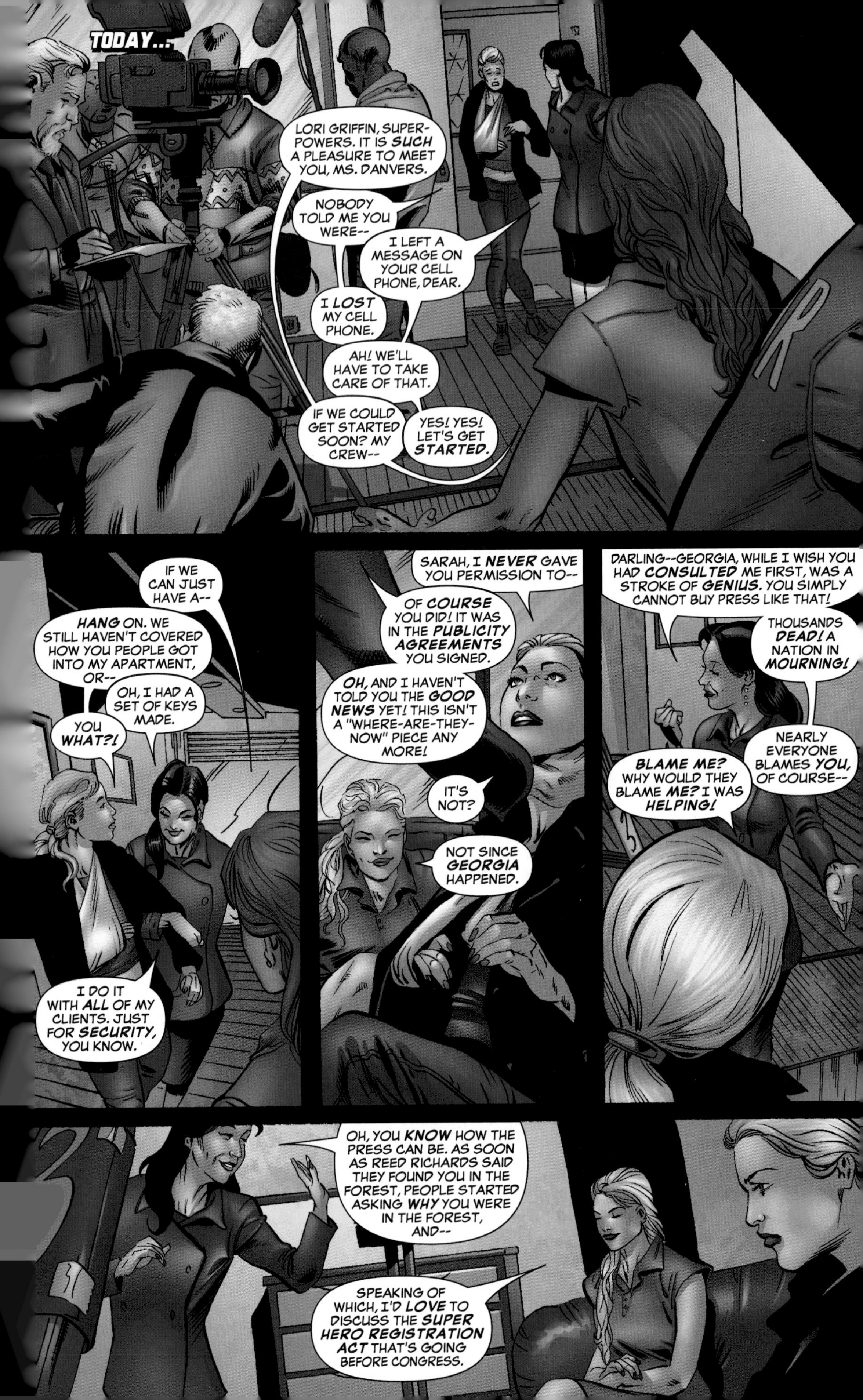
TODAY...
LORI GRIFFIN, SUPER-POWERS. IT IS SUCH A PLEASURE TO MEET YOU, MS. DANVERS.
NOBODY TOLD ME YOU WERE--
I LEFT A MESSAGE ON YOUR CELL PHONE, DEAR.
I LOST MY CELL PHONE.
AH! WE'LL HAVE TO TAKE CARE OF THAT.
IF WE COULD GET STARTED SOON? MY CREW--
YES! YES! LET'S GET STARTED.
IF WE CAN JUST HAVE A--
HANG ON. WE STILL HAVEN'T COVERED HOW YOU PEOPLE GOT INTO MY APARTMENT, OR--
OH, I HAD A SET OF KEYS MADE.
YOU WHAT?!
I DO IT WITH ALL OF MY CLIENTS. JUST FOR SECURITY, YOU KNOW.
SARAH, I NEVER GAVE YOU PERMISSION TO--
OF COURSE YOU DID! IT WAS IN THE PUBLICITY AGREEMENTS YOU SIGNED.
OH, AND I HAVEN'T TOLD YOU THE GOOD NEWS YET! THIS ISN'T A "WHERE-ARE-THEY-NOW" PIECE ANY MORE!
IT'S NOT?
NOT SINCE GEORGIA HAPPENED.
DARLING--GEORGIA, WHILE I WISH YOU HAD CONSULTED ME FIRST, WAS A STROKE OF GENIUS. YOU SIMPLY CANNOT BUY PRESS LIKE THAT!
THOUSANDS DEAD! A NATION IN MOURNING!
NEARLY EVERYONE BLAMES YOU, OF COURSE--
BLAME ME? WHY WOULD THEY BLAME ME? I WAS HELPING!
OH, YOU KNOW HOW THE PRESS CAN BE. AS SOON AS REED RICHARDS SAID THEY FOUND YOU IN THE FOREST, PEOPLE STARTED ASKING WHY YOU WERE IN THE FOREST, AND--
SPEAKING OF WHICH, I'D LOVE TO DISCUSS THE SUPER HERO REGISTRATION ACT THAT'S GOING BEFORE CONGRESS.

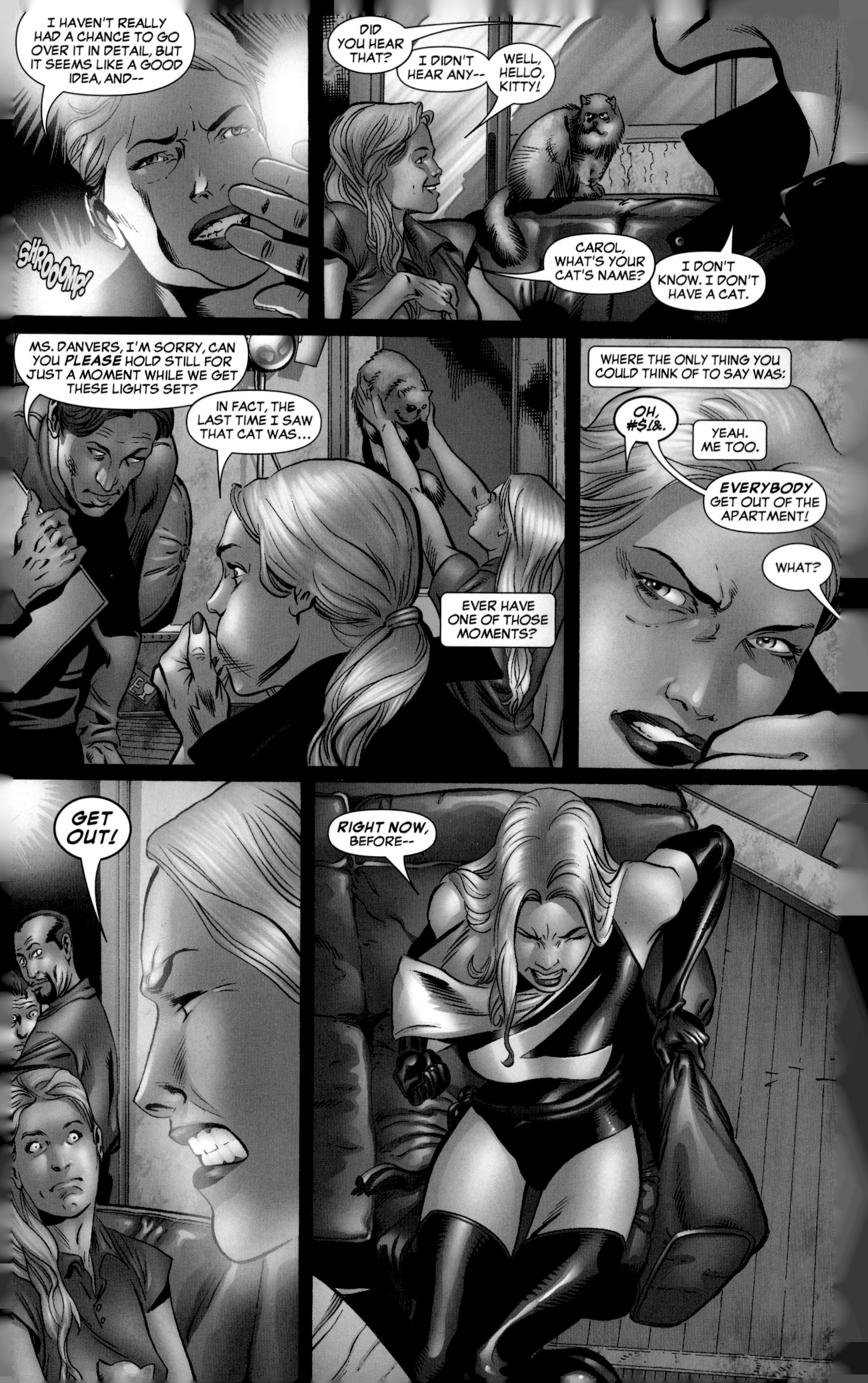
I HAVEN'T REALLY HAD A CHANCE TO GO OVER IT IN DETAIL, BUT IT SEEMS LIKE A GOOD IDEA, AND--
SHROOOMP!
DID YOU HEAR THAT?
I DIDN'T HEAR ANY--
WELL, HELLO, KITTY!
CAROL, WHAT'S YOUR CAT'S NAME?
I DON'T KNOW. I DON'T HAVE A CAT.
MS. DANVERS, I'M SORRY, CAN YOU PLEASE HOLD STILL FOR JUST A MOMENT WHILE WE GET THESE LIGHTS SET?
IN FACT, THE LAST TIME I SAW THAT CAT WAS...
EVER HAVE ONE OF THOSE MOMENTS?
WHERE THE ONLY THING YOU COULD THINK OF TO SAY WAS:
OH, #$!&.
YEAH. ME TOO.
EVERYBODY GET OUT OF THE APARTMENT!
WHAT?
GET OUT!
RIGHT NOW, BEFORE--

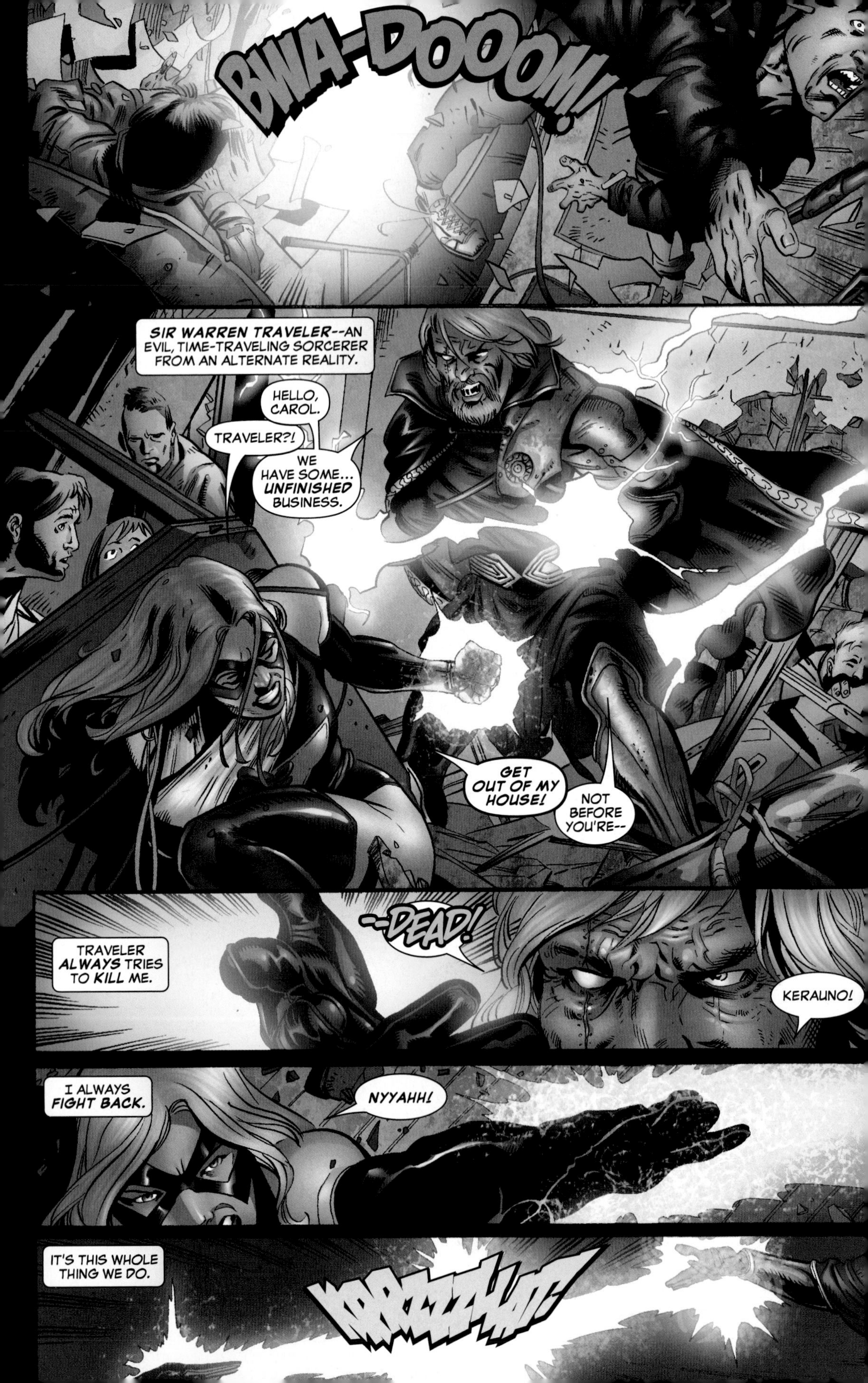
BWA-DOOOOM!!
SIR WARREN TRAVELER--AN EVIL, TIME-TRAVELING SORCERER FROM AN ALTERNATE REALITY.
HELLO, CAROL.
TRAVELER?!
WE HAVE SOME... UNFINISHED BUSINESS.
GET OUT OF MY HOUSE!
NOT BEFORE YOU'RE--
--DEAD!
TRAVELER ALWAYS TRIES TO KILL ME.
KERAUNO!
I ALWAYS FIGHT BACK.
NYYAHH!
IT'S THIS WHOLE THING WE DO.

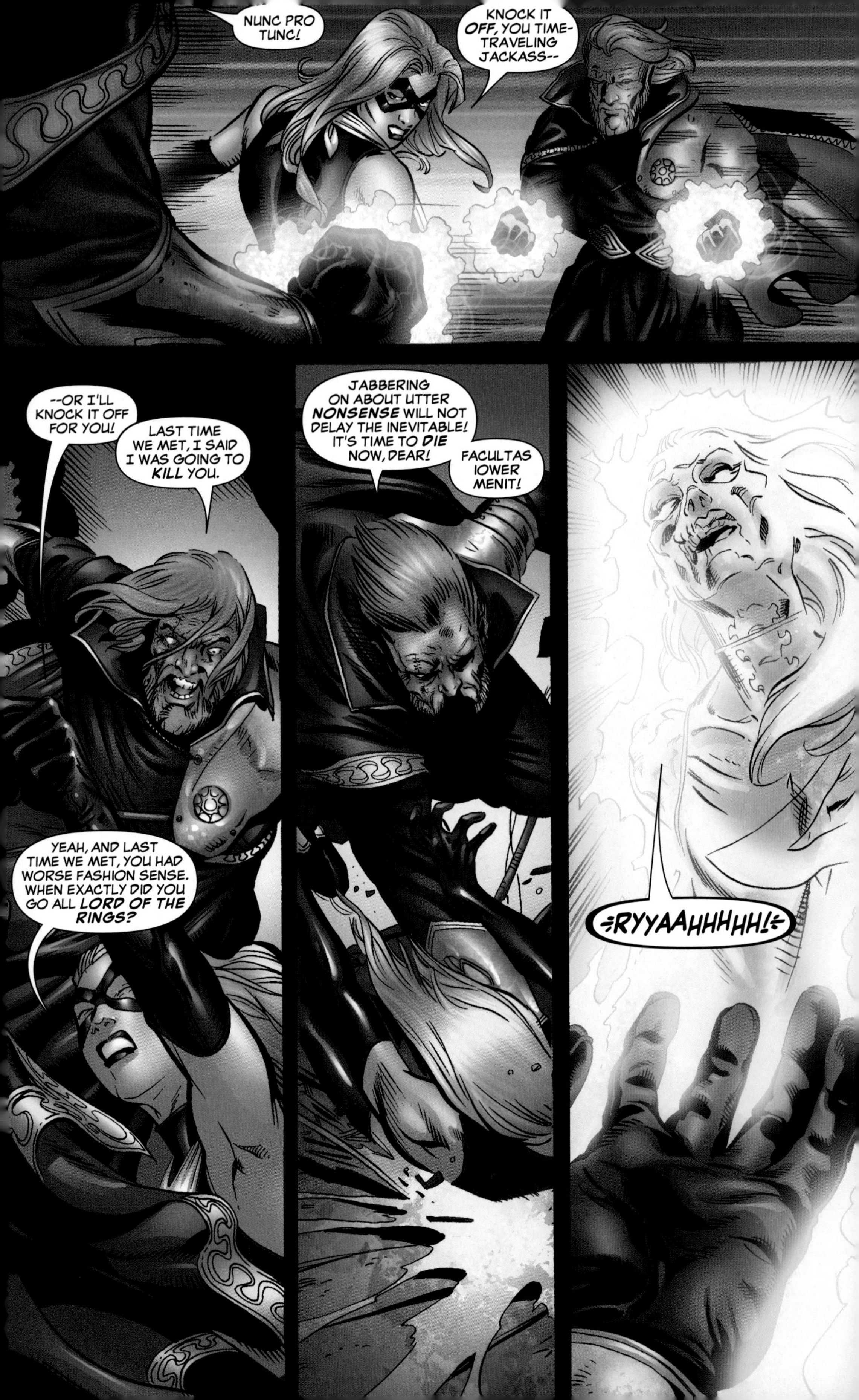
NUNC PRO TUNC!
KNOCK IT OFF, YOU TIME-TRAVELING JACKASS--
--OR I'LL KNOCK IT OFF FOR YOU!
LAST TIME WE MET, I SAID I WAS GOING TO KILL YOU.
YEAH, AND LAST TIME WE MET, YOU HAD WORSE FASHION SENSE. WHEN EXACTLY DID YOU GO ALL LORD OF THE RINGS?
JABBERING ON ABOUT UTTER NONSENSE WILL NOT DELAY THE INEVITABLE! IT'S TIME TO DIE NOW, DEAR!
FACULTAS IOWER MENIT!
RYYAAHHHHH!

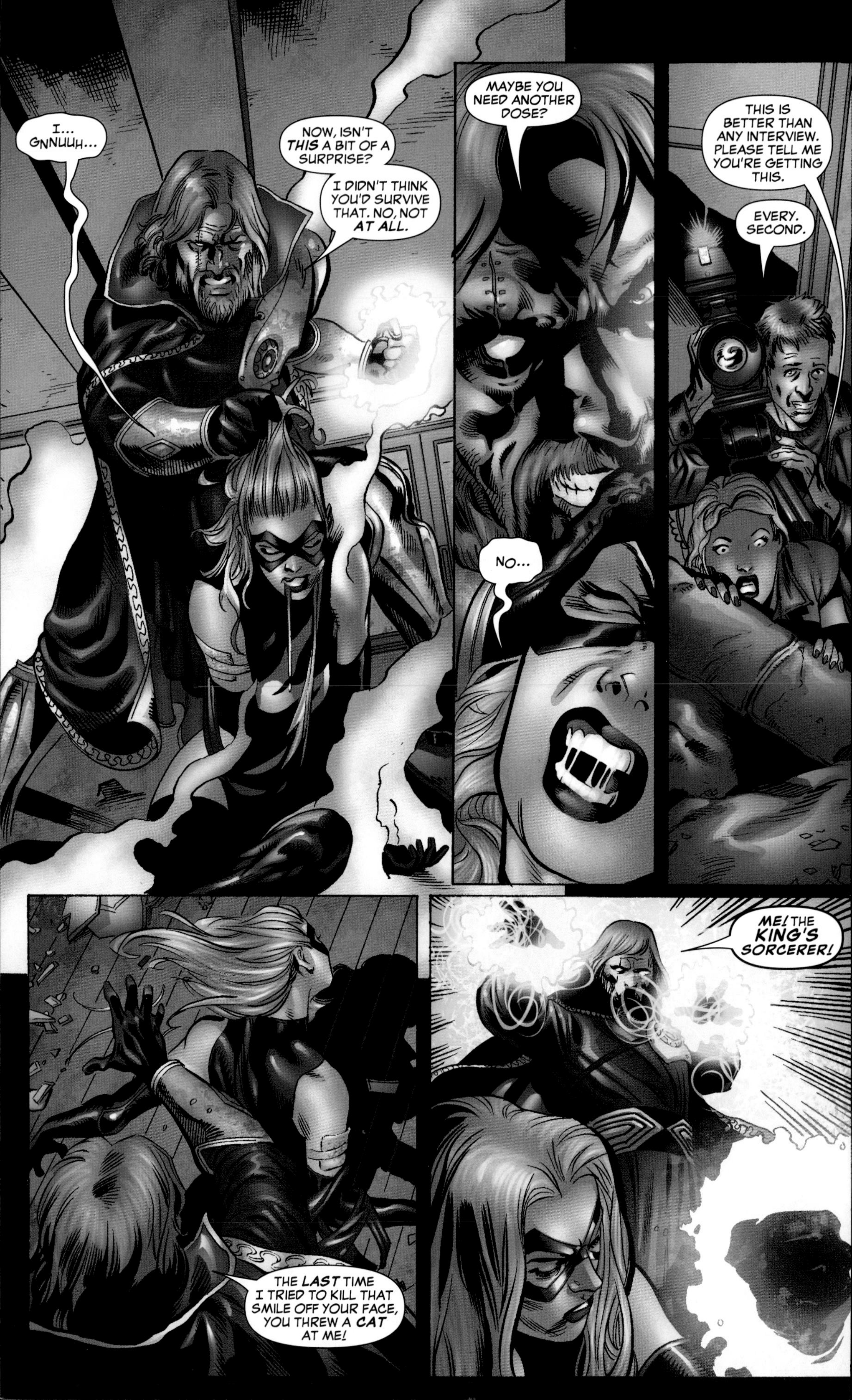
I... GNNUUH...
NOW, ISN'T *THIS* A BIT OF A SURPRISE?
I DIDN'T THINK YOU'D SURVIVE THAT. NO, NOT *AT ALL.*
MAYBE YOU NEED ANOTHER DOSE?
NO...
THIS IS BETTER THAN ANY INTERVIEW. PLEASE TELL ME YOU'RE GETTING THIS.
EVERY. SECOND.
THE *LAST* TIME I TRIED TO KILL THAT SMILE OFF YOUR FACE, YOU THREW A *CAT* AT ME!
ME! THE *KING'S SORCERER!*

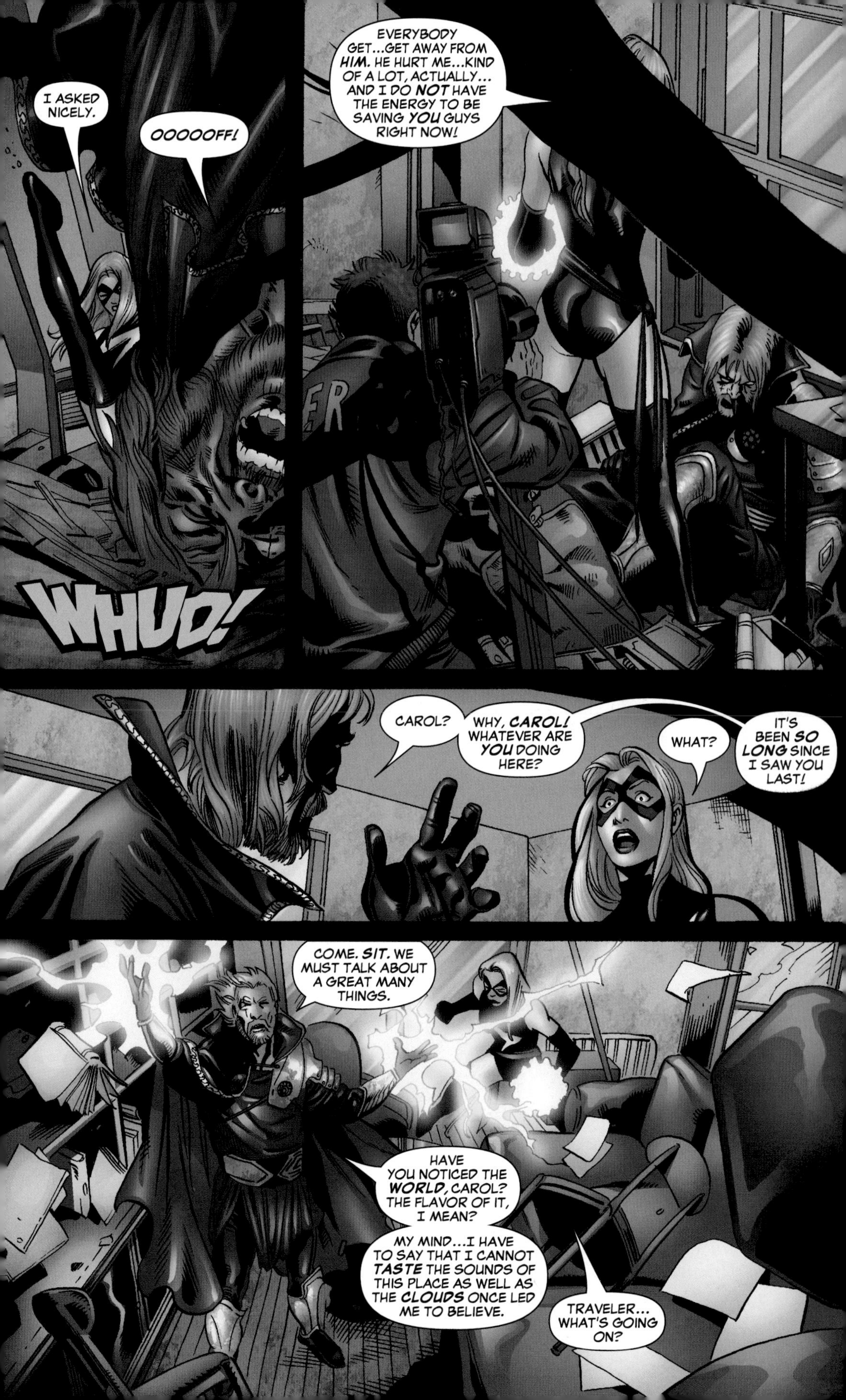
I ASKED NICELY.
OOOOOFF!
WHUD!
EVERYBODY GET...GET AWAY FROM HIM. HE HURT ME...KIND OF A LOT, ACTUALLY... AND I DO NOT HAVE THE ENERGY TO BE SAVING YOU GUYS RIGHT NOW!
CAROL?
WHY, CAROL! WHATEVER ARE YOU DOING HERE?
WHAT?
IT'S BEEN SO LONG SINCE I SAW YOU LAST!
COME. SIT. WE MUST TALK ABOUT A GREAT MANY THINGS.
HAVE YOU NOTICED THE WORLD, CAROL? THE FLAVOR OF IT, I MEAN?
MY MIND...I HAVE TO SAY THAT I CANNOT TASTE THE SOUNDS OF THIS PLACE AS WELL AS THE CLOUDS ONCE LED ME TO BELIEVE.
TRAVELER... WHAT'S GOING ON?

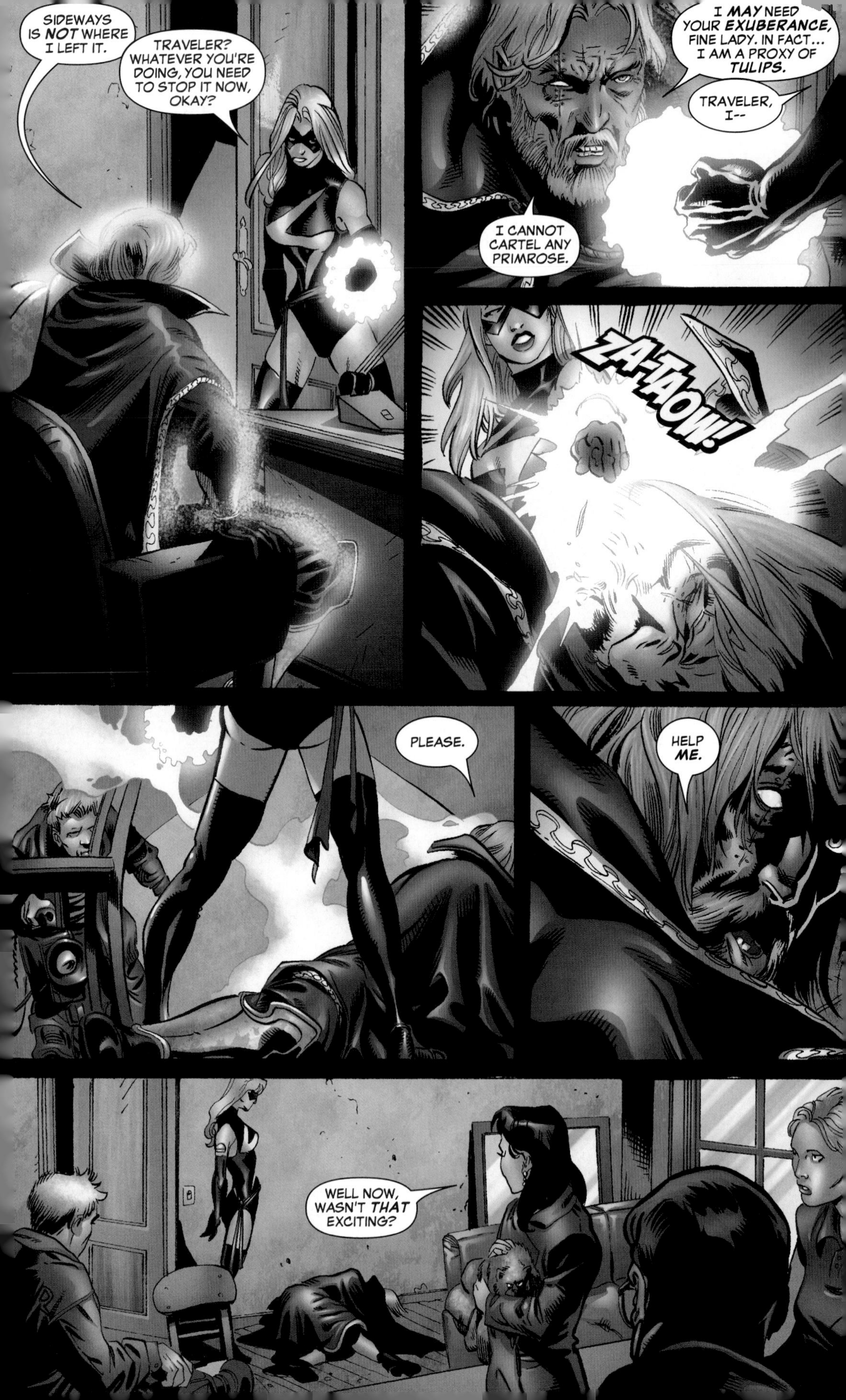
SIDEWAYS IS NOT WHERE I LEFT IT.
TRAVELER? WHATEVER YOU'RE DOING, YOU NEED TO STOP IT NOW, OKAY?
I MAY NEED YOUR EXUBERANCE, FINE LADY. IN FACT... I AM A PROXY OF TULIPS.
TRAVELER, I--
I CANNOT CARTEL ANY PRIMROSE.
ZA-TAOW!
PLEASE.
HELP ME.
WELL NOW, WASN'T THAT EXCITING?

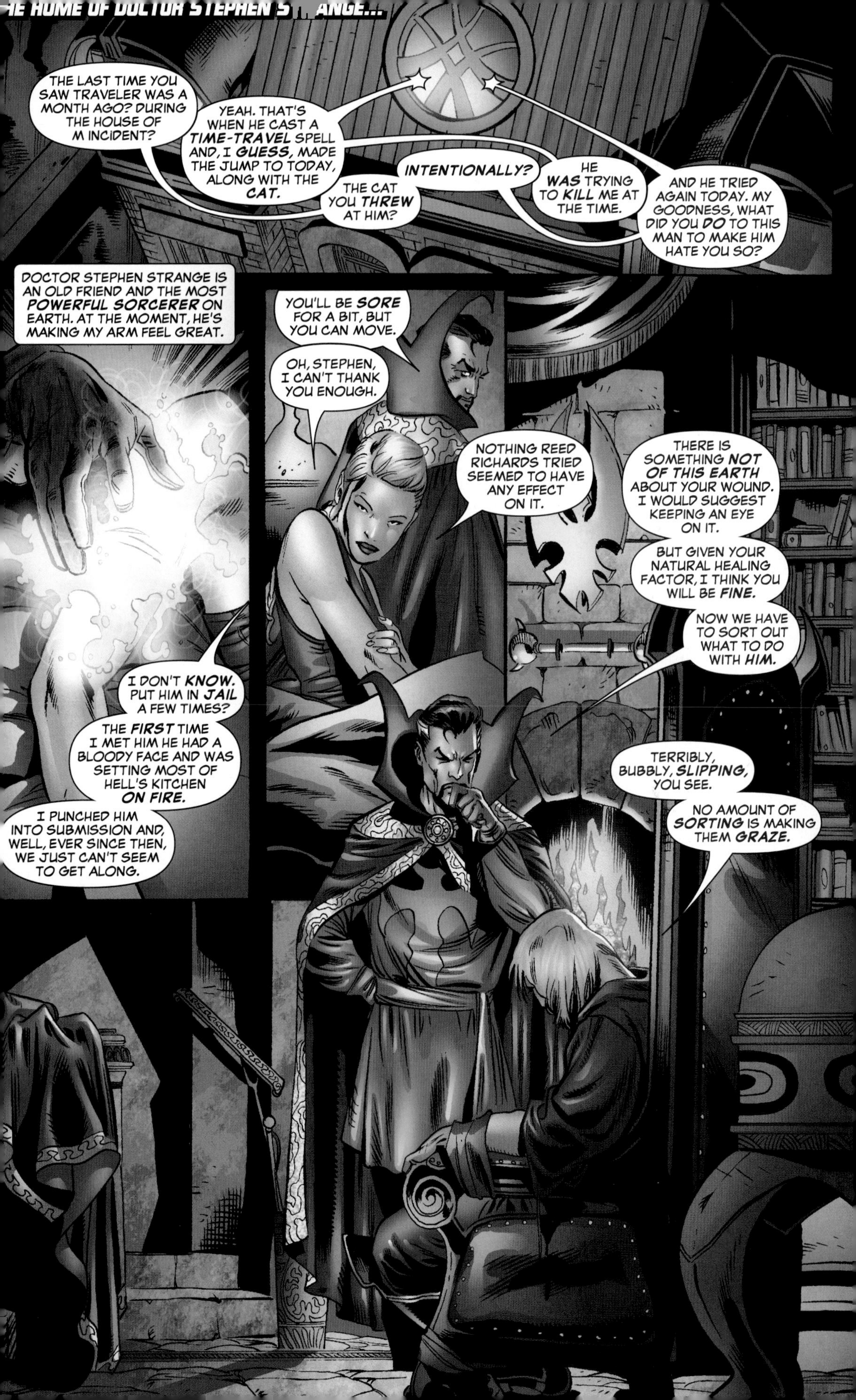

THE HOME OF DOCTOR STEPHEN STRANGE...
THE LAST TIME YOU SAW TRAVELER WAS A MONTH AGO? DURING THE HOUSE OF M INCIDENT?
YEAH. THAT'S WHEN HE CAST A TIME-TRAVEL SPELL AND, I GUESS, MADE THE JUMP TO TODAY, ALONG WITH THE CAT.
THE CAT YOU THREW AT HIM?
INTENTIONALLY?
HE WAS TRYING TO KILL ME AT THE TIME.
AND HE TRIED AGAIN TODAY. MY GOODNESS, WHAT DID YOU DO TO THIS MAN TO MAKE HIM HATE YOU SO?
DOCTOR STEPHEN STRANGE IS AN OLD FRIEND AND THE MOST POWERFUL SORCERER ON EARTH. AT THE MOMENT, HE'S MAKING MY ARM FEEL GREAT.
YOU'LL BE SORE FOR A BIT, BUT YOU CAN MOVE.
OH, STEPHEN, I CAN'T THANK YOU ENOUGH.
NOTHING REED RICHARDS TRIED SEEMED TO HAVE ANY EFFECT ON IT.
THERE IS SOMETHING NOT OF THIS EARTH ABOUT YOUR WOUND. I WOULD SUGGEST KEEPING AN EYE ON IT.
BUT GIVEN YOUR NATURAL HEALING FACTOR, I THINK YOU WILL BE FINE.
NOW WE HAVE TO SORT OUT WHAT TO DO WITH HIM.
I DON'T KNOW. PUT HIM IN JAIL A FEW TIMES?
THE FIRST TIME I MET HIM HE HAD A BLOODY FACE AND WAS SETTING MOST OF HELL'S KITCHEN ON FIRE.
I PUNCHED HIM INTO SUBMISSION AND, WELL, EVER SINCE THEN, WE JUST CAN'T SEEM TO GET ALONG.
TERRIBLY, BUBBLY, SLIPPING, YOU SEE.
NO AMOUNT OF SORTING IS MAKING THEM GRAZE.

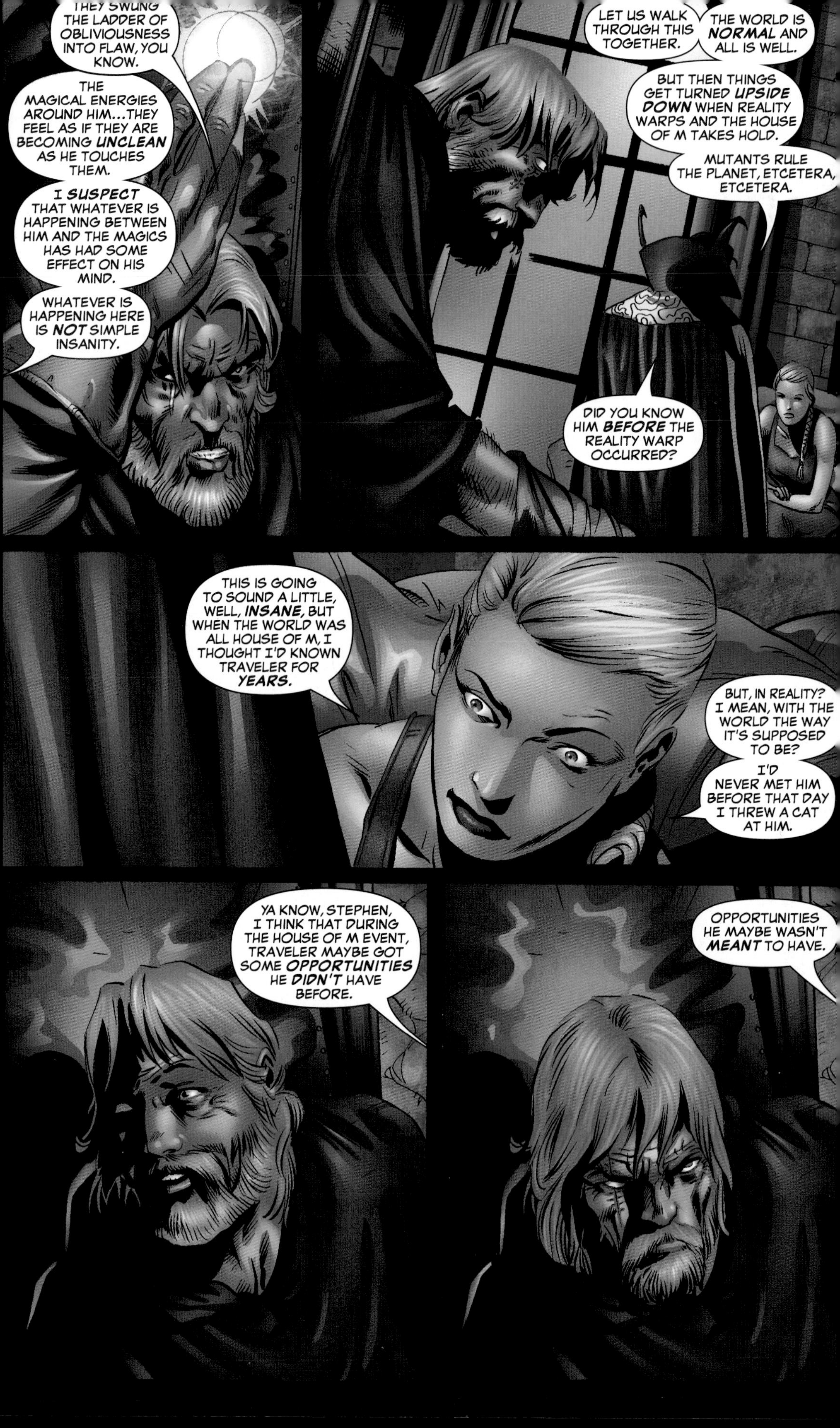

THEY SWUNG THE LADDER OF OBLIVIOUSNESS INTO FLAW, YOU KNOW.
THE MAGICAL ENERGIES AROUND HIM...THEY FEEL AS IF THEY ARE BECOMING UNCLEAN AS HE TOUCHES THEM.
I SUSPECT THAT WHATEVER IS HAPPENING BETWEEN HIM AND THE MAGICS HAS HAD SOME EFFECT ON HIS MIND.
WHATEVER IS HAPPENING HERE IS NOT SIMPLE INSANITY.
LET US WALK THROUGH THIS TOGETHER.
THE WORLD IS NORMAL AND ALL IS WELL.
BUT THEN THINGS GET TURNED UPSIDE DOWN WHEN REALITY WARPS AND THE HOUSE OF M TAKES HOLD.
MUTANTS RULE THE PLANET, ETCETERA, ETCETERA.
DID YOU KNOW HIM BEFORE THE REALITY WARP OCCURRED?
THIS IS GOING TO SOUND A LITTLE, WELL, INSANE, BUT WHEN THE WORLD WAS ALL HOUSE OF M, I THOUGHT I'D KNOWN TRAVELER FOR YEARS.
BUT, IN REALITY? I MEAN, WITH THE WORLD THE WAY IT'S SUPPOSED TO BE?
I'D NEVER MET HIM BEFORE THAT DAY I THREW A CAT AT HIM.
YA KNOW, STEPHEN, I THINK THAT DURING THE HOUSE OF M EVENT, TRAVELER MAYBE GOT SOME OPPORTUNITIES HE DIDN'T HAVE BEFORE.
OPPORTUNITIES HE MAYBE WASN'T MEANT TO HAVE.

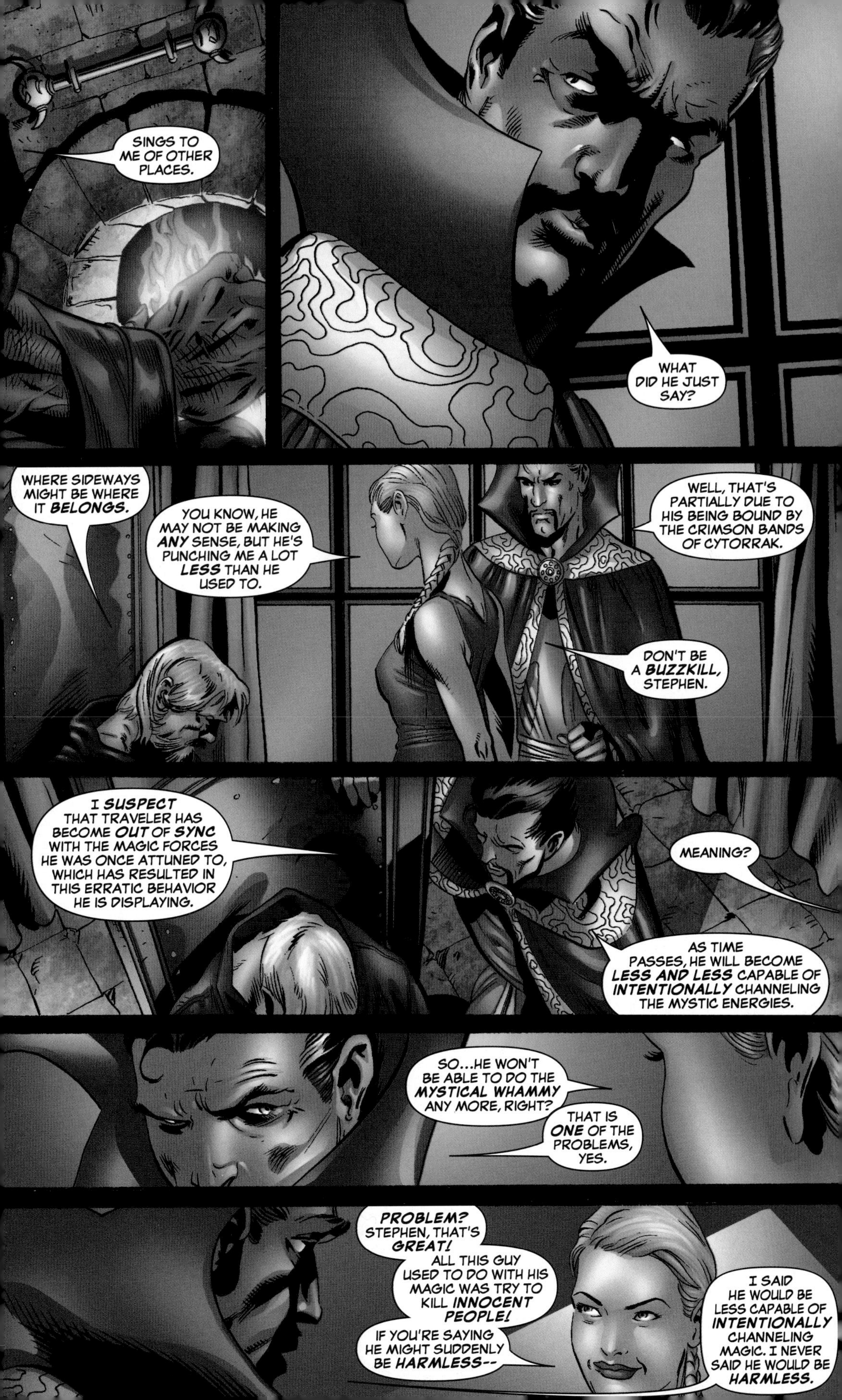
SINGS TO ME OF OTHER PLACES.
WHAT DID HE JUST SAY?
WHERE SIDEWAYS MIGHT BE WHERE IT BELONGS.
YOU KNOW, HE MAY NOT BE MAKING ANY SENSE, BUT HE'S PUNCHING ME A LOT LESS THAN HE USED TO.
WELL, THAT'S PARTIALLY DUE TO HIS BEING BOUND BY THE CRIMSON BANDS OF CYTORRAK.
DON'T BE A BUZZKILL, STEPHEN.
I SUSPECT THAT TRAVELER HAS BECOME OUT OF SYNC WITH THE MAGIC FORCES HE WAS ONCE ATTUNED TO, WHICH HAS RESULTED IN THIS ERRATIC BEHAVIOR HE IS DISPLAYING.
MEANING?
AS TIME PASSES, HE WILL BECOME LESS AND LESS CAPABLE OF INTENTIONALLY CHANNELING THE MYSTIC ENERGIES.
SO...HE WON'T BE ABLE TO DO THE MYSTICAL WHAMMY ANY MORE, RIGHT?
THAT IS ONE OF THE PROBLEMS, YES.
PROBLEM? STEPHEN, THAT'S GREAT!
ALL THIS GUY USED TO DO WITH HIS MAGIC WAS TRY TO KILL INNOCENT PEOPLE!
IF YOU'RE SAYING HE MIGHT SUDDENLY BE HARMLESS--
I SAID HE WOULD BE LESS CAPABLE OF INTENTIONALLY CHANNELING MAGIC. I NEVER SAID HE WOULD BE HARMLESS.

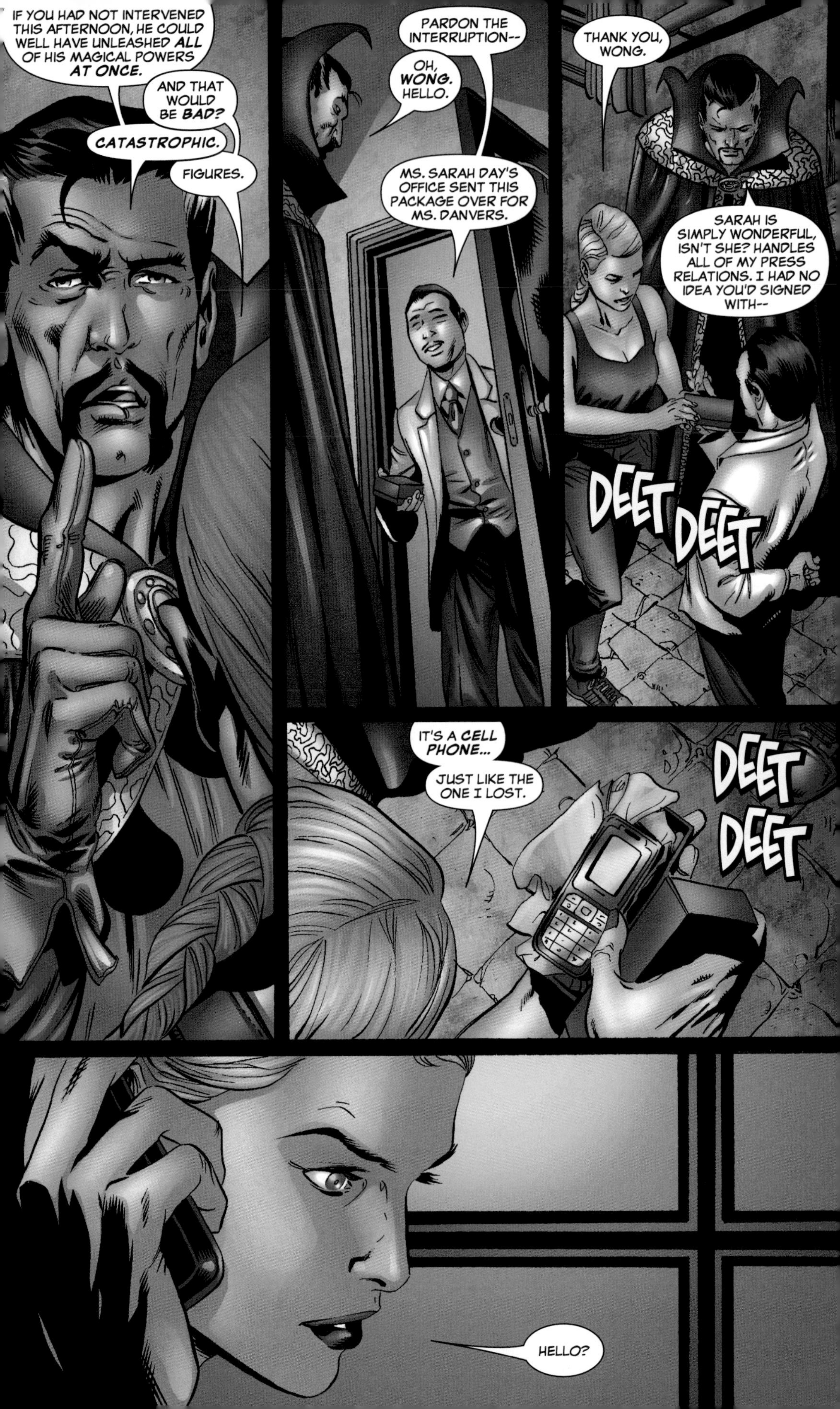
IF YOU HAD NOT INTERVENED THIS AFTERNOON, HE COULD WELL HAVE UNLEASHED ALL OF HIS MAGICAL POWERS AT ONCE.
AND THAT WOULD BE BAD?
CATASTROPHIC.
FIGURES.
PARDON THE INTERRUPTION--
OH, WONG. HELLO.
MS. SARAH DAY'S OFFICE SENT THIS PACKAGE OVER FOR MS. DANVERS.
THANK YOU, WONG.
SARAH IS SIMPLY WONDERFUL, ISN'T SHE? HANDLES ALL OF MY PRESS RELATIONS. I HAD NO IDEA YOU'D SIGNED WITH--
DEET DEET
IT'S A CELL PHONE...
JUST LIKE THE ONE I LOST.
DEET DEET
HELLO?

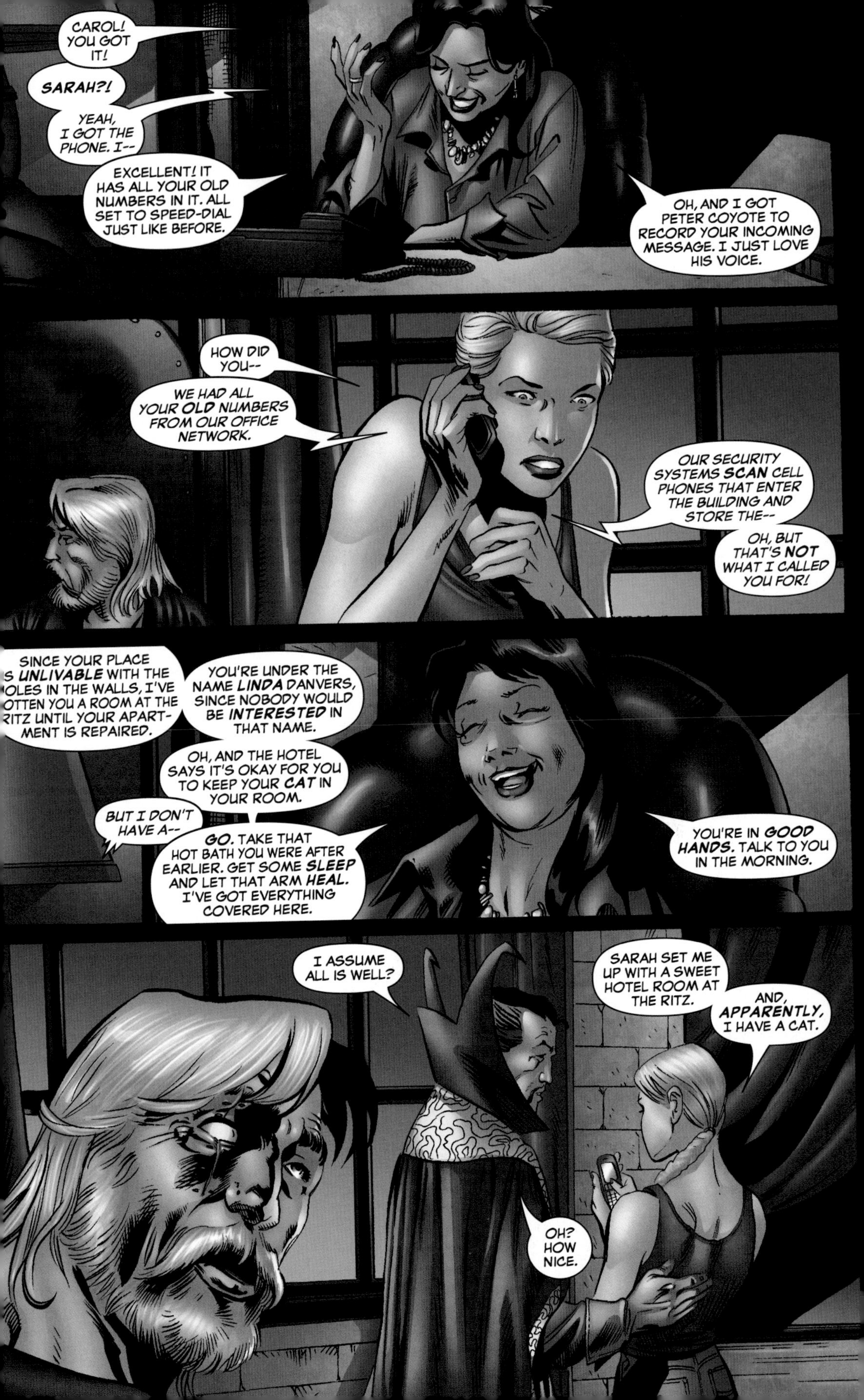
CAROL! YOU GOT IT!
SARAH?!
YEAH, I GOT THE PHONE. I--
EXCELLENT! IT HAS ALL YOUR OLD NUMBERS IN IT. ALL SET TO SPEED-DIAL JUST LIKE BEFORE.
OH, AND I GOT PETER COYOTE TO RECORD YOUR INCOMING MESSAGE. I JUST LOVE HIS VOICE.
HOW DID YOU--
WE HAD ALL YOUR OLD NUMBERS FROM OUR OFFICE NETWORK.
OUR SECURITY SYSTEMS SCAN CELL PHONES THAT ENTER THE BUILDING AND STORE THE--
OH, BUT THAT'S NOT WHAT I CALLED YOU FOR!
SINCE YOUR PLACE IS UNLIVABLE WITH THE HOLES IN THE WALLS, I'VE GOTTEN YOU A ROOM AT THE RITZ UNTIL YOUR APARTMENT IS REPAIRED.
YOU'RE UNDER THE NAME LINDA DANVERS, SINCE NOBODY WOULD BE INTERESTED IN THAT NAME.
OH, AND THE HOTEL SAYS IT'S OKAY FOR YOU TO KEEP YOUR CAT IN YOUR ROOM.
BUT I DON'T HAVE A--
GO. TAKE THAT HOT BATH YOU WERE AFTER EARLIER. GET SOME SLEEP AND LET THAT ARM HEAL. I'VE GOT EVERYTHING COVERED HERE.
YOU'RE IN GOOD HANDS. TALK TO YOU IN THE MORNING.
I ASSUME ALL IS WELL?
SARAH SET ME UP WITH A SWEET HOTEL ROOM AT THE RITZ.
AND, APPARENTLY, I HAVE A CAT.
OH? HOW NICE.

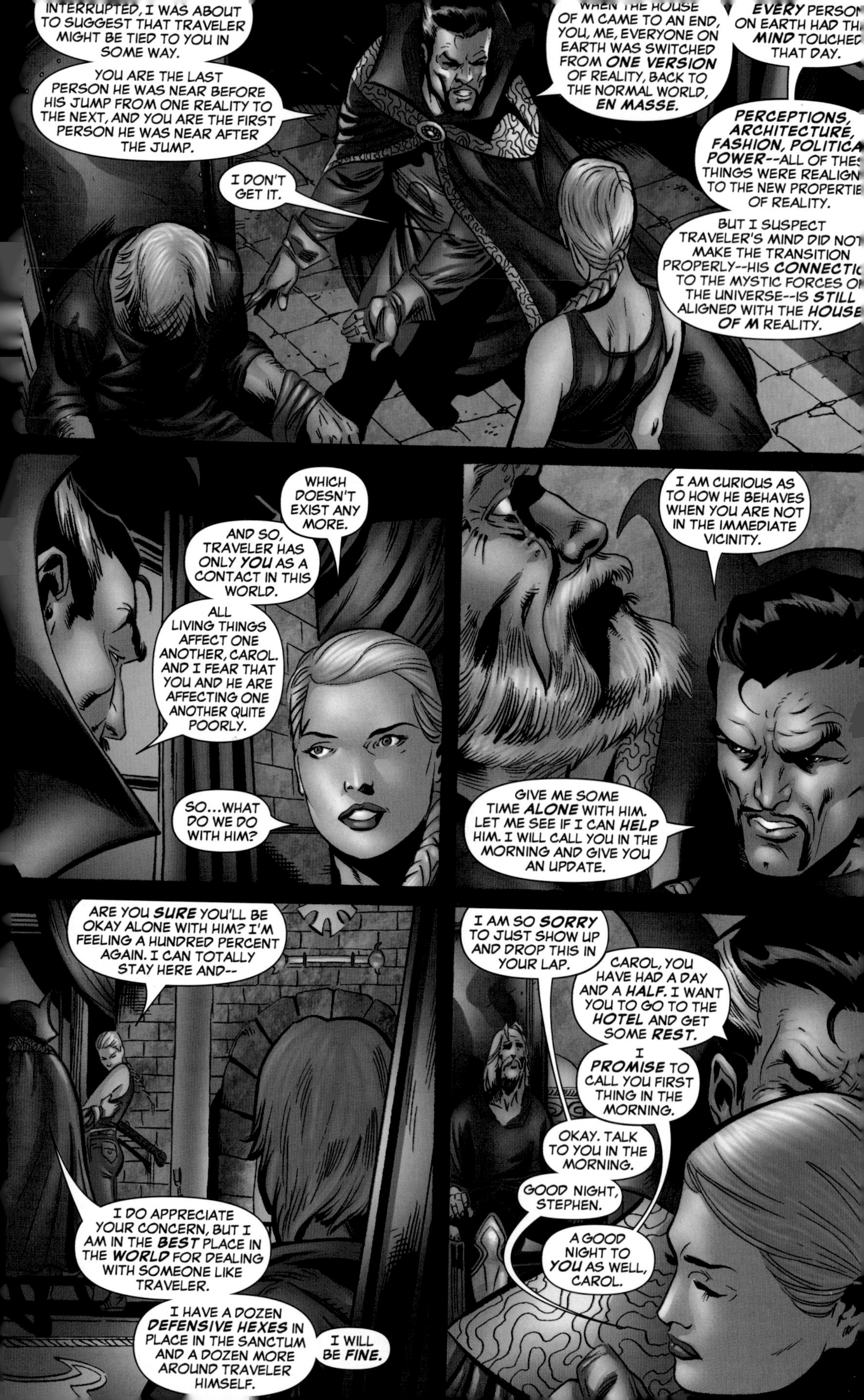
INTERRUPTED, I WAS ABOUT TO SUGGEST THAT TRAVELER MIGHT BE TIED TO YOU IN SOME WAY.
YOU ARE THE LAST PERSON HE WAS NEAR BEFORE HIS JUMP FROM ONE REALITY TO THE NEXT, AND YOU ARE THE FIRST PERSON HE WAS NEAR AFTER THE JUMP.
I DON'T GET IT.
WHEN THE HOUSE OF M CAME TO AN END, YOU, ME, EVERYONE ON EARTH WAS SWITCHED FROM ONE VERSION OF REALITY, BACK TO THE NORMAL WORLD, EN MASSE.
EVERY PERSO ON EARTH HAD TH MIND TOUCHED THAT DAY.
PERCEPTIONS, ARCHITECTURE, FASHION, POLITICA POWER--ALL OF THES THINGS WERE REALIGN TO THE NEW PROPERTIE OF REALITY.
BUT I SUSPECT TRAVELER'S MIND DID NOT MAKE THE TRANSITION PROPERLY--HIS CONNECTI TO THE MYSTIC FORCES O THE UNIVERSE--IS STILL ALIGNED WITH THE HOUSE OF M REALITY.
WHICH DOESN'T EXIST ANY MORE.
AND SO, TRAVELER HAS ONLY YOU AS A CONTACT IN THIS WORLD.
ALL LIVING THINGS AFFECT ONE ANOTHER, CAROL. AND I FEAR THAT YOU AND HE ARE AFFECTING ONE ANOTHER QUITE POORLY.
SO...WHAT DO WE DO WITH HIM?
I AM CURIOUS AS TO HOW HE BEHAVES WHEN YOU ARE NOT IN THE IMMEDIATE VICINITY.
GIVE ME SOME TIME ALONE WITH HIM. LET ME SEE IF I CAN HELP HIM. I WILL CALL YOU IN THE MORNING AND GIVE YOU AN UPDATE.
ARE YOU SURE YOU'LL BE OKAY ALONE WITH HIM? I'M FEELING A HUNDRED PERCENT AGAIN. I CAN TOTALLY STAY HERE AND--
I DO APPRECIATE YOUR CONCERN, BUT I AM IN THE BEST PLACE IN THE WORLD FOR DEALING WITH SOMEONE LIKE TRAVELER.
I HAVE A DOZEN DEFENSIVE HEXES IN PLACE IN THE SANCTUM AND A DOZEN MORE AROUND TRAVELER HIMSELF.
I WILL BE FINE.
I AM SO SORRY TO JUST SHOW UP AND DROP THIS IN YOUR LAP.
CAROL, YOU HAVE HAD A DAY AND A HALF. I WANT YOU TO GO TO THE HOTEL AND GET SOME REST.
I PROMISE TO CALL YOU FIRST THING IN THE MORNING.
OKAY. TALK TO YOU IN THE MORNING.
GOOD NIGHT, STEPHEN.
A GOOD NIGHT TO YOU AS WELL, CAROL.

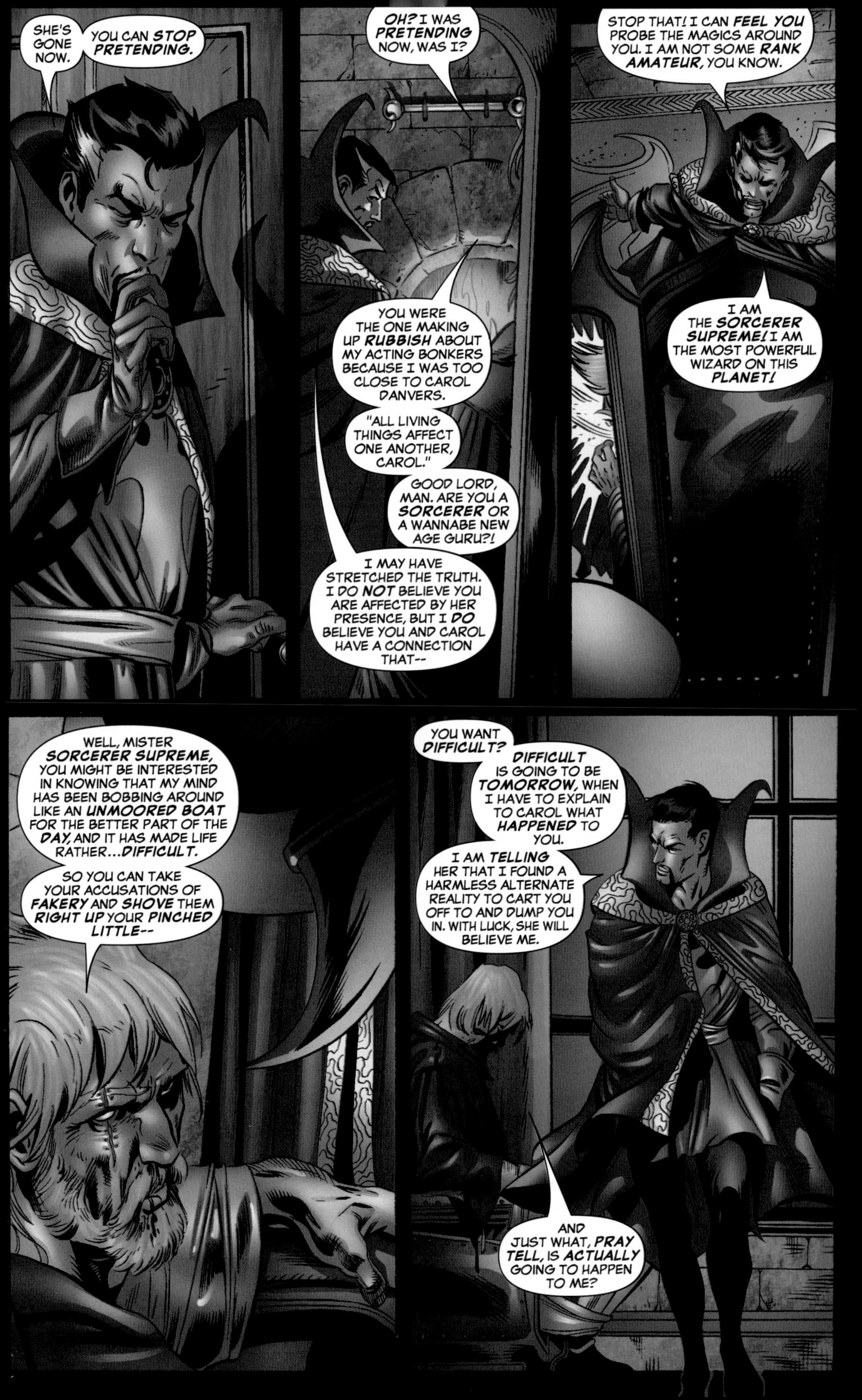
SHE'S GONE NOW.
YOU CAN STOP PRETENDING.
OH? I WAS PRETENDING NOW, WAS I?
YOU WERE THE ONE MAKING UP RUBBISH ABOUT MY ACTING BONKERS BECAUSE I WAS TOO CLOSE TO CAROL DANVERS.
"ALL LIVING THINGS AFFECT ONE ANOTHER, CAROL."
GOOD LORD, MAN. ARE YOU A SORCERER OR A WANNABE NEW AGE GURU?!
I MAY HAVE STRETCHED THE TRUTH. I DO NOT BELIEVE YOU ARE AFFECTED BY HER PRESENCE, BUT I DO BELIEVE YOU AND CAROL HAVE A CONNECTION THAT--
STOP THAT! I CAN FEEL YOU PROBE THE MAGICS AROUND YOU. I AM NOT SOME RANK AMATEUR, YOU KNOW.
I AM THE SORCERER SUPREME! I AM THE MOST POWERFUL WIZARD ON THIS PLANET!
WELL, MISTER SORCERER SUPREME, YOU MIGHT BE INTERESTED IN KNOWING THAT MY MIND HAS BEEN BOBBING AROUND LIKE AN UNMOORED BOAT FOR THE BETTER PART OF THE DAY, AND IT HAS MADE LIFE RATHER...DIFFICULT.
SO YOU CAN TAKE YOUR ACCUSATIONS OF FAKERY AND SHOVE THEM RIGHT UP YOUR PINCHED LITTLE--
YOU WANT DIFFICULT?
DIFFICULT IS GOING TO BE TOMORROW, WHEN I HAVE TO EXPLAIN TO CAROL WHAT HAPPENED TO YOU.
I AM TELLING HER THAT I FOUND A HARMLESS ALTERNATE REALITY TO CART YOU OFF TO AND DUMP YOU IN. WITH LUCK, SHE WILL BELIEVE ME.
AND JUST WHAT, PRAY TELL, IS ACTUALLY GOING TO HAPPEN TO ME?

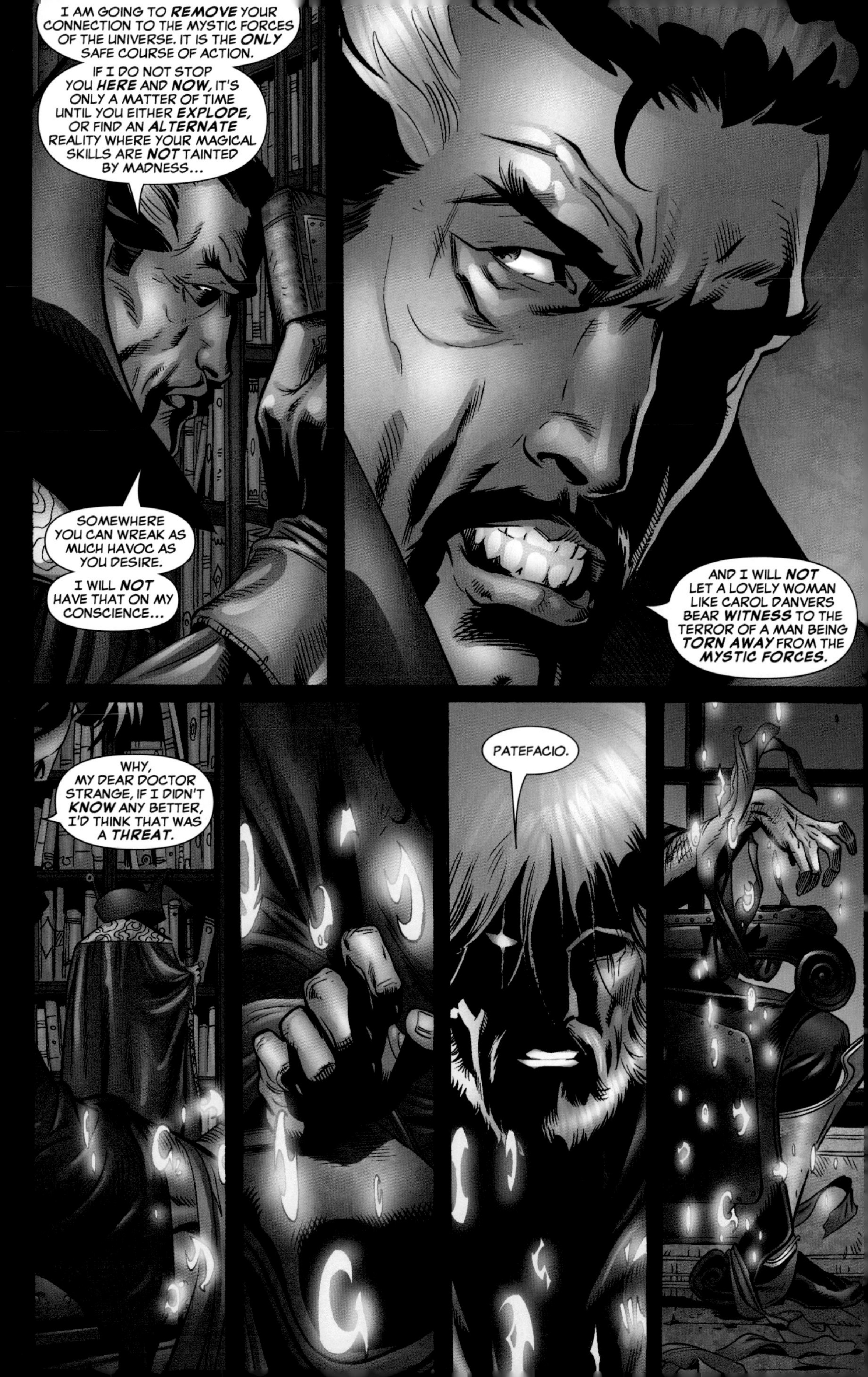
I AM GOING TO REMOVE YOUR CONNECTION TO THE MYSTIC FORCES OF THE UNIVERSE. IT IS THE ONLY SAFE COURSE OF ACTION.
IF I DO NOT STOP YOU HERE AND NOW, IT'S ONLY A MATTER OF TIME UNTIL YOU EITHER EXPLODE, OR FIND AN ALTERNATE REALITY WHERE YOUR MAGICAL SKILLS ARE NOT TAINTED BY MADNESS...
SOMEWHERE YOU CAN WREAK AS MUCH HAVOC AS YOU DESIRE.
I WILL NOT HAVE THAT ON MY CONSCIENCE...
AND I WILL NOT LET A LOVELY WOMAN LIKE CAROL DANVERS BEAR WITNESS TO THE TERROR OF A MAN BEING TORN AWAY FROM THE MYSTIC FORCES.
WHY, MY DEAR DOCTOR STRANGE, IF I DIDN'T KNOW ANY BETTER, I'D THINK THAT WAS A THREAT.
PATEFACIO.

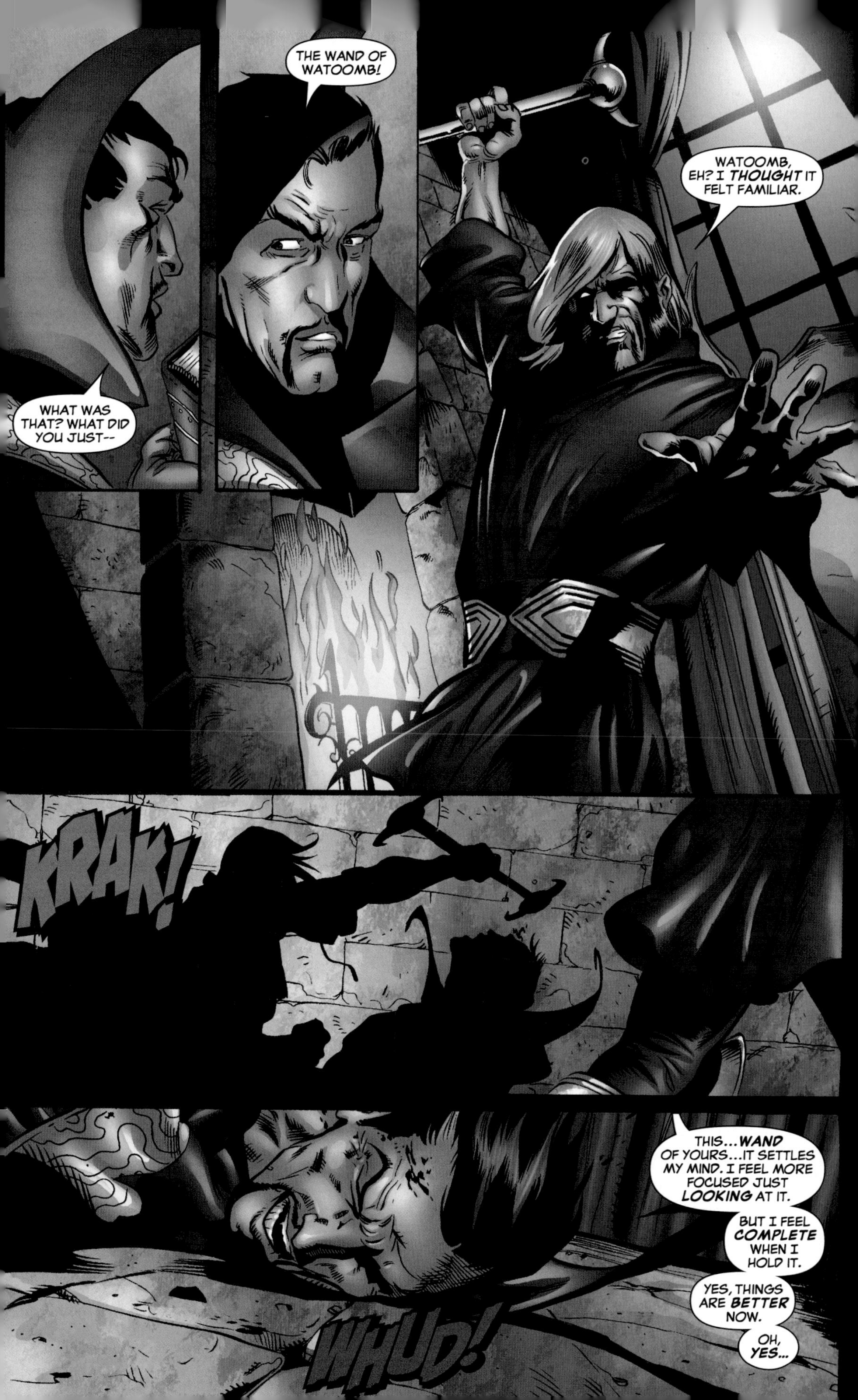
WHAT WAS THAT? WHAT DID YOU JUST--
THE WAND OF WATOOMB!
WATOOMB, EH? I THOUGHT IT FELT FAMILIAR.
KRAK!
THIS...WAND OF YOURS...IT SETTLES MY MIND. I FEEL MORE FOCUSED JUST LOOKING AT IT.
BUT I FEEL COMPLETE WHEN I HOLD IT.
YES, THINGS ARE BETTER NOW.
OH, YES...
WHUD!

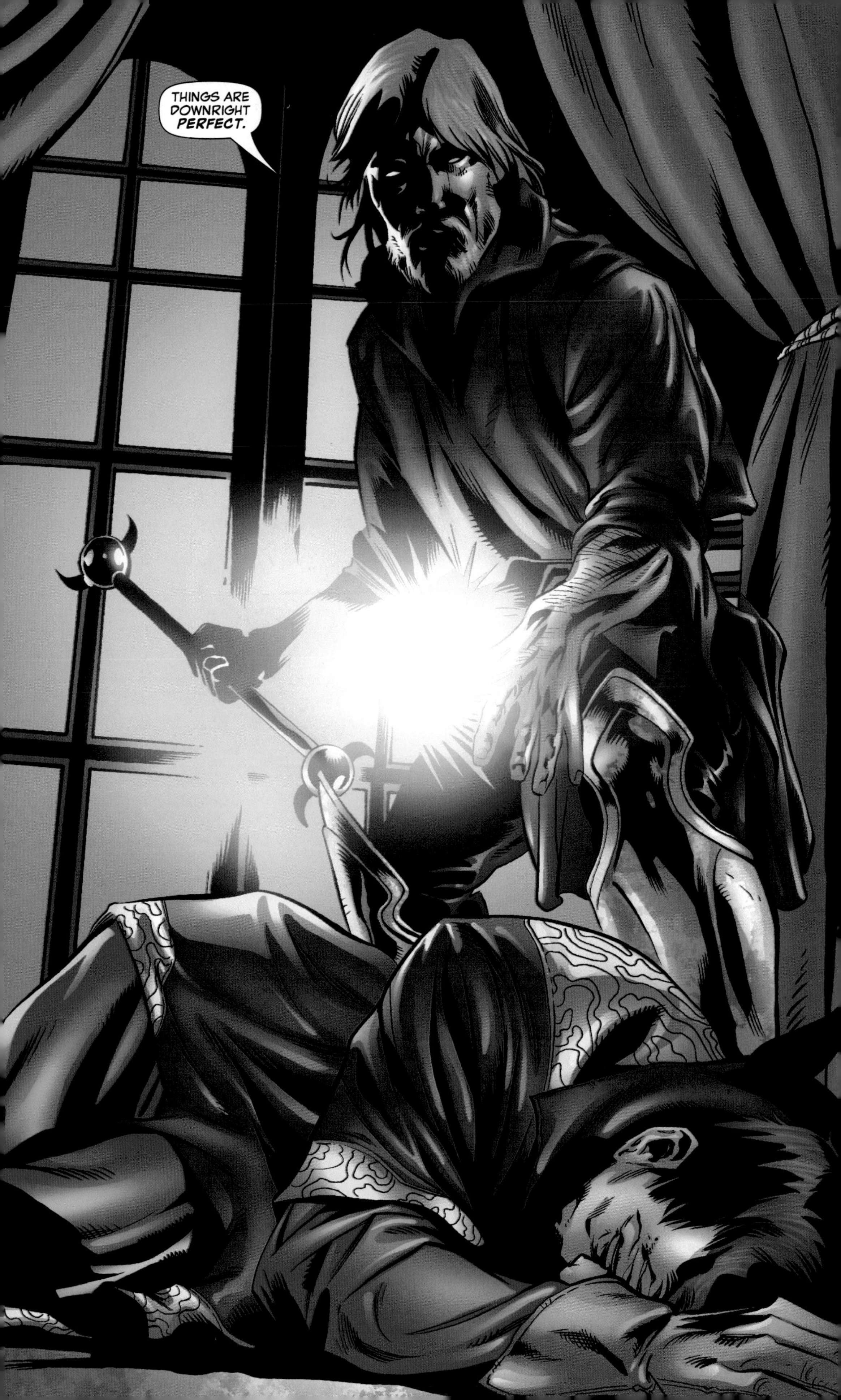
THINGS ARE DOWNRIGHT PERFECT.

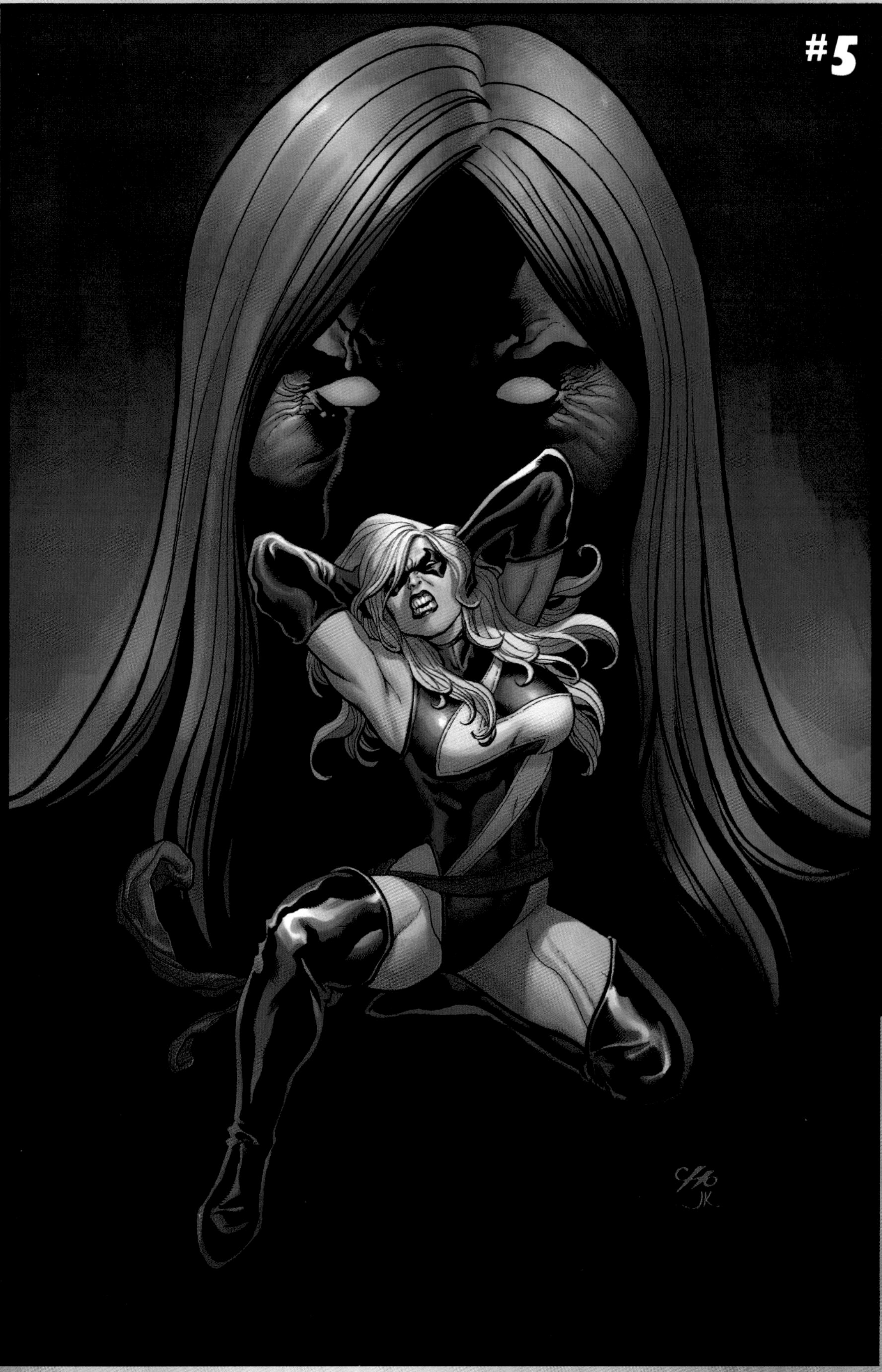
#5

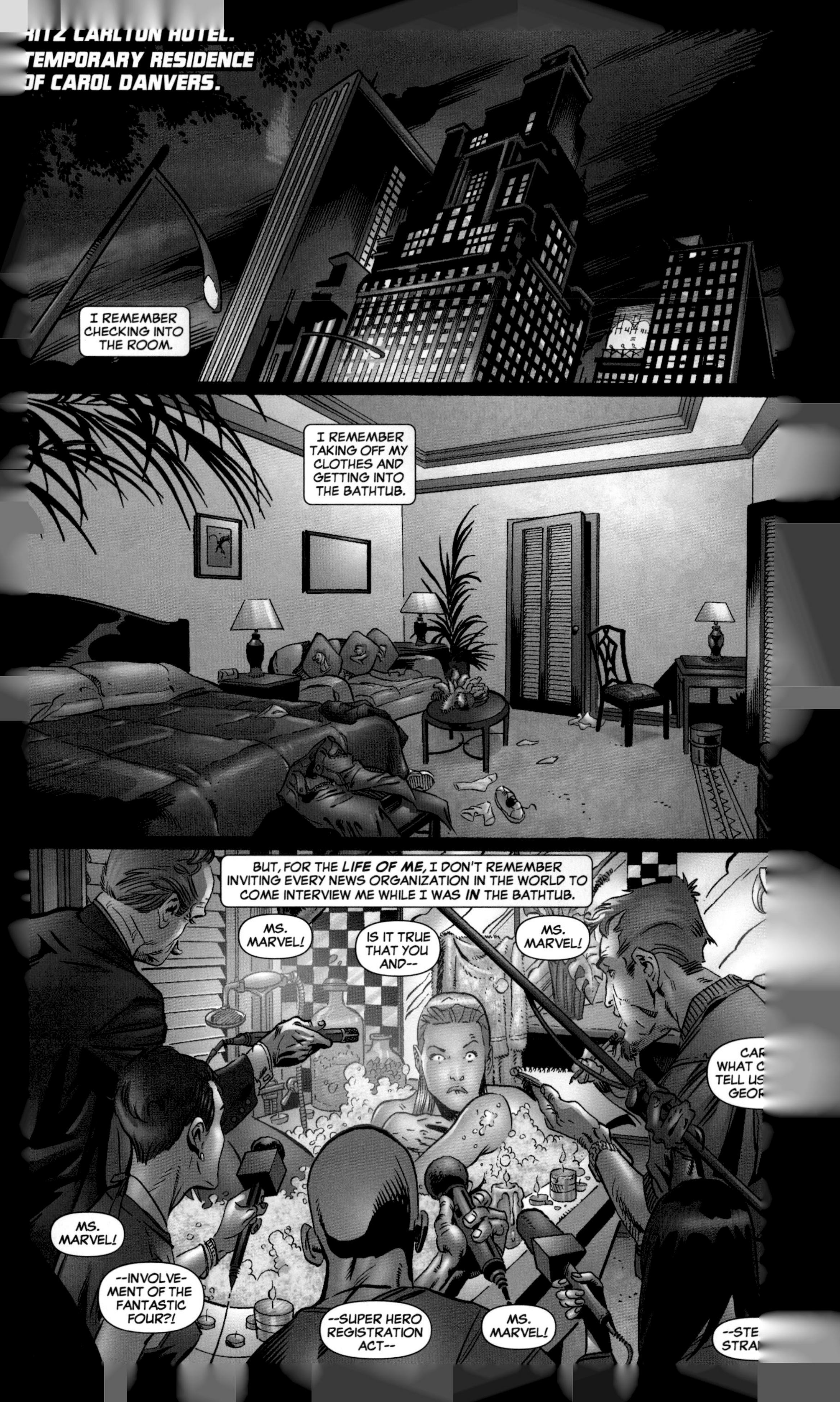

ITZ CARLTON HOTEL.
TEMPORARY RESIDENCE
OF CAROL DANVERS.
I REMEMBER CHECKING INTO THE ROOM.
I REMEMBER TAKING OFF MY CLOTHES AND GETTING INTO THE BATHTUB.
BUT, FOR THE *LIFE OF ME*, I DON'T REMEMBER INVITING EVERY NEWS ORGANIZATION IN THE WORLD TO COME INTERVIEW ME WHILE I WAS *IN* THE BATHTUB.
MS. MARVEL!
IS IT TRUE THAT YOU AND--
MS. MARVEL!
CAR WHAT C TELL US GEOR
MS. MARVEL!
--INVOLVEMENT OF THE FANTASTIC FOUR?!
--SUPER HERO REGISTRATION ACT--
MS. MARVEL!
--STE STRA

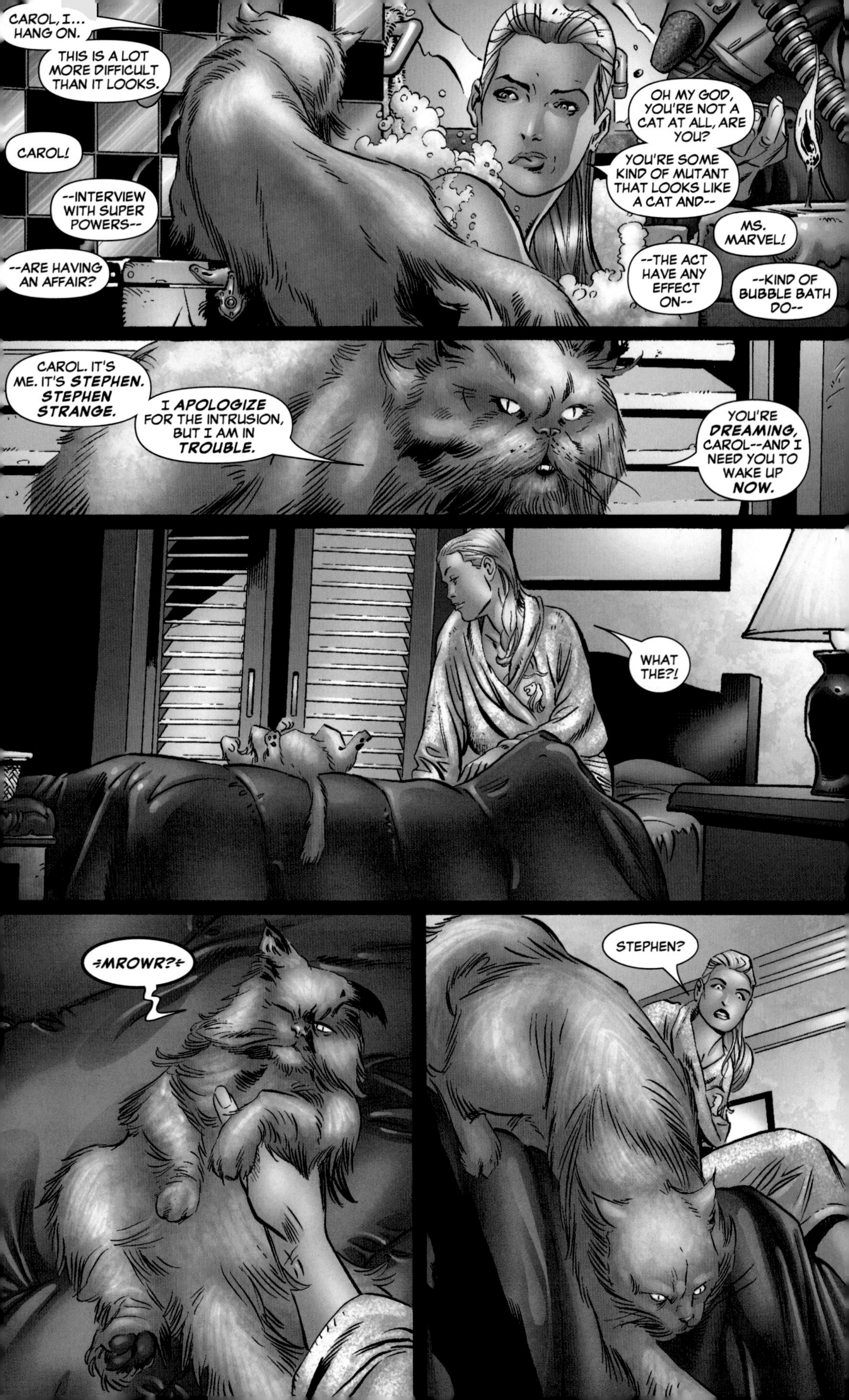

CAROL, I... HANG ON.
THIS IS A LOT MORE DIFFICULT THAN IT LOOKS.
CAROL!
--INTERVIEW WITH SUPER POWERS--
--ARE HAVING AN AFFAIR?
OH MY GOD, YOU'RE NOT A CAT AT ALL, ARE YOU?
YOU'RE SOME KIND OF MUTANT THAT LOOKS LIKE A CAT AND--
MS. MARVEL!
--THE ACT HAVE ANY EFFECT ON--
--KIND OF BUBBLE BATH DO--
CAROL. IT'S ME. IT'S STEPHEN. STEPHEN STRANGE.
I APOLOGIZE FOR THE INTRUSION, BUT I AM IN TROUBLE.
YOU'RE DREAMING, CAROL--AND I NEED YOU TO WAKE UP NOW.
WHAT THE?!
MROWR?
STEPHEN?

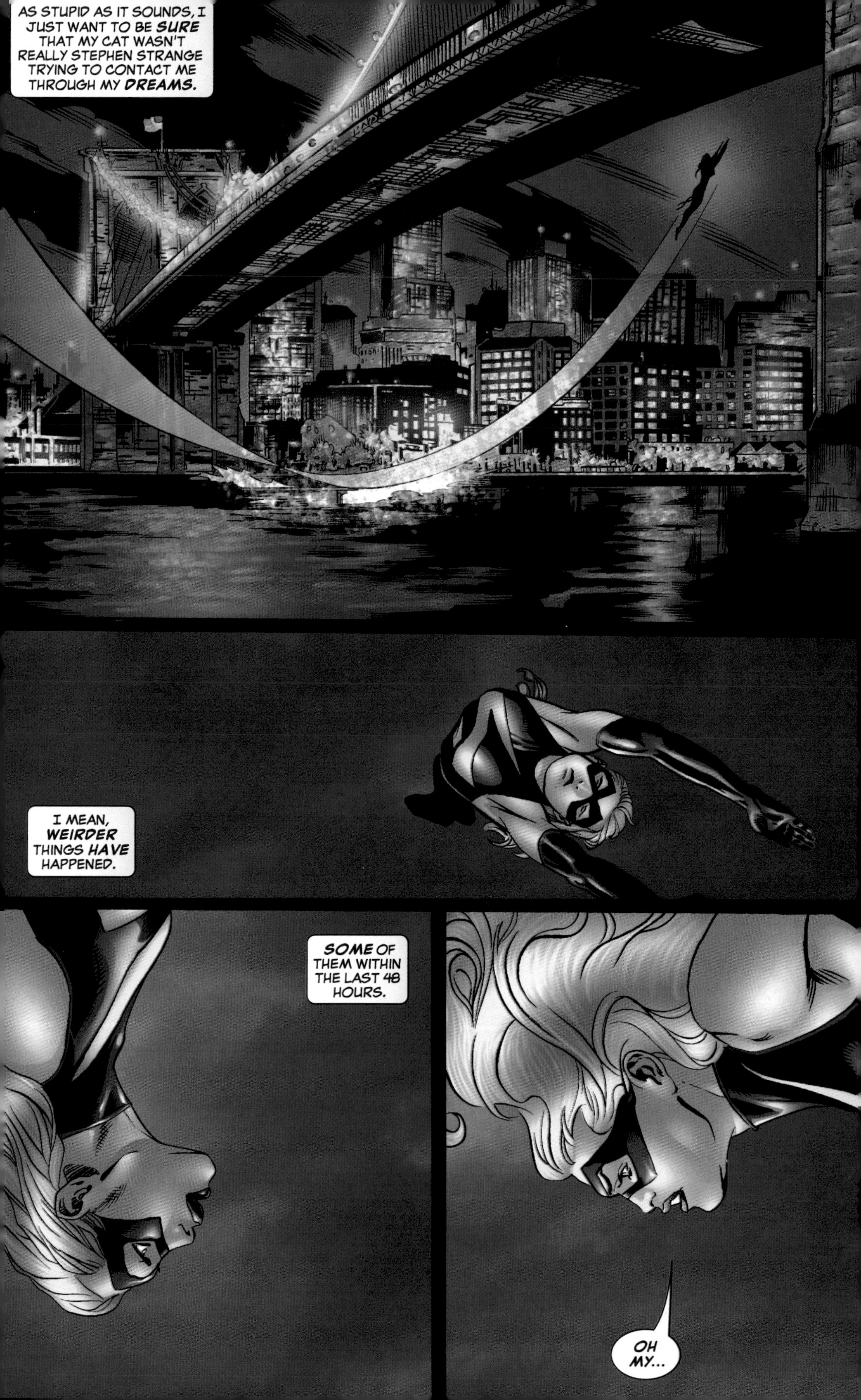
AS STUPID AS IT SOUNDS, I JUST WANT TO BE SURE THAT MY CAT WASN'T REALLY STEPHEN STRANGE TRYING TO CONTACT ME THROUGH MY DREAMS.
I MEAN, WEIRDER THINGS HAVE HAPPENED.
SOME OF THEM WITHIN THE LAST 48 HOURS.
OH MY...

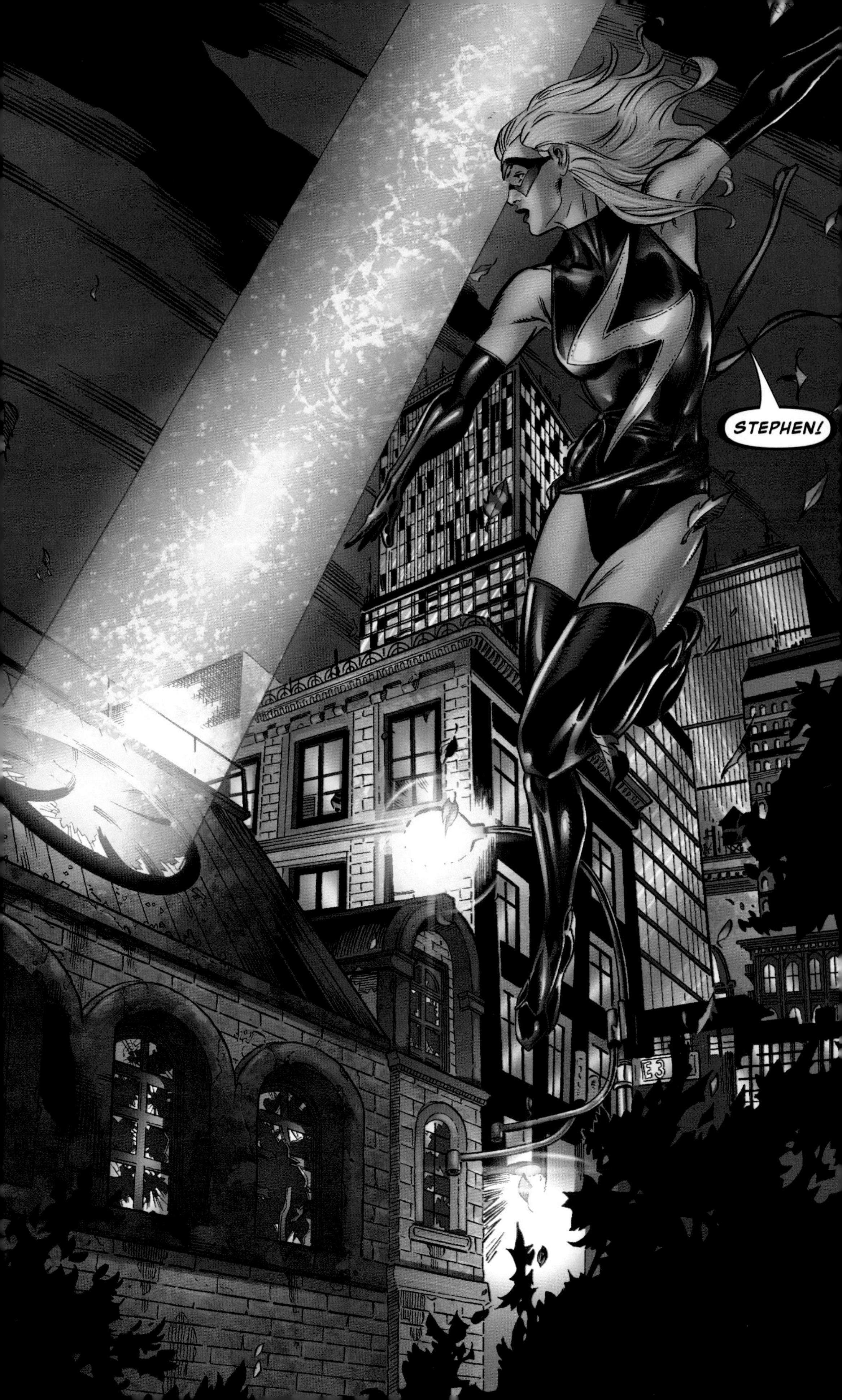
STEPHEN!

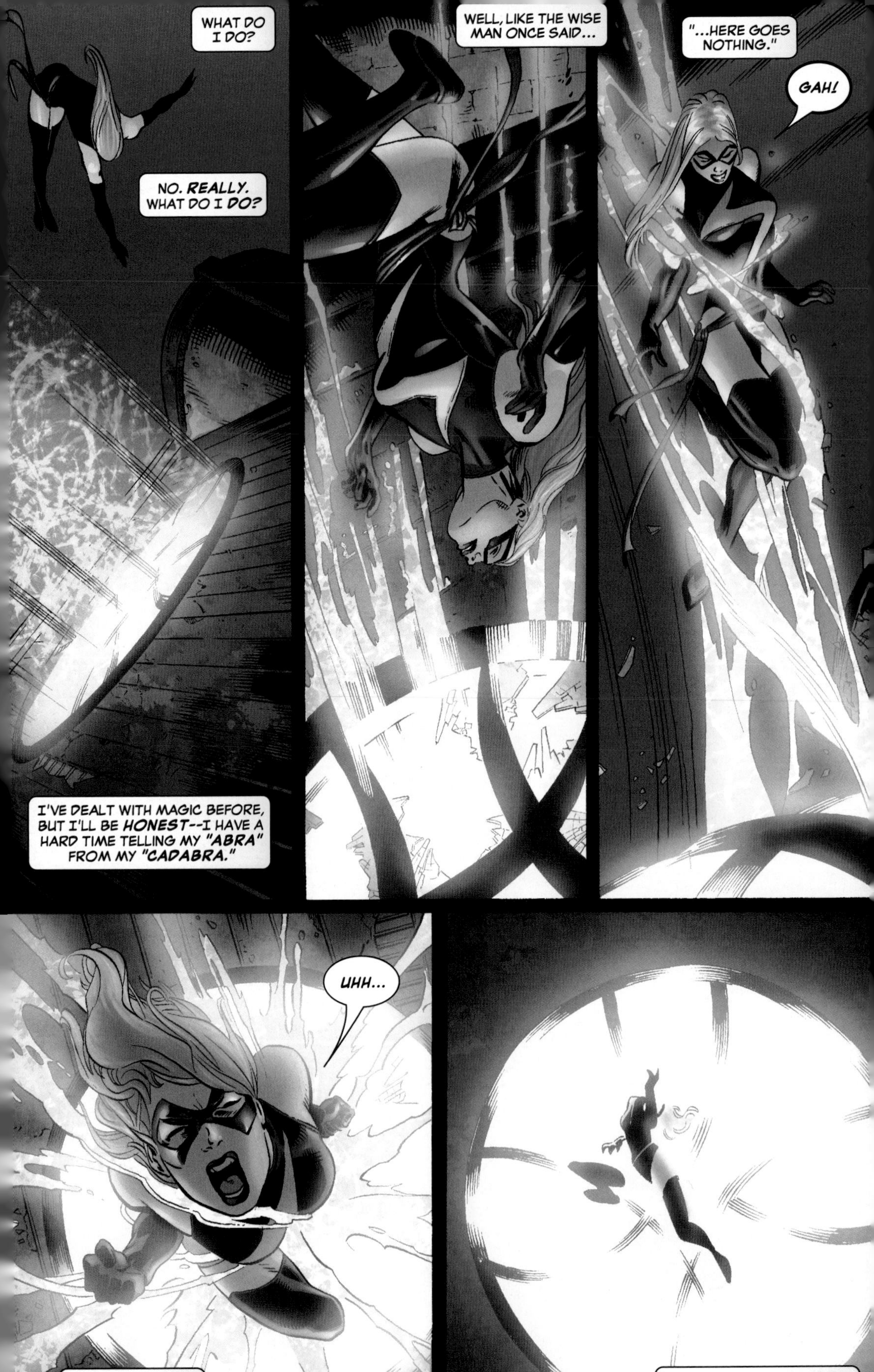
WHAT DO I DO?
NO. REALLY. WHAT DO I DO?
I'VE DEALT WITH MAGIC BEFORE, BUT I'LL BE HONEST--I HAVE A HARD TIME TELLING MY "ABRA" FROM MY "CADABRA."
WELL, LIKE THE WISE MAN ONCE SAID...
"...HERE GOES NOTHING."
GAH!
UHH...
...ABSORB AS MUCH AS I CAN--
MAYBE THIS WASN'T SUCH A GOOD IDEA AFTER ALL.

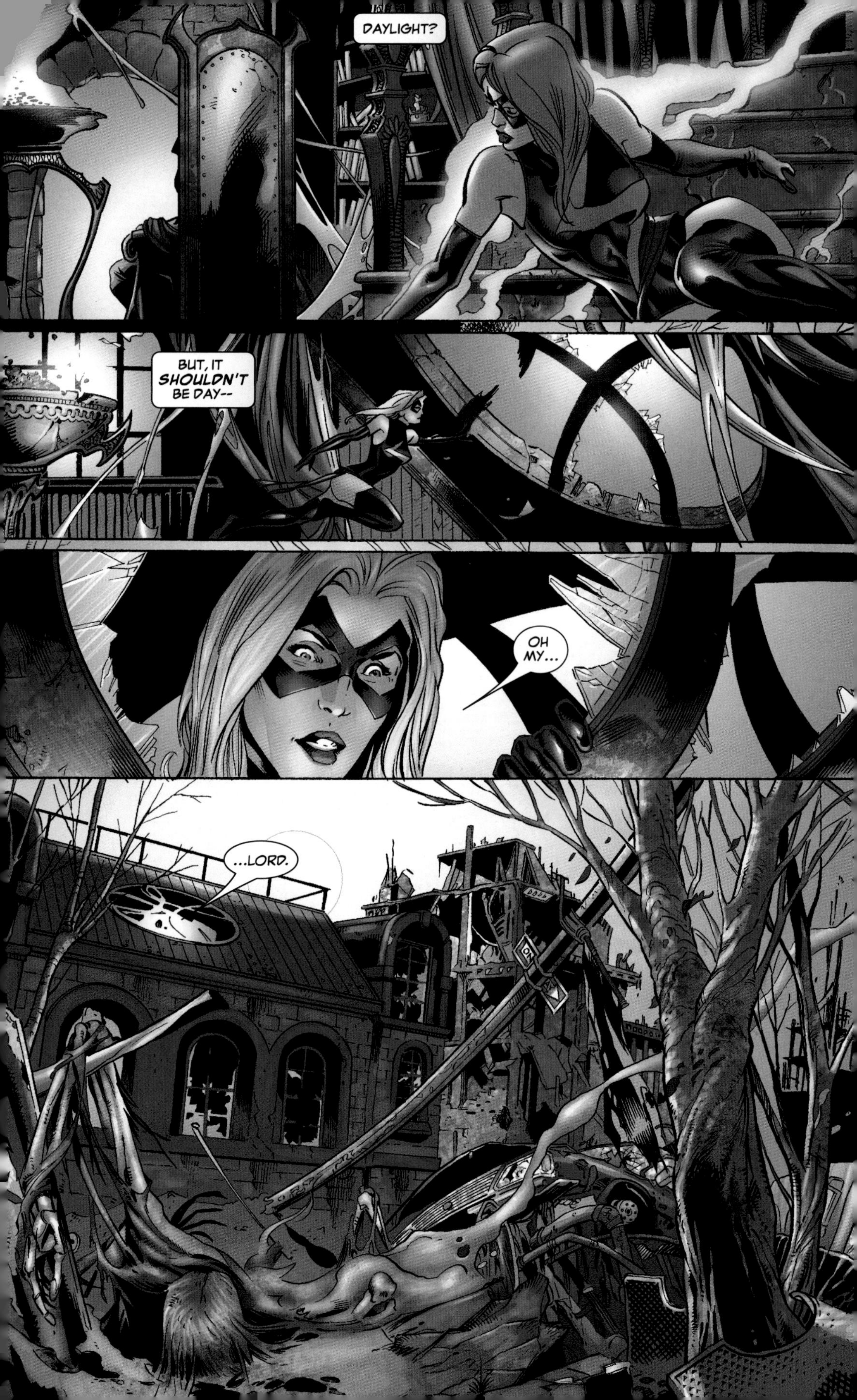
DAYLIGHT?
BUT, IT SHOULDN'T BE DAY--
OH MY...
...LORD.

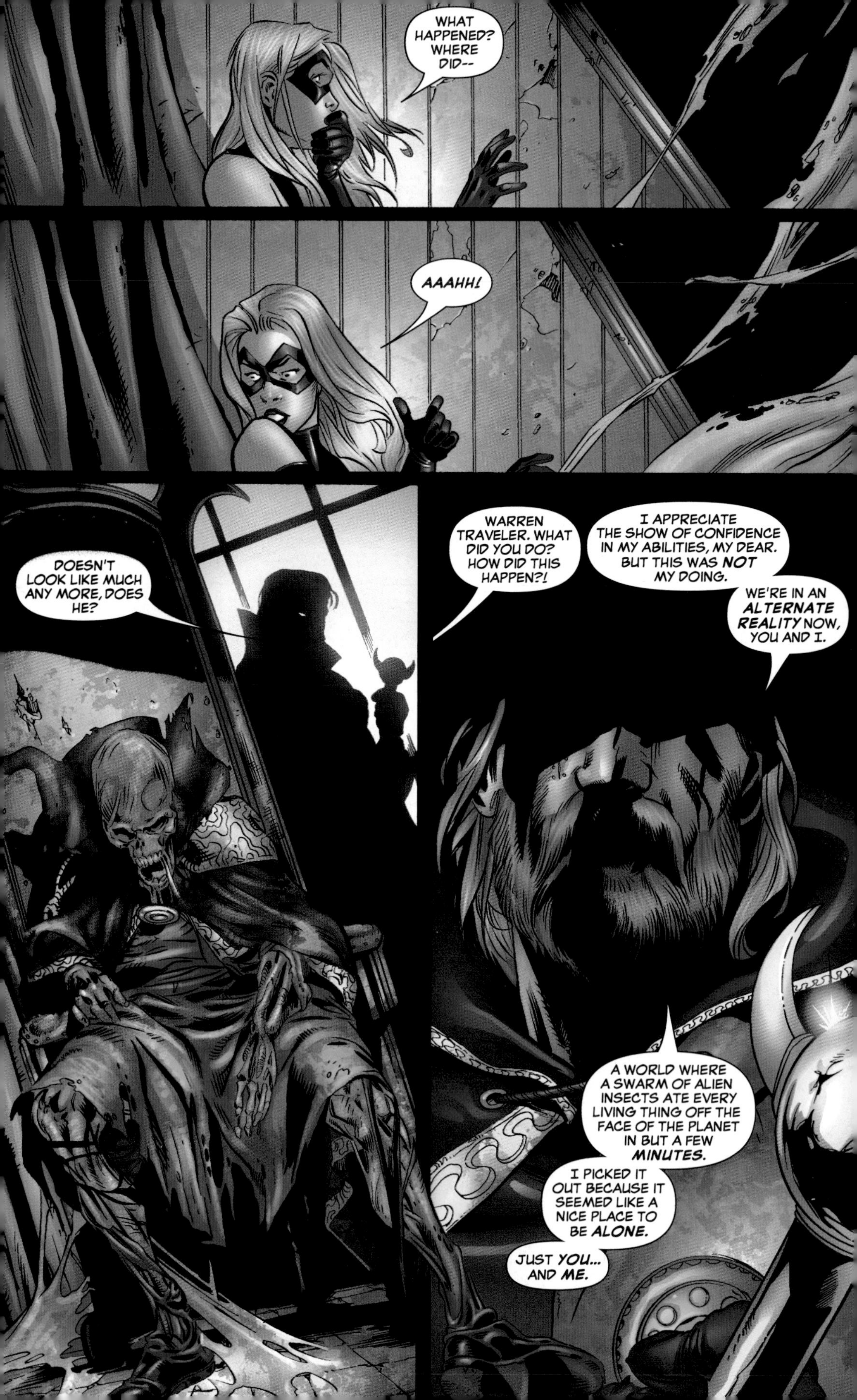

WHAT HAPPENED? WHERE DID--
AAAHH!
DOESN'T LOOK LIKE MUCH ANY MORE, DOES HE?
WARREN TRAVELER. WHAT DID YOU DO? HOW DID THIS HAPPEN?!
I APPRECIATE THE SHOW OF CONFIDENCE IN MY ABILITIES, MY DEAR. BUT THIS WAS NOT MY DOING.
WE'RE IN AN ALTERNATE REALITY NOW, YOU AND I.
A WORLD WHERE A SWARM OF ALIEN INSECTS ATE EVERY LIVING THING OFF THE FACE OF THE PLANET IN BUT A FEW MINUTES.
I PICKED IT OUT BECAUSE IT SEEMED LIKE A NICE PLACE TO BE ALONE.
JUST YOU... AND ME.

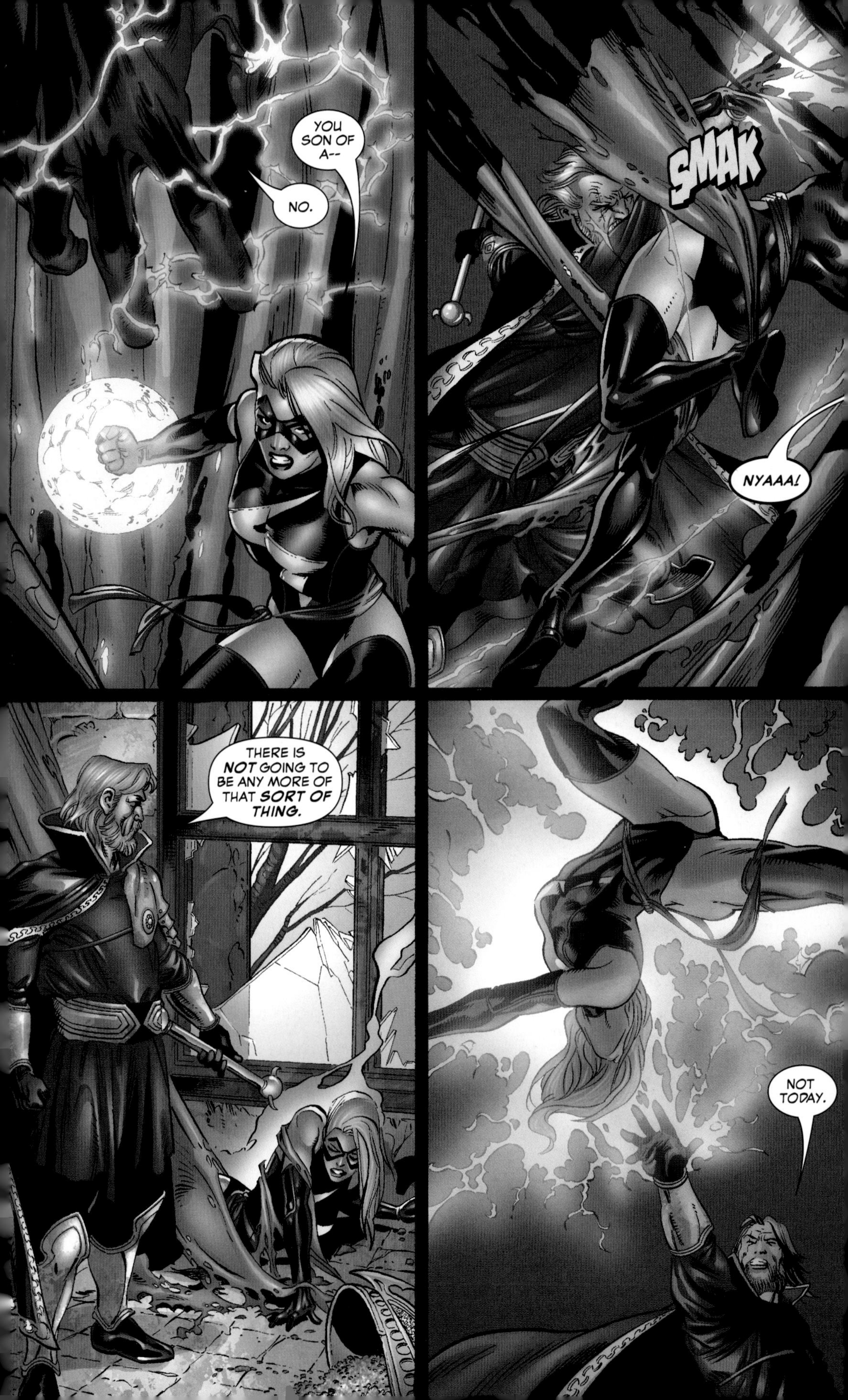
YOU SON OF A--
NO.
SMAK
NYAAA!
THERE IS **NOT** GOING TO BE ANY MORE OF THAT **SORT OF THING.**
NOT TODAY.

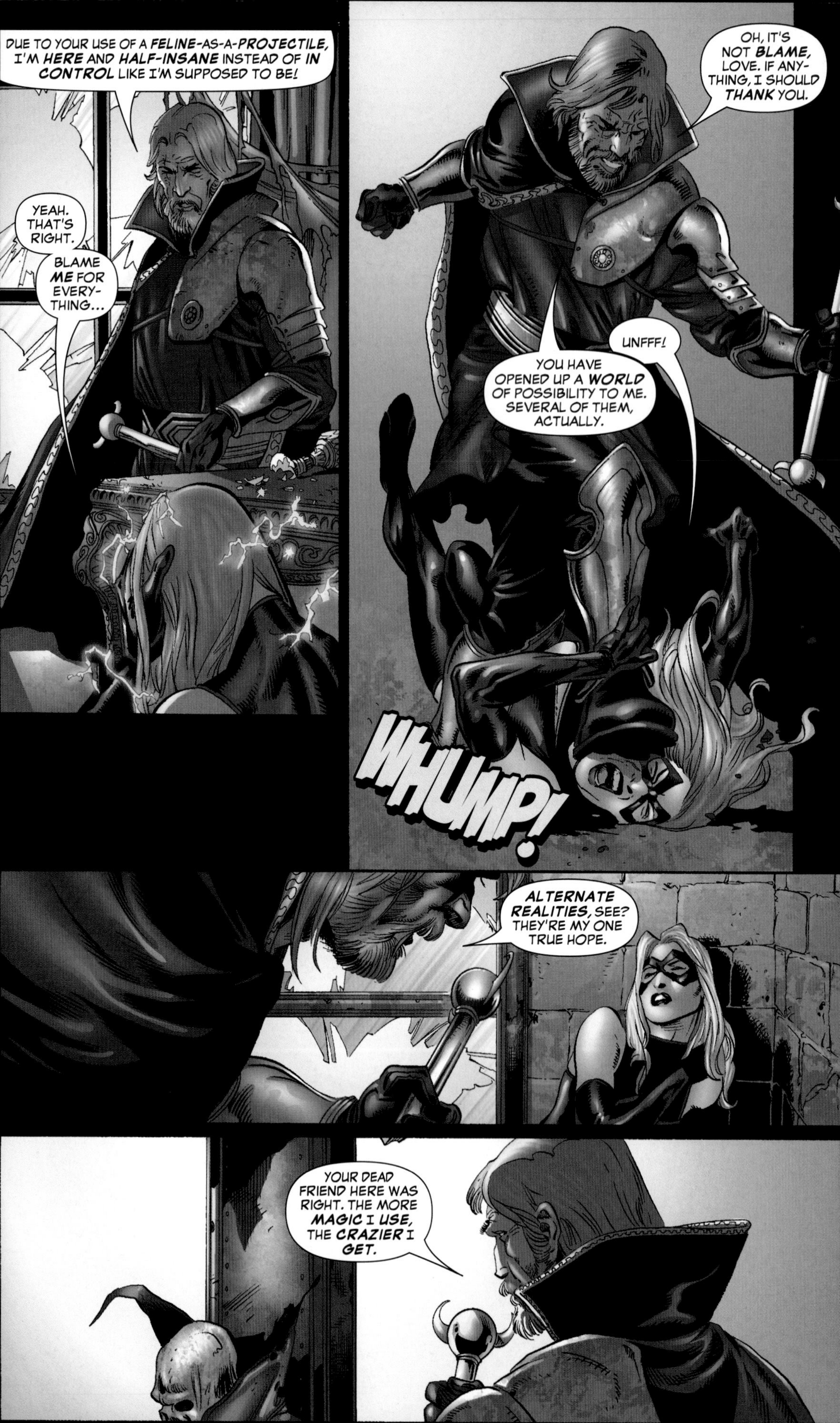

DUE TO YOUR USE OF A FELINE-AS-A-PROJECTILE, I'M HERE AND HALF-INSANE INSTEAD OF IN CONTROL LIKE I'M SUPPOSED TO BE!
YEAH. THAT'S RIGHT.
BLAME ME FOR EVERY-THING...
OH, IT'S NOT BLAME, LOVE. IF ANY-THING, I SHOULD THANK YOU.
UNFFF!
YOU HAVE OPENED UP A WORLD OF POSSIBILITY TO ME. SEVERAL OF THEM, ACTUALLY.
WHUMP!
ALTERNATE REALITIES, SEE? THEY'RE MY ONE TRUE HOPE.
YOUR DEAD FRIEND HERE WAS RIGHT. THE MORE MAGIC I USE, THE CRAZIER I GET.

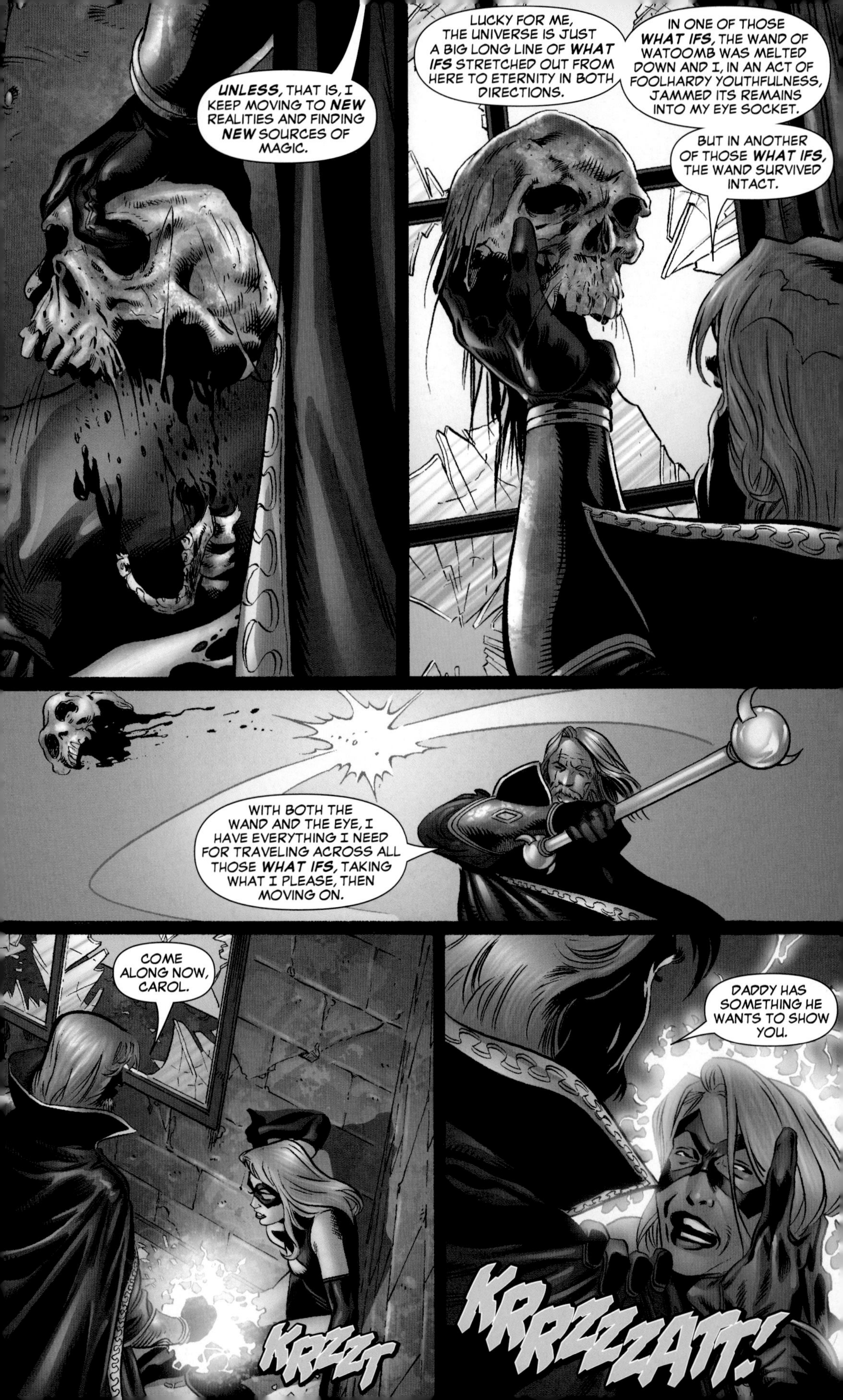
UNLESS, THAT IS, I KEEP MOVING TO NEW REALITIES AND FINDING NEW SOURCES OF MAGIC.
LUCKY FOR ME, THE UNIVERSE IS JUST A BIG LONG LINE OF WHAT IFS STRETCHED OUT FROM HERE TO ETERNITY IN BOTH DIRECTIONS.
IN ONE OF THOSE WHAT IFS, THE WAND OF WATOOMB WAS MELTED DOWN AND I, IN AN ACT OF FOOLHARDY YOUTHFULNESS, JAMMED ITS REMAINS INTO MY EYE SOCKET.
BUT IN ANOTHER OF THOSE WHAT IFS, THE WAND SURVIVED INTACT.
WITH BOTH THE WAND AND THE EYE, I HAVE EVERYTHING I NEED FOR TRAVELING ACROSS ALL THOSE WHAT IFS, TAKING WHAT I PLEASE, THEN MOVING ON.
COME ALONG NOW, CAROL.
KRZZZT
DADDY HAS SOMETHING HE WANTS TO SHOW YOU.
KRRZZZZATT!

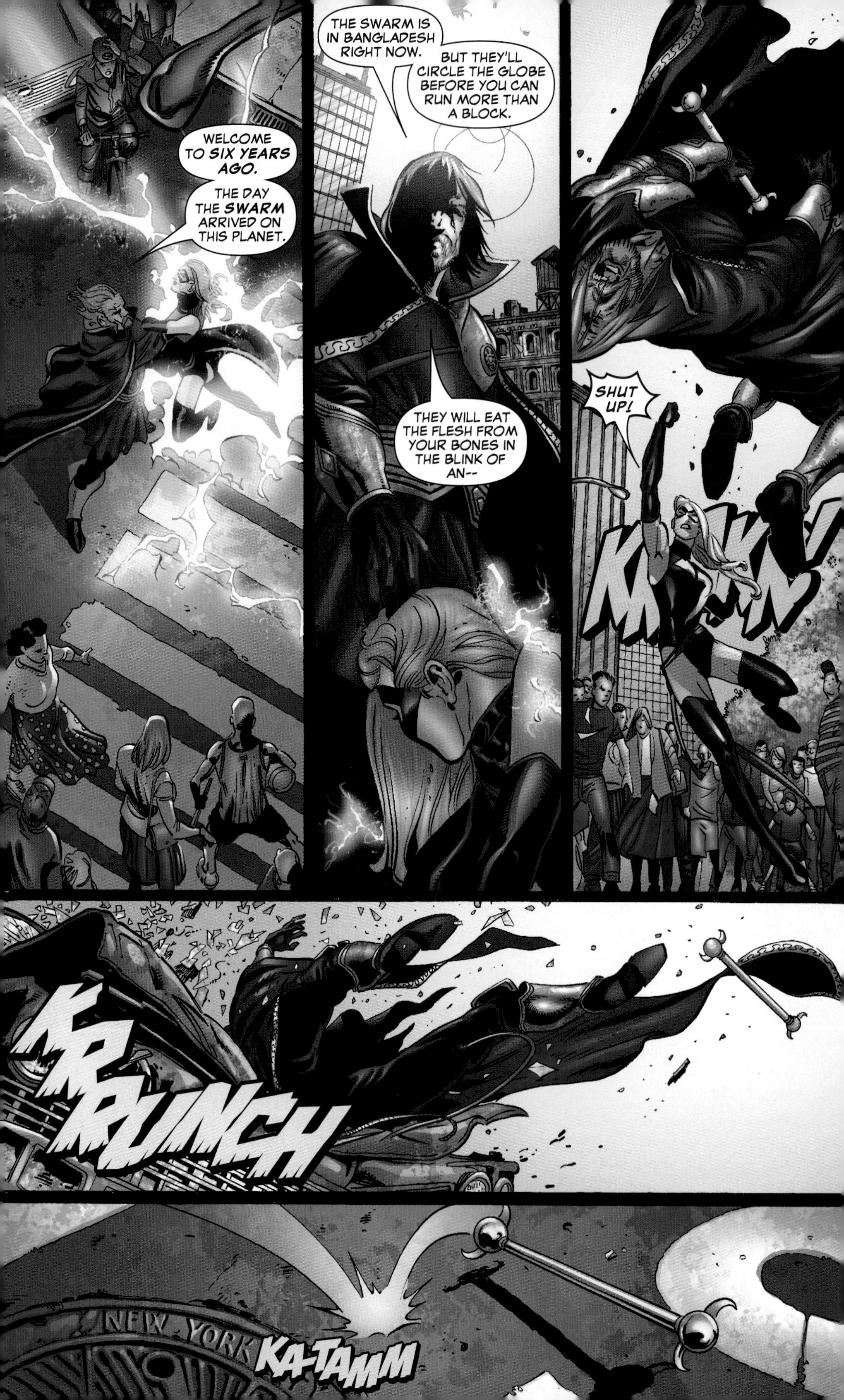
WELCOME TO SIX YEARS AGO.
THE DAY THE SWARM ARRIVED ON THIS PLANET.
THE SWARM IS IN BANGLADESH RIGHT NOW.
BUT THEY'LL CIRCLE THE GLOBE BEFORE YOU CAN RUN MORE THAN A BLOCK.
THEY WILL EAT THE FLESH FROM YOUR BONES IN THE BLINK OF AN--
SHUT UP!
KRUNCH
NEW YORK
KA-TAMM

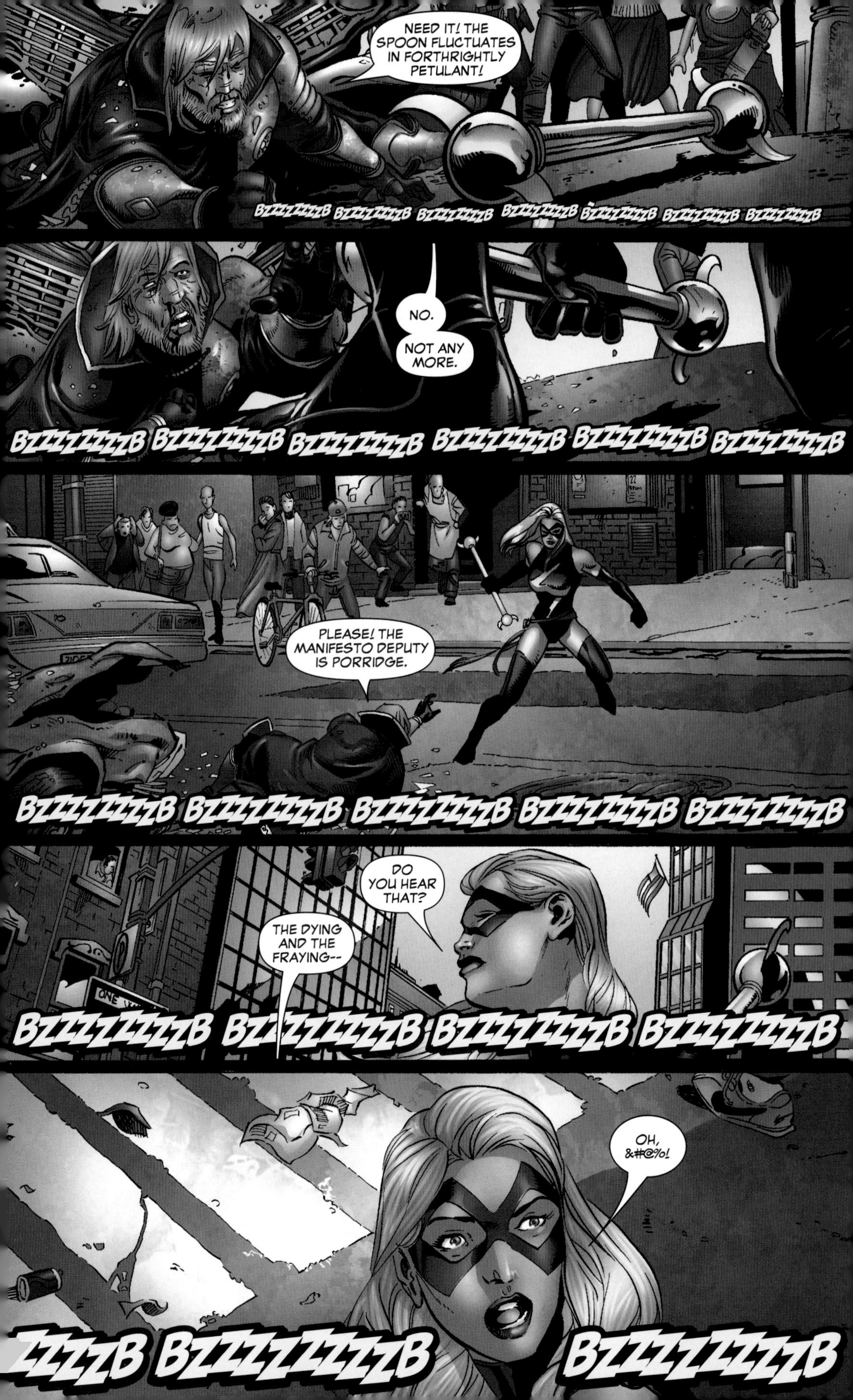
NEED IT! THE SPOON FLUCTUATES IN FORTHRIGHTLY PETULANT!
BZZZZZZZZB BZZZZZZZZB BZZZZZZZZB BZZZZZZZZB BZZZZZZZZB BZZZZZZZZB BZZZZZZZZB
NO.
NOT ANY MORE.
BZZZZZZZZB BZZZZZZZZB BZZZZZZZZB BZZZZZZZZB BZZZZZZZZB BZZZZZZZZB
PLEASE! THE MANIFESTO DEPUTY IS PORRIDGE.
BZZZZZZZZB BZZZZZZZZB BZZZZZZZZB BZZZZZZZZB BZZZZZZZZB
DO YOU HEAR THAT?
THE DYING AND THE FRAYING--
BZZZZZZZZB BZZZZZZZZB BZZZZZZZZB BZZZZZZZZB
OH, &#@%!
ZZZZB BZZZZZZZZZB BZZZZZZZZB

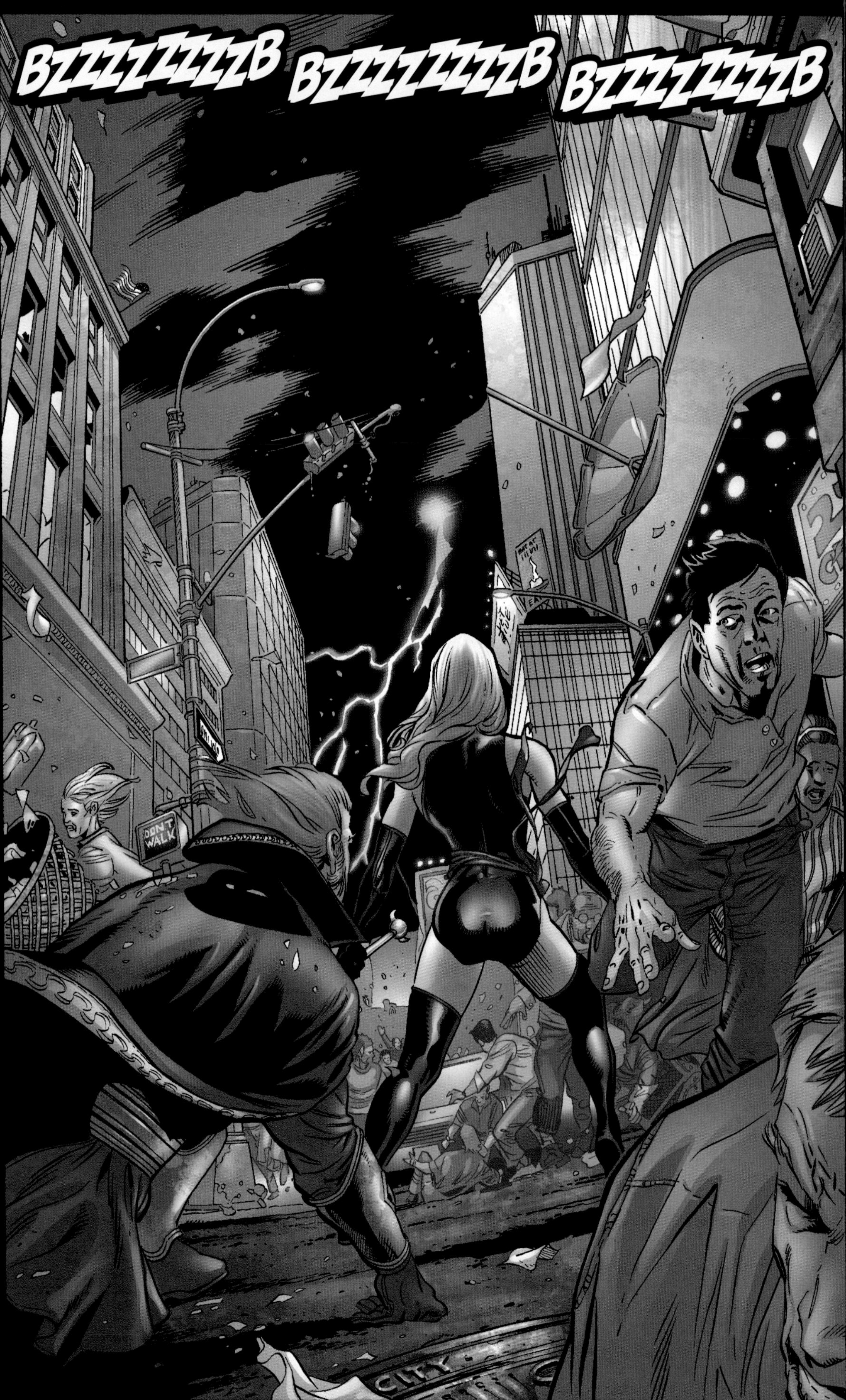
BZZZZZZZZZB
BZZZZZZZZZB
BZZZZZZZZZB
DON'T WALK
CITY

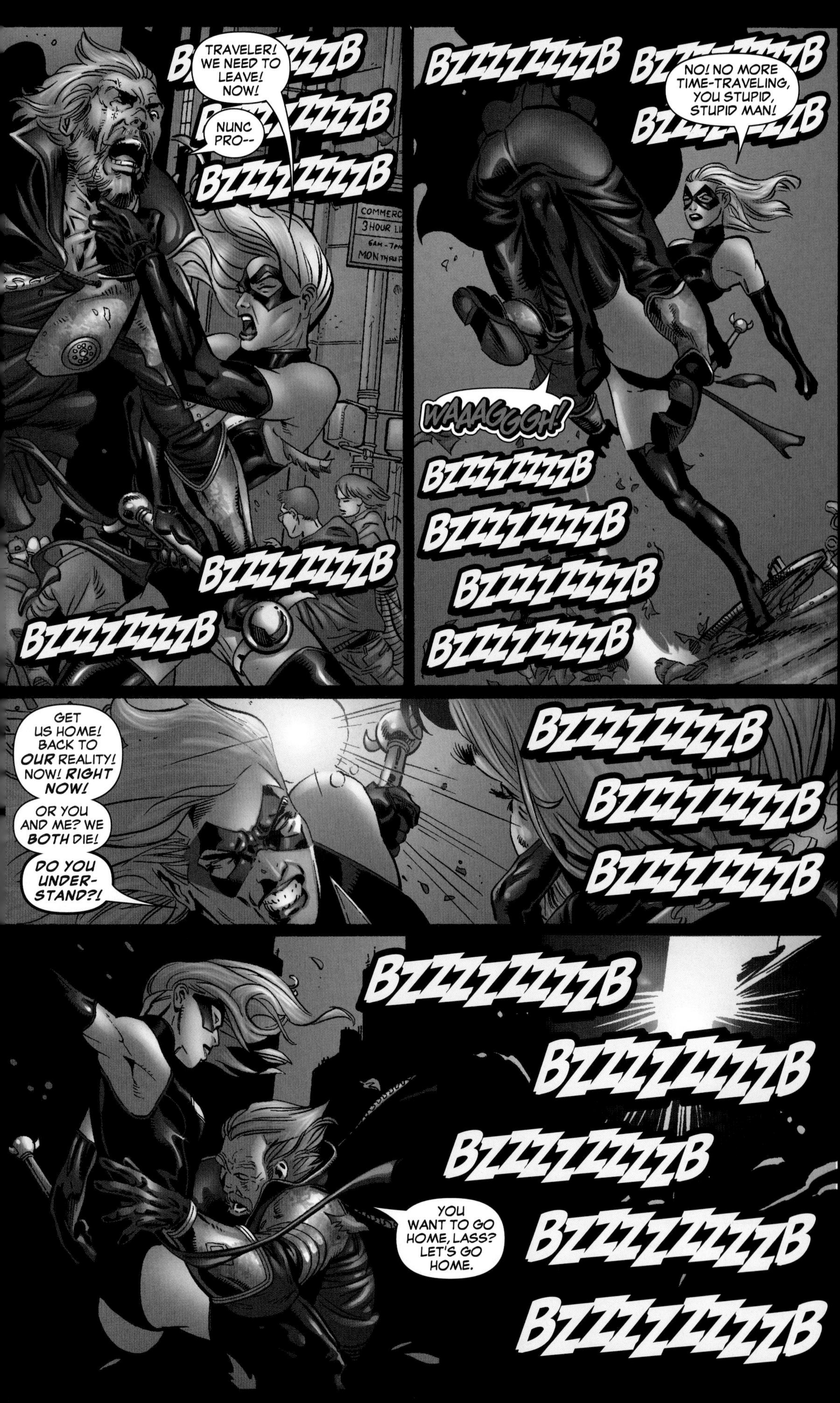

BZZZZZZZZZB
TRAVELER! WE NEED TO LEAVE! NOW!
BZZZZZZZZZB
NUNC PRO--
BZZZZZZZZZB
BZZZZZZZZZB
BZZZZZZZZZB
BZZZZZZZZZB
BZZZZZZZZZB
NO! NO MORE TIME-TRAVELING, YOU STUPID, STUPID MAN!
BZZZZZZZZZB
WAAAGGGH!
BZZZZZZZZZB
BZZZZZZZZZB
BZZZZZZZZZB
BZZZZZZZZZB
GET US HOME! BACK TO OUR REALITY! NOW! RIGHT NOW!
OR YOU AND ME? WE BOTH DIE!
DO YOU UNDER-STAND?!
BZZZZZZZZZB
BZZZZZZZZZB
BZZZZZZZZZB
BZZZZZZZZZB
BZZZZZZZZZB
BZZZZZZZZZB
YOU WANT TO GO HOME, LASS? LET'S GO HOME.
BZZZZZZZZZB
BZZZZZZZZZB

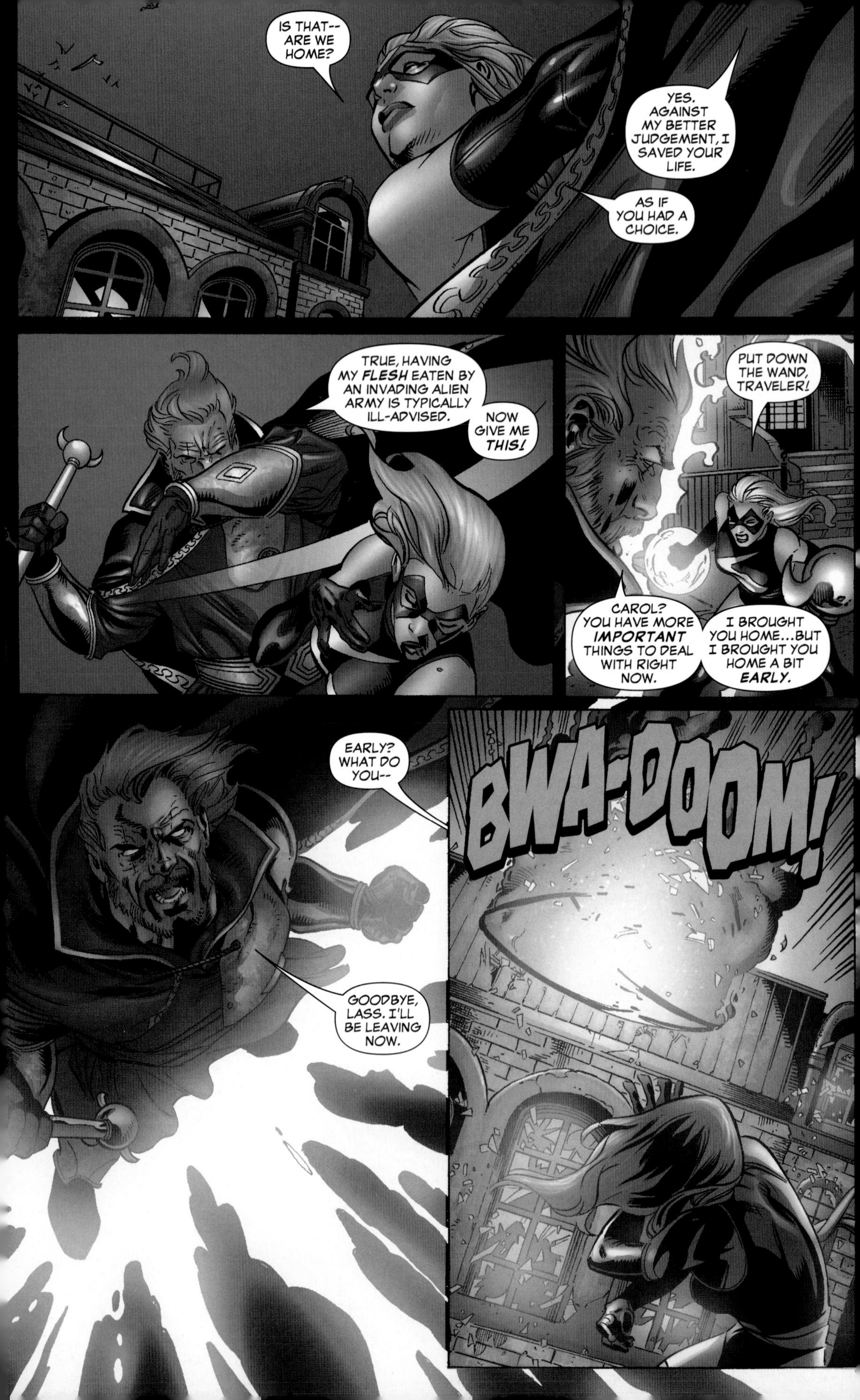
IS THAT-- ARE WE HOME?
YES. AGAINST MY BETTER JUDGEMENT, I SAVED YOUR LIFE.
AS IF YOU HAD A CHOICE.
TRUE, HAVING MY FLESH EATEN BY AN INVADING ALIEN ARMY IS TYPICALLY ILL-ADVISED.
NOW GIVE ME THIS!
PUT DOWN THE WAND, TRAVELER!
CAROL? YOU HAVE MORE IMPORTANT THINGS TO DEAL WITH RIGHT NOW.
I BROUGHT YOU HOME...BUT I BROUGHT YOU HOME A BIT EARLY.
EARLY? WHAT DO YOU--
GOODBYE, LASS. I'LL BE LEAVING NOW.
BWA-DOOM!

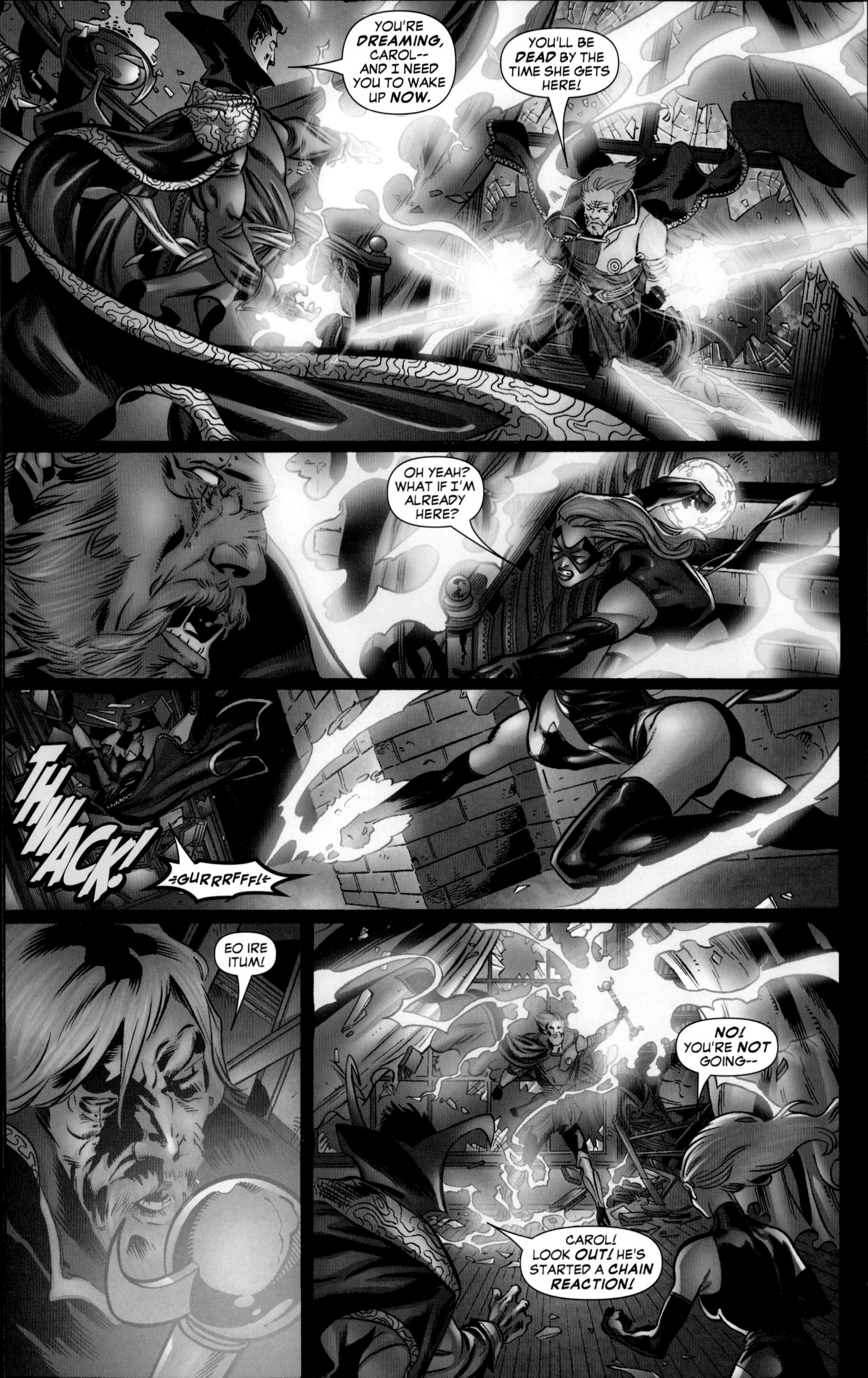
YOU'RE DREAMING, CAROL-- AND I NEED YOU TO WAKE UP NOW.
YOU'LL BE DEAD BY THE TIME SHE GETS HERE!
OH YEAH? WHAT IF I'M ALREADY HERE?
THWACK!
GURRRFFF!
EO IRE ITUM!
NO! YOU'RE NOT GOING--
CAROL! LOOK OUT! HE'S STARTED A CHAIN REACTION!

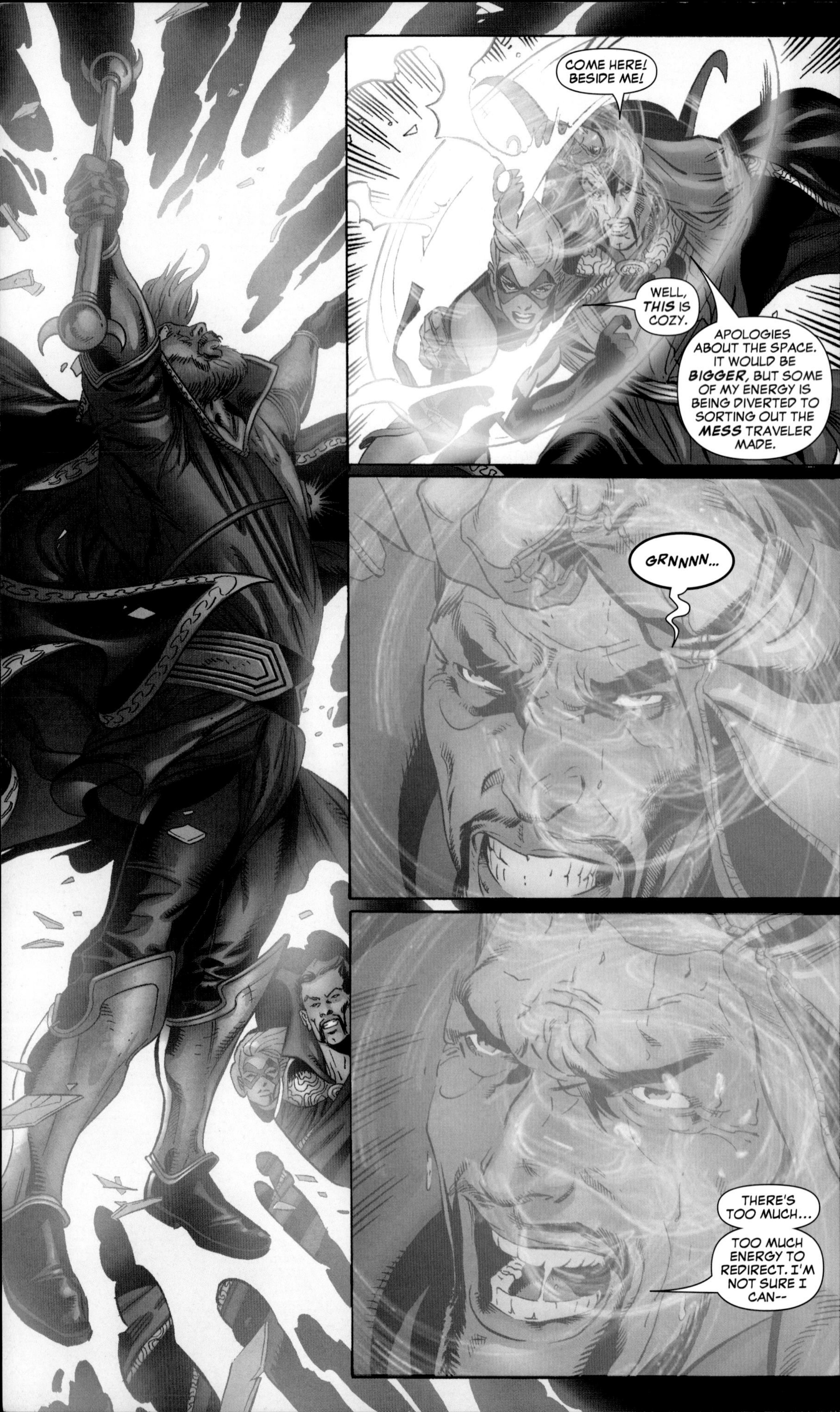
COME HERE! BESIDE ME!
WELL, THIS IS COZY.
APOLOGIES ABOUT THE SPACE. IT WOULD BE BIGGER, BUT SOME OF MY ENERGY IS BEING DIVERTED TO SORTING OUT THE MESS TRAVELER MADE.
GRNNNN...
THERE'S TOO MUCH...
TOO MUCH ENERGY TO REDIRECT. I'M NOT SURE I CAN--

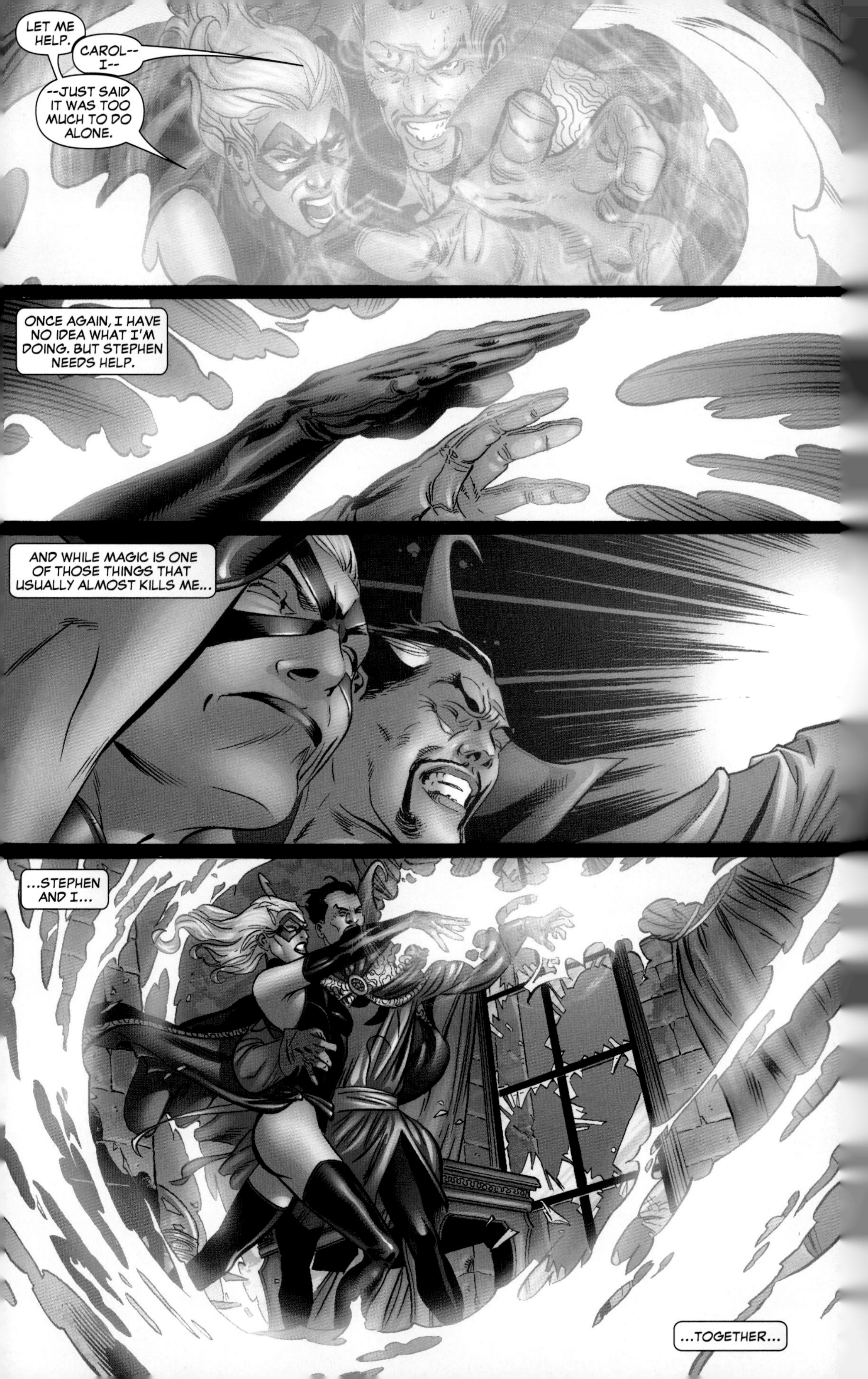
LET ME HELP.
CAROL-- I--
--JUST SAID IT WAS TOO MUCH TO DO ALONE.
ONCE AGAIN, I HAVE NO IDEA WHAT I'M DOING. BUT STEPHEN NEEDS HELP.
AND WHILE MAGIC IS ONE OF THOSE THINGS THAT USUALLY ALMOST KILLS ME...
...STEPHEN AND I...
...TOGETHER...

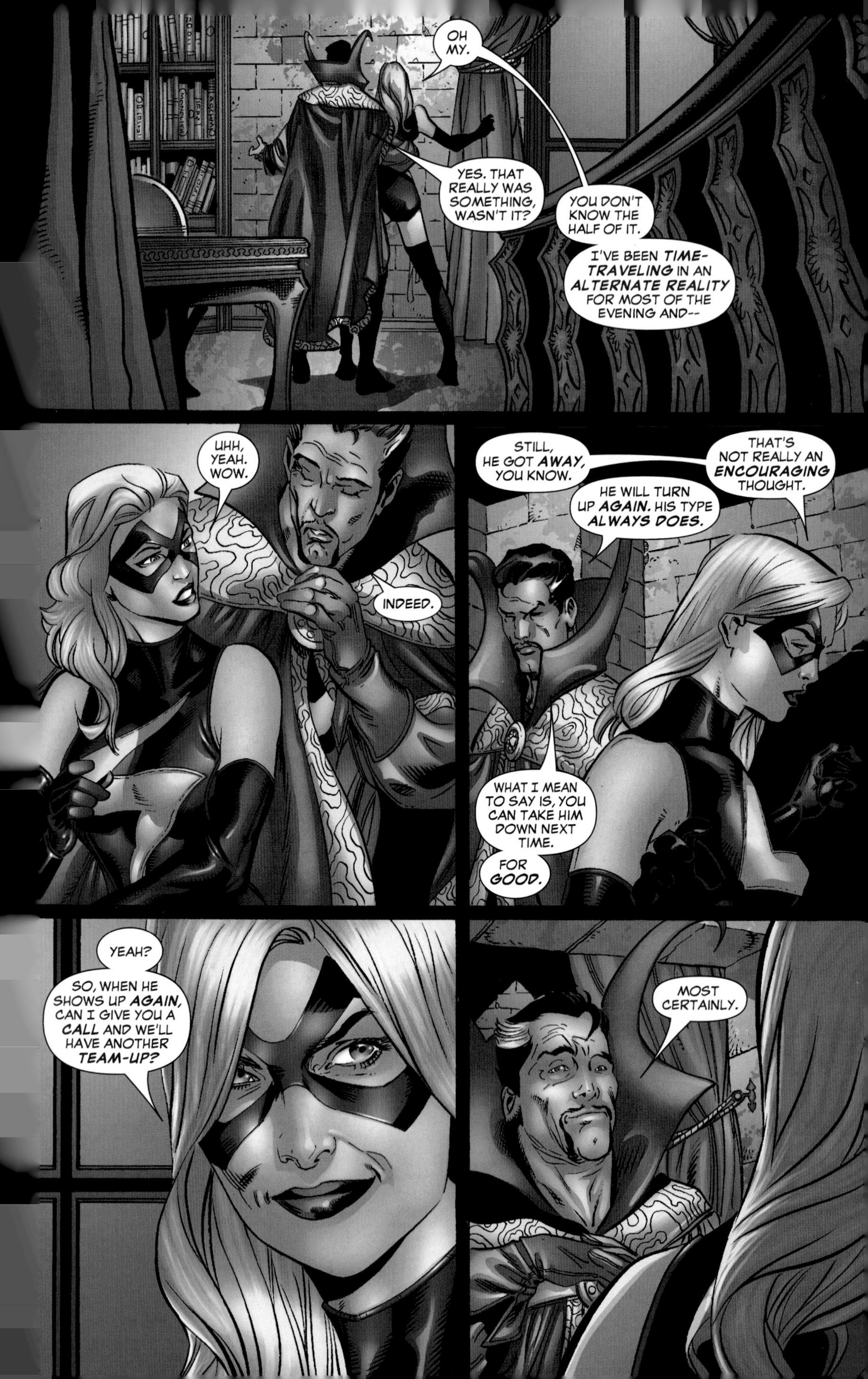

OH MY.
YES. THAT REALLY WAS SOMETHING, WASN'T IT?
YOU DON'T KNOW THE HALF OF IT.
I'VE BEEN TIME-TRAVELING IN AN ALTERNATE REALITY FOR MOST OF THE EVENING AND--
UHH, YEAH. WOW.
INDEED.
STILL, HE GOT AWAY, YOU KNOW.
THAT'S NOT REALLY AN ENCOURAGING THOUGHT.
HE WILL TURN UP AGAIN. HIS TYPE ALWAYS DOES.
WHAT I MEAN TO SAY IS, YOU CAN TAKE HIM DOWN NEXT TIME.
FOR GOOD.
YEAH?
SO, WHEN HE SHOWS UP AGAIN, CAN I GIVE YOU A CALL AND WE'LL HAVE ANOTHER TEAM-UP?
MOST CERTAINLY.

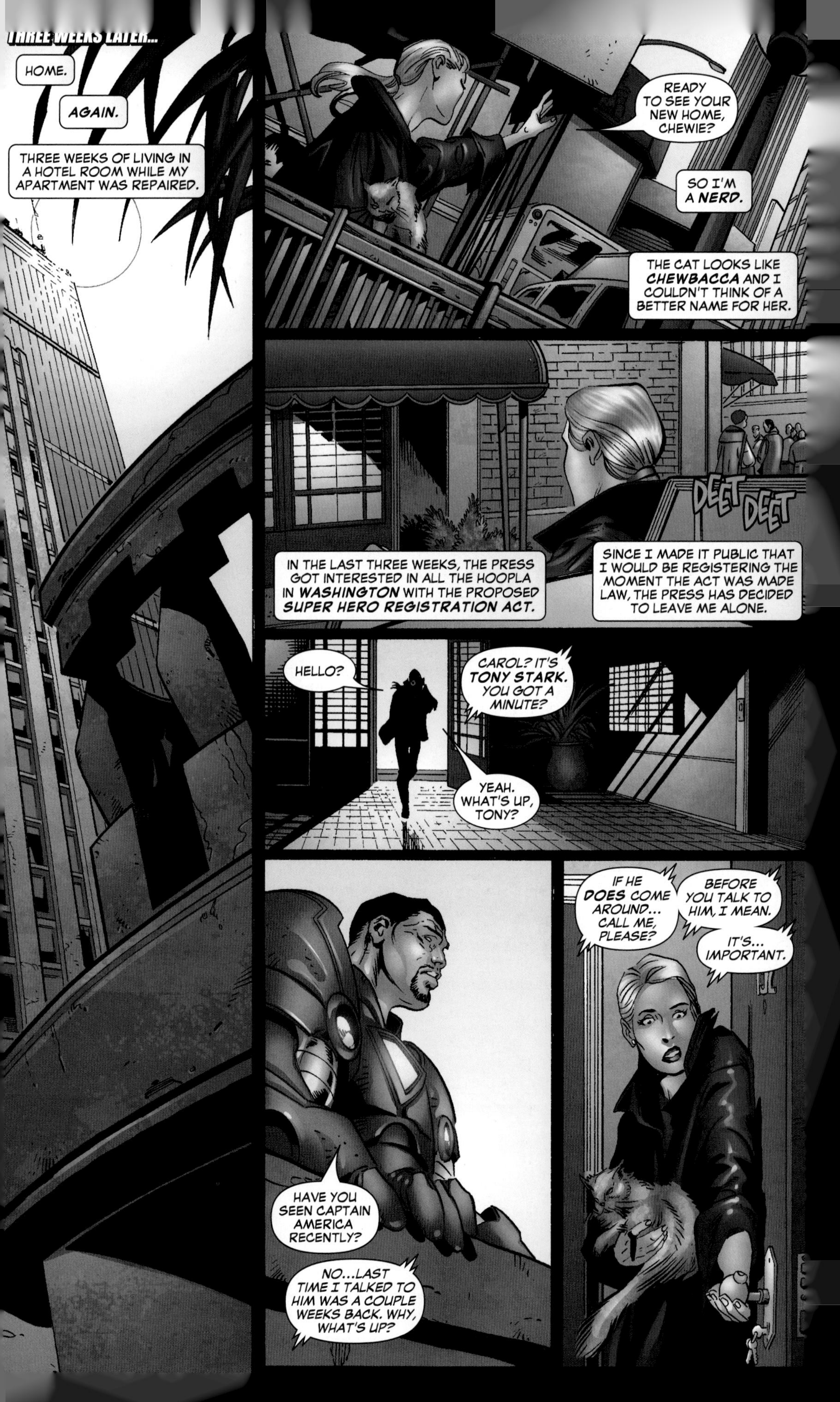
THREE WEEKS LATER...
HOME.
AGAIN.
THREE WEEKS OF LIVING IN A HOTEL ROOM WHILE MY APARTMENT WAS REPAIRED.
READY TO SEE YOUR NEW HOME, CHEWIE?
SO I'M A NERD.
THE CAT LOOKS LIKE CHEWBACCA AND I COULDN'T THINK OF A BETTER NAME FOR HER.
DEET DEET
IN THE LAST THREE WEEKS, THE PRESS GOT INTERESTED IN ALL THE HOOPLA IN WASHINGTON WITH THE PROPOSED SUPER HERO REGISTRATION ACT.
SINCE I MADE IT PUBLIC THAT I WOULD BE REGISTERING THE MOMENT THE ACT WAS MADE LAW, THE PRESS HAS DECIDED TO LEAVE ME ALONE.
HELLO?
CAROL? IT'S TONY STARK. YOU GOT A MINUTE?
YEAH. WHAT'S UP, TONY?
HAVE YOU SEEN CAPTAIN AMERICA RECENTLY?
NO...LAST TIME I TALKED TO HIM WAS A COUPLE WEEKS BACK. WHY, WHAT'S UP?
IF HE DOES COME AROUND... CALL ME, PLEASE?
BEFORE YOU TALK TO HIM, I MEAN.
IT'S... IMPORTANT.

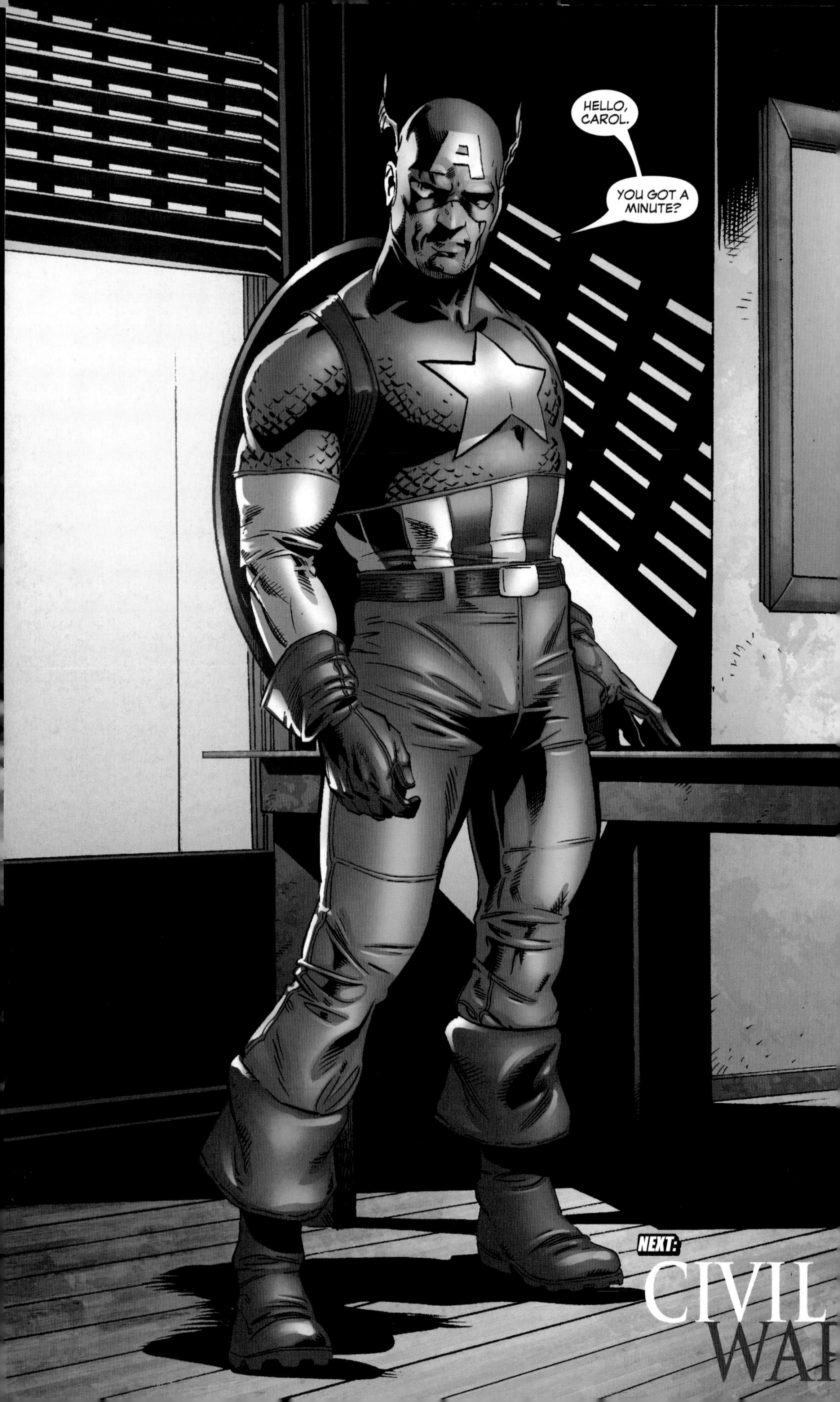
HELLO, CAROL.
YOU GOT A MINUTE?
NEXT:
CIVIL WAR

Ms. Marvel #1 Variant Cover by Michael Turner

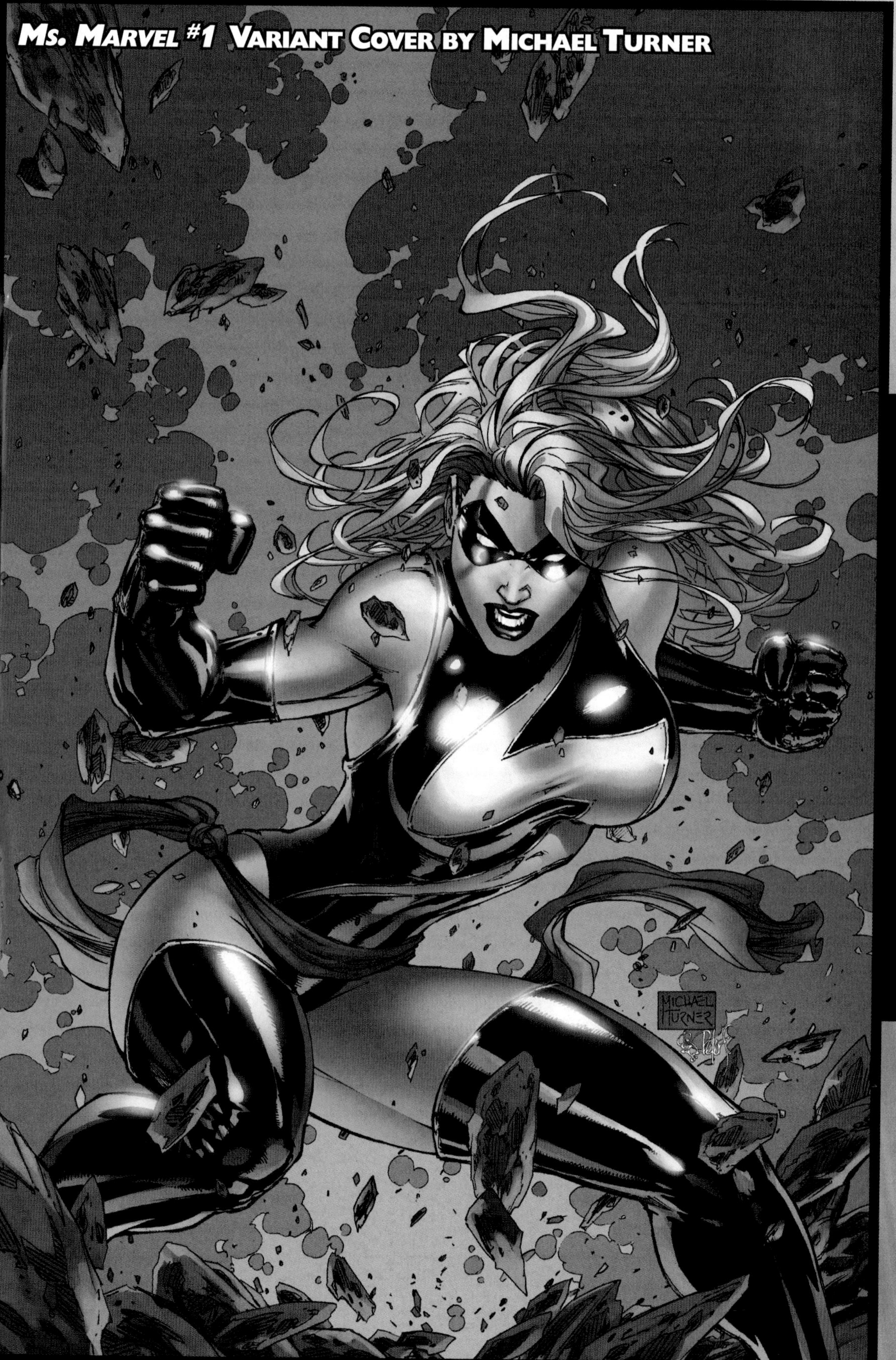
MICHAEL TURNER

Concept Sketches by Roberto De La Torre

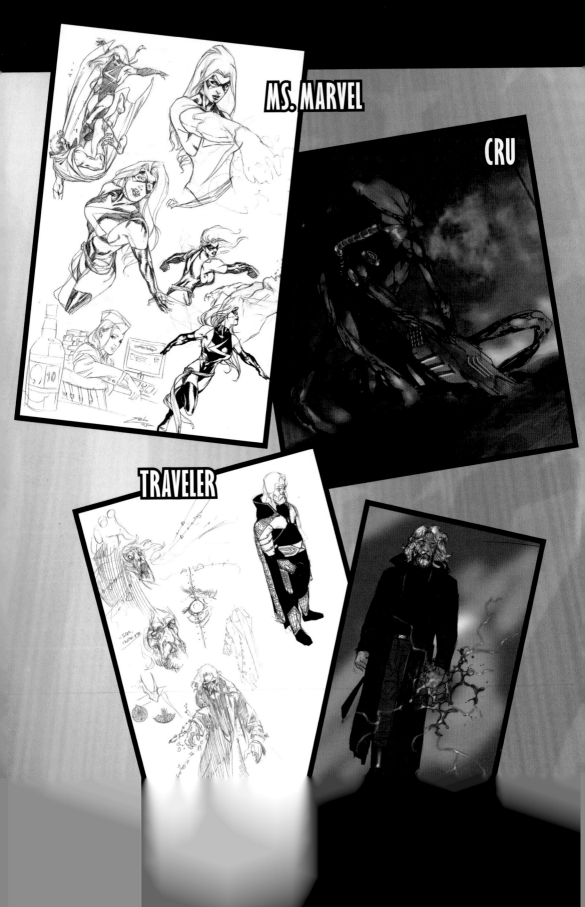

MS. MARVEL

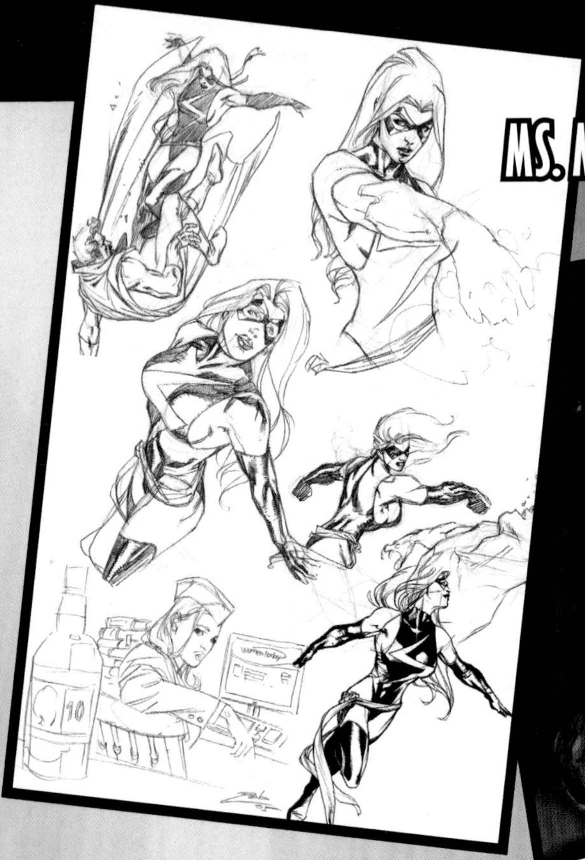

CRU

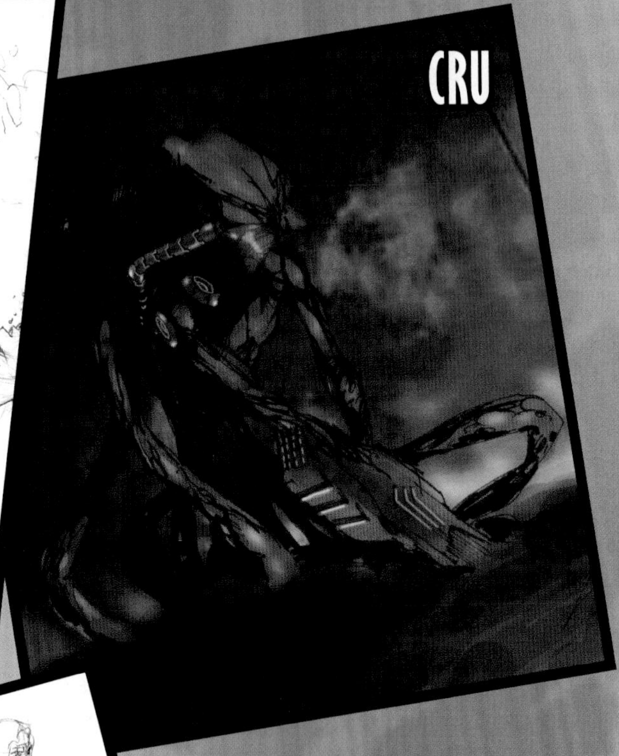

TRAVELER

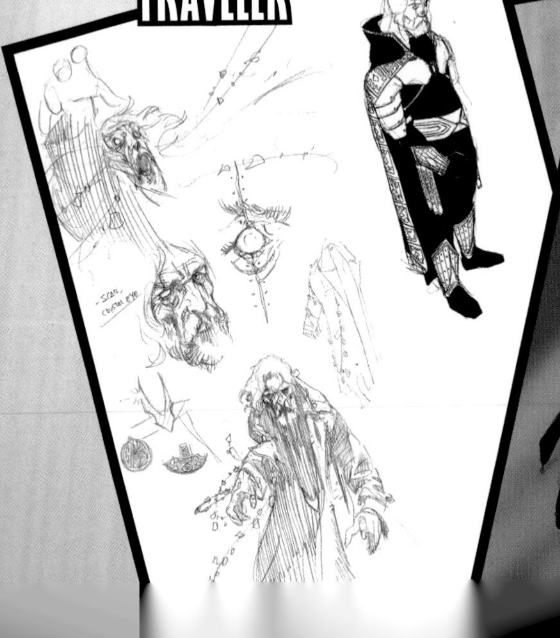

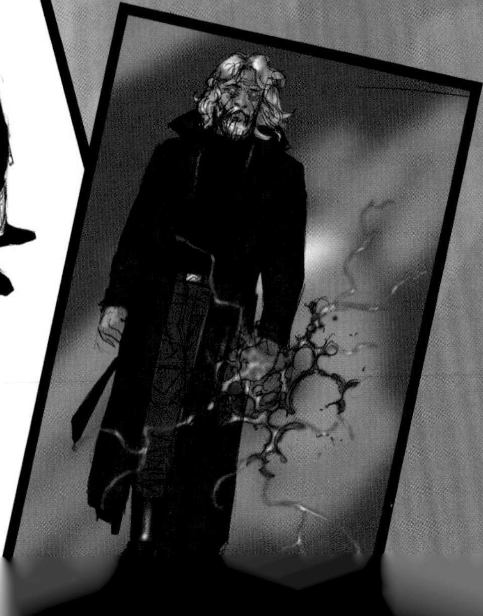